# AMAZING SUPER HERO GUIDE

LONDON, NEW YORK, MELBOURNE,
MUNICH AND DELHI

Senior Editors  Laura Gilbert and Helen Murray
Editorial Assistant  Emma Grange
Designers  Owen Bennett and Lauren Rosier
Art editors  Nico Alba, Akanksha Gupta, and Lisa Sodeau
Design Assistant  Rhys Thomas
Senior Art Editors  Guy Harvey and Rajnish Kashyap
Senior Designer and Brand Manager  Robert Perry
Design Manager  Ron Stobbart
Publishing Manager  Julie Ferris
Art Director  Lisa Lanzarini
Publishing Director  Simon Beecroft

Jacket Designer Mark Penfound
DTP Designer Kavita Varma
Senior Producer Charlotte Oliver

This edition published in 2014
First published in Great Britain in 2014 by Dorling Kindersley Limited
80 Strand, London WC2R 0RL
A Penguin Random House Company

First published in the UK 2009 - 2013 as three separate titles: Spider-Man Inside the
World of Your Friendly Neighbourhood Hero *2013,* Iron Man The Ultimate Guide to the
Armoured Super Hero *2010,* Wolverine Inside the World of the Living Weapon *2009.*

001-266546-Mar/2014

A CIP catalogue record for this book is available from the British Library.

ISBN: 978-1-4093-5373-7

Colour reproduction by Altaimage
Printed and bound in China by Hung Hing

The publisher would like to thank Shari Last for the index and editorial assistance; Neil
Kelly for editorial assistance; Anjan Dey and Era Chawla for design assistance;
Chelsea Alon, Rich Thomas, Scott Piehl, and Lauren Kressel from Disney Publishing;
Ruwan Jayatilleke and Kelly Lamy from Marvel.

marvel.com
© 2014 MARVEL

Discover more at
www.dk.com

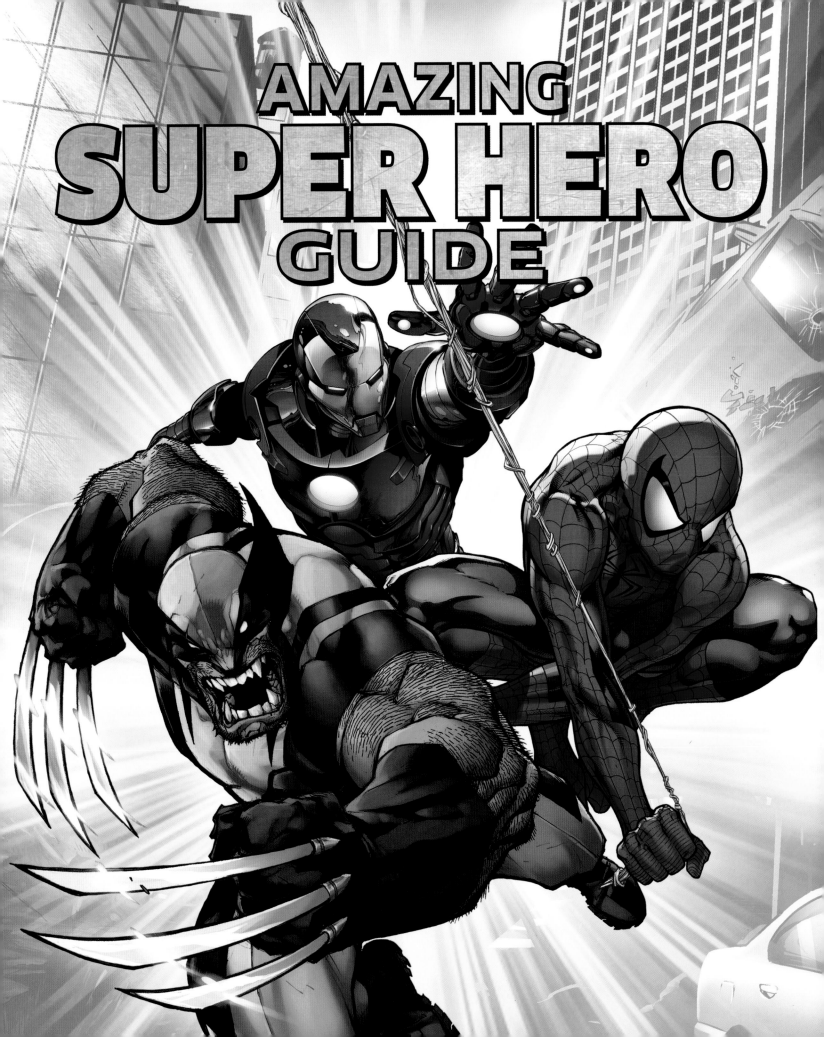

# Contents

*Wolverine. James Howlett. Logan. Skunk-Bear. Runt. Weapon X. Death. The ol' Canucklehead. He goes by many names, but no matter his moniker, one thing remains a constant: Wolverine is the best there is at what he does.*

One of the most iconic Super Heroes of all time, Spider-Man has leapt off the comic book page and into the mainstream. From big budget Hollywood films to action figures, from T-shirts to theme park attractions, from cartoons to a Broadway musical, Spider-Man's popularity is an indisputable fact, as is his status as Marvel's most notable creation.

## INTRODUCING...

# SPIDER-MAN

He swings through the air on merely a thin strand of webbing. He can climb up the side of a building as easily as he can walk down the street. Due to the irradiated bite of a spider, he has the proportionate strength of an arachnid, and can effortlessly lift nearly ten tons. He has an unexplainable precognitive sense of when danger is approaching. His reflexes, agility, and endurance pale the accomplishments of even the most dedicated athlete. He is the amazing Spider-Man.

But although Spider-Man possesses more power than most people could dream of, his alter ego, Peter Parker, is just a regular guy trying to make ends meet. Imbued with a strict moral code and a heightened sense of responsibility, Peter is always struggling to do the right thing, no matter the sacrifice involved. More than just the sum of his abilities, Spider-Man's strength and longevity come from the man beneath the mask, a man whose often-heard mantra dictates his every decision: "With great power there must also come—great responsibility!"

# THE STORY OF SPIDER-MAN

*"THIS SURE BEATS WAITING FOR A BUS!"*

**Stan Lee was toying with the idea of leaving comics. Fed up with the stagnant Super Hero format, Lee decided that before he quit, he'd take a whack at writing comics his way. From that simple idea sprang the Marvel Age of comics, and its main attraction—Spider-Man.**

Stan Lee knew that he'd chanced upon something special when he concocted the idea of the Super Hero Spider-Man and his teenage alter ego Peter Parker. Before that time, almost every teenager in comics served as a sidekick. They were meant to be a younger voice that kids could relate to in order to better enjoy the adventures of the sidekick's mentor, the comic's star. Stan never liked sidekicks, but he saw potential in the concept of having a young lead character that a newer generation could claim as their own. So Lee placed Peter Parker squarely in high school, and to go even further, he decided to make Peter a bit of a bookworm. This in turn made the hero even more relatable. Peter Parker wasn't the type of high school student to try out for the football team, he was the kind who was more comfortable sitting on the sidelines reading a good book—or comic book, as the case may be.

Knowing he had a home run on his hands, Lee put a lot of consideration into deciding which artist to pair with. Although he usually partnered with the legendary Jack Kirby, after seeing Kirby's Spider-Man artwork, Lee decided Jack was making the character too heroic, and not the underdog Lee wanted to portray. While Jack sketched the cover, Lee turned to the brilliant Steve Ditko for the interiors, and everything fell smoothly into place. With the debut of *Amazing Fantasy* #15 in August 1962, the world met the amazing Spider-Man.

**THE MAN-SPIDER?**
Marvel had actually toyed with the idea of a Spider-Man before. In a story drawn by Jack Kirby called "Where Will You Be, When… the Spider Strikes!" and featured in *Journey Into Mystery* #73 (October 1961), an ordinary house spider is exposed to radiation and gains the abilities of a human. This monstrous spider even shot webbing, just like Spider-Man, but he was very different to the web-slinger we know and love.

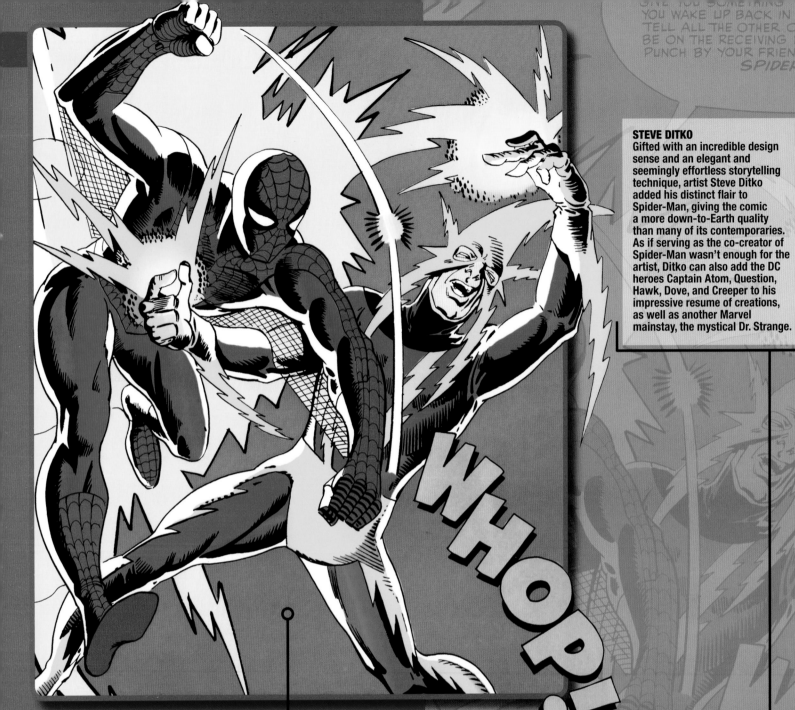

**STEVE DITKO**
Gifted with an incredible design sense and an elegant and seemingly effortless storytelling technique, artist Steve Ditko added his distinct flair to Spider-Man, giving the comic a more down-to-Earth quality than many of its contemporaries. As if serving as the co-creator of Spider-Man wasn't enough for the artist, Ditko can also add the DC heroes Captain Atom, Question, Hawk, Dove, and Creeper to his impressive resume of creations, as well as another Marvel mainstay, the mystical Dr. Strange.

## THE CREATORS

"AND NOW, YOU HIGH-VOLTAGE HEEL, I'LL GIVE YOU SOMETHING TO TALK ABOUT WHEN YOU WAKE UP BACK IN YOUR CELL! YOU CAN TELL THE OTHER CONS HOW IT FEELS TO BE ON THE RECEIVING END OF A KNOCKOUT PUNCH BY YOUR FRIENDLY NEIGHBORHOOD SPIDER-MAN!!"

SPIDER-MAN TO ELECTRO

**STAN LEE**
Stan "The Man" Lee might just be comics' biggest celebrity. Responsible for changing the face of Marvel, as well as the entire comic book industry in the 1960s, Lee has co-created hundreds of characters alongside landmark artists like Jack Kirby and Steve Ditko. The writer behind nearly all of Marvel's iconic heroes, from the Fantastic Four to Spider-Man to the Incredible Hulk to the X-Men, Lee worked at Marvel as a writer, editor, president, and chairman. Even when not acting as Marvel's guiding force, he has continued to serve as the company's inspiration.

August 1962

# AMAZING FANTASY #15

*"Okay, world—better hang onto your hat! Here comes the **Spider-Man!**"*

PETER PARKER

**EDITOR-IN-CHIEF**
Stan Lee

**COVER ARTISTS**
Jack Kirby and Steve Ditko

**WRITER**
Stan Lee

**PENCILER**
Steve Ditko

**INKER**
Steve Ditko

**LETTERER**
Art Simek

**MAIN CHARACTERS: Spider-Man; Aunt May Parker; Uncle Ben Parker; The Burglar**
**MAIN SUPPORTING CHARACTERS: Sally; Flash Thompson; Crusher Hogan**
**MAIN LOCATIONS: Midtown High School; the Parker residence; Science exhibit, New York City; wrestling arena, New York City; TV studio, New York City; Acme warehouse, Queens, New York**

## BACKGROUND

Faced with the prospect of cancellation, the publisher of *Amazing Fantasy*, a comic packed with alien and monster stories, had nothing to lose when he agreed to let Stan Lee and Steve Ditko introduce a new and unconventional Super Hero to the world. In a mere eleven pages, writer-editor Stan Lee and artist Steve Ditko spun a tale that would take most current comic book writers around six issues to weave. It was to become the most famous story in Spider-Man's history: his origin.

Lee, together with Ditko, set the stage for Spider-Man's career by focusing on the true star, Peter Parker. Unlike many other comics of the day, which relied on super-heroics to lure in readers, Lee wanted his protagonist to be an everyman, an easily relatable high school student, who had to deal with the typical problems and troubles of adolescence outside of the hectic world of crime fighting.

And Lee and Ditko were right. Something in this tidy little piece of storytelling and artistry struck a chord with the readers, and although this was the last issue of *Amazing Fantasy*, the web-slinger proved so popular that less than a year later he was granted his own ongoing comic, *The Amazing Spider-Man*.

"If only I had stopped him when I **could** have! But I **didn't**—and now—Uncle Ben—is dead..."

**PETER PARKER**

## THE STORY

**When bitten by a radioactive spider at a science exhibit, bookworm Peter Parker is transformed into the mysterious teen powerhouse sensation known as the amazing Spider-Man.**

His classmates called him a "professional wallflower." The girls rejected him and the boys ridiculed and berated him every chance they got. But little did the students of Midtown High realize that soon enough they'd be calling Peter Parker "amazing."

But Peter's life wasn't all bad. Back in his modest Forest Hills home, Peter Parker had a support system in the form of his elderly Uncle Ben and Aunt May (**1**). Their kindness meant the world to him, and with their guidance, he often buried himself in his schoolwork, trying his best to ignore the cruel taunts of his high school peers (**2**).

On one such day, Peter was escaping his troubles at a science exhibit in New York City on radiology. Unbeknownst to the teen, a spider dangled into an active experiment, got doused by radioactive rays, and then bit Peter Parker on his hand (**3**). Feeling strange, Peter left the exhibit and wandered into the street, not noticing a car careering toward him. As if by instinct, the young man suddenly leapt out of the way, and managed to adhere to the side of a neighboring building (**4**).

After he accidentally crunched a steel pipe in his hand as if it were paper, Peter realized that the dying spider must have gifted him with an amazing new set of abilities (**5**). This was the opportunity he'd waited his entire life for. He quickly began to take advantage of his new powers, entering himself in an open-call wrestling match against a hulking brute called Crusher Hogan (**6**). Not wanting to reveal his identity to the general public, Peter donned a cheap mask as a disguise, and then easily defeated the wrestler in true showboat fashion. The match led to the cash prize, which led to Peter nabbing a publicity agent, which in turn led to the next big chapter in his life.

Peter crafted a bright costume and used his scientific knowledge to concoct wrist shooters and a revolutionary web-like adhesive (**7**). He dubbed himself Spider-Man and it wasn't long before he was starring in his own TV special. Happily strolling backstage after the first day's filming, Peter ignored the cries for help from a nearby policeman, and allowed a fleeing burglar to run right past him, unimpeded (**8**). It was a small incident, and Peter Parker assumed that it wasn't his problem.

Instead, Peter continued his career as Spider-Man, becoming a TV star and a national sensation. However, one night, when Peter was returning home from a personal appearance as Spider-Man, he was startled to find a police car parked in front of his house. The young man soon discovered his beloved Uncle Ben had been murdered (**9**), and that the culprit was held up at the Acme warehouse at the waterfront. In a fit of rage, Peter donned his Spider-Man costume, and swung across town to the dilapidated old building. The warehouse was surrounded by police, but they were powerless—the killer had plenty of places to hide and he would be able to pick them off one by one if they charged. Realizing it was only a matter of time before darkness fell, Spider-Man sprang into action. He quickly used his powers to capture and beat the criminal (**10**), only to discover that the man was the same burglar he had let escape from the TV studio just a few days earlier.

After webbing up the criminal for the police to find, Peter Parker walked slowly into the moonlight, overwhelmed with grief and guilt (**11**) and learning the most important lesson of his life: "With great power there must also come—great responsibility!"

# THE COSTUME

It was originally supposed to be just a simple stage costume. But when Spider-Man made the transition from show business to Super Hero, his famous red and blue attire soon became one of the most recognizable and celebrated costumes in the world. Peter Parker used his scientific expertise to create an ingenious costume with complex web-shooters and mask, and a belt packed with essential gadgets.

## THE FIRST SPIDEY SUIT

When Peter Parker first designed his costume it wasn't for crime fighting. He essentially just needed an exciting look for his stage act. After learning that Midtown High's dance class was throwing out some old bodysuits, he slipped into the school after dark and found one that fit him. A few hours later, he had silk-screened a web pattern on the suit and made a skintight pair of gloves and boots. And Spider-Man was born.

As it turned out, Peter's knack for science was arguably rivaled by his design sense.

Peter Parker created eyepieces using one-way mirrors he found in his school's drama class's prop box. These eyepieces hide Spider-Man's identity without hindering his vision.

While a full mask hides Peter's face from the world, it also plants a seed of distrust in the minds of the general public.

## THE MASK

Born out of a need to hide his true identity, Spider-Man's mask might just be the most essential part of his uniform. The mask is thin and light, composed of a synthetic stretch fabric that matches the rest of his costume. While the lightweight material may come in handy on hot summer days, it can be prone to ripping, which is a problem that Peter always has to keep at the back of his mind while battling foes. A close encounter with the Lizard's claws or Kraven the Hunter's knife could expose his identity for the world to see, and put the lives of his loved ones in jeopardy.

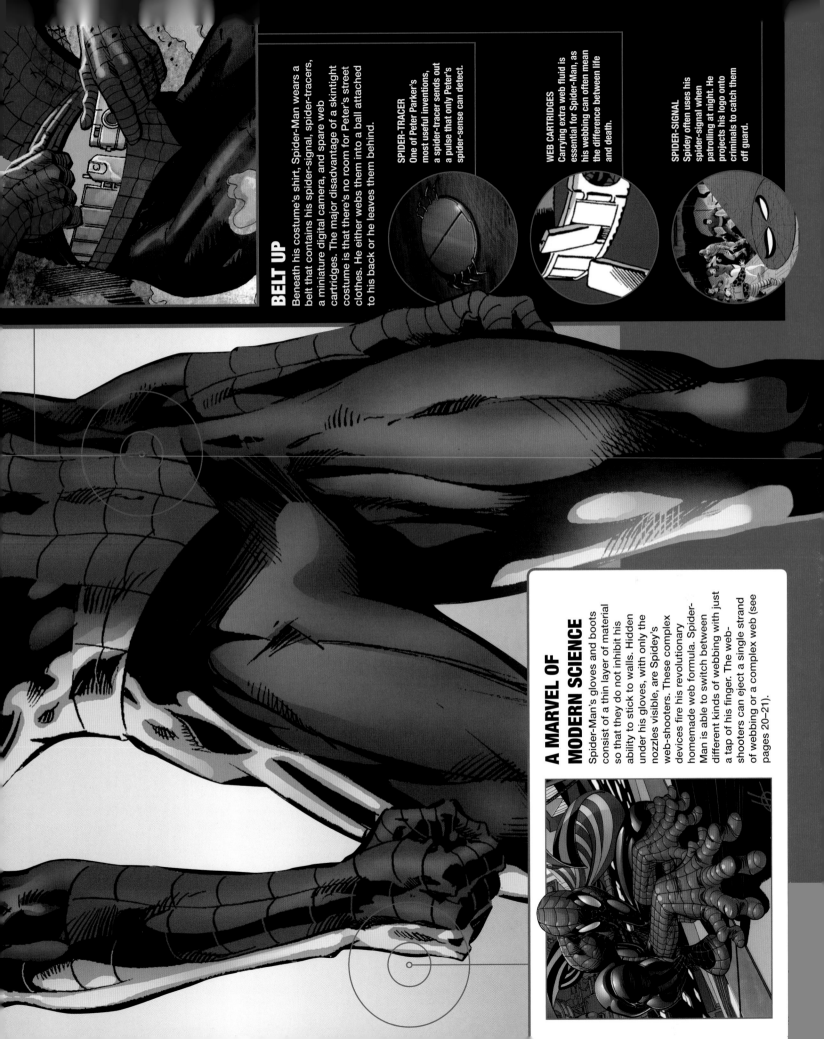

## BELT UP

Beneath his costume's shirt, Spider-Man wears a belt that contains his spider-signal, spider-tracers, a miniature digital camera, and spare web cartridges. The major disadvantage of a skintight costume is that there's no room for Peter's street clothes. He either webs them into a ball attached to his back or he leaves them behind.

**SPIDER-TRACER**
One of Peter Parker's most useful inventions, a spider-tracer sends out a pulse that only Peter's spider-sense can detect.

**WEB CARTRIDGES**
Carrying extra web fluid is essential for Spider-Man, as his webbing can often mean the difference between life and death.

**SPIDER-SIGNAL**
Spidey often uses his spider-signal when patrolling at night. He projects his logo onto criminals to catch them off guard.

## A MARVEL OF MODERN SCIENCE

Spider-Man's gloves and boots consist of a thin layer of material so that they do not inhibit his ability to stick to walls. Hidden under his gloves, with only the nozzles visible, are Spidey's web-shooters. These complex devices fire his revolutionary homemade web formula. Spider-Man is able to switch between different kinds of webbing with just a tap of his finger. The web-shooters can eject a single strand of webbing or a complex web (see pages 20–21).

With one of the most eye-catching costumes in all of Super Hero-dom, one would think Spider-Man wouldn't need to alter his uniform's iconic appearance. However, Peter Parker isn't above adopting a new suit if it will give him an advantage in a fight. From an insulated costume to protect himself from electricity, to a suit made of a living alien creature, Spider-Man's wardrobe has seen as many changes as the hero himself.

## ARMORED COSTUME

Peter once donned a steel-plated version of his costume to battle a heavily armed team of villains known as the New Enforcers. The uniform was actually a pseudo-metallic composition that Peter created in the laboratories of Empire State University. But while the armor protected Spider-Man from heavy-caliber firearms, it greatly hindered his agility, and slowed him down. The suit was eventually destroyed by acid in battle.

## STEALTH SUIT

Using the technology at Horizon Labs, Spider-Man developed a version of his costume that could be completely invisible by warping light and sound. The costume came equipped with lenses that allowed Spider-Man to see his own hands and feet, making movements much easier. The stealth suit was also completely impervious to sonic attacks.

## BULLETPROOF COSTUME

After losing his spider-sense and getting shot with a bullet, Spider-Man used the facilities at Horizon Labs to create a bulletproof version of his costume. Flexible enough to not hinder Spider-Man's movement, the suit also employed magnetic webbing that fired out of the top of Spider-Man's wrists and blocked all radio frequencies.

## FF UNIFORM

After Johnny Storm died, Spider-Man took his place as the fourth core member of the FF (the Future Foundation—the new incarnation of the Fantastic Four). Spidey was given a costume made of third generation unstable molecules, which could change design at will and had a black and white default setting. Although Spider-Man thought that the costume looked too much like the symbiote worn by his enemy Anti-Venom, being on the team meant so much to Spidey that he continued to wear the FF suit, keeping his complaints to a bare minimum.

## WRESTLER COSTUME

Before Peter Parker had devised the costume and concept of Spider-Man, he first donned a mesh mask to hide his identity when he entered an open call wrestling match against hulking brute Crusher Hogan. Although the mesh mask worked as a disguise, it wouldn't cut it in the glamorous world of show business, and Peter went on to create his iconic blue and red costume.

## COSMIC SPIDER-MAN

When a lab accident exposed Peter to an unknown energy source, his powers were upgraded and so was his costume. His new powers included flight, enhanced strength and senses, and the ability to shoot energy from his fingertips. In reality, the mysterious extra-dimensional entity known as the Enigma Force had bestowed upon Spider-Man its fabled Uni-Power, briefly turning Spidey into the latest in a long line of champions dubbed Captain Universe.

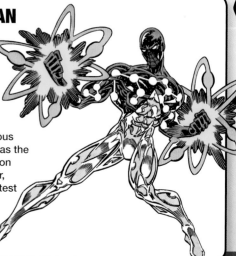

## THE KNOCKOFF

On one occasion, when he was without his actual costume, Peter Parker was forced to take on the villain Overdrive while wearing a store-bought Halloween version of his famous uniform.

## ALIEN COSTUME

Peter acquired his black costume while fighting on a far-off planet called Battleworld. This suit had a seemingly endless supply of webbing, and could change its appearance instantly. It seemed to respond to Peter's thoughts, and would slip over him whenever he wanted to go out web-swinging. But Peter eventually learned that the costume was an alien symbiote that wanted to form a permanent attachment to him. Even though he ultimately abandoned the alien suit, Spider-Man wore a cloth version for a time, given to him by the Black Cat.

## AMAZING BAG-MAN

Stranded without clothes after discovering that his black costume was actually an alien symbiote, Peter found himself at the mercy of Human Torch. Unable to resist a joke at Spidey's expense, Johnny Storm let Spider-Man borrow a uniform that wasn't quite up to the wall-crawler's usual standards—although Johnny had a spare Fantastic Four costume, they were apparently short on masks.

## SCARLET SPIDER

When Spider-Man's clone Ben Reilly returned to New York after years of travelling, he decided he couldn't escape his responsibility, and took up the identity of the Scarlet Spider. With a modified spider hoodie he'd purchased from a museum gift shop, and exterior web-shooters with a matching cartridge belt, Ben made his triumphant return to the Super Hero scene.

## REILLY'S COSTUME

Peter Parker retired from costumed crime fighting for a brief time and turned over his duties to his clone Ben Reilly. Ben designed his own version of Peter's classic costume, with a much larger spider on his chest and a different design on his pants. As well as redesigning the web-shooters, he invented new weapons to add to his personal arsenal.

## SIX-ARMED SPIDEY

At one point in his career, Peter's image drastically changed. In an attempt to live a normal life, Peter had developed a formula to remove his powers. Even though it hadn't been tested, he drank the liquid. When he came around, Peter felt a pain in his sides. He looked down as four extra arms burst through his costume! Peter turned to his friend Dr. Curt Connors, who helped him to develop a cure.

## IRON SPIDER

In a campaign to win Peter Parker's favor, Tony Stark developed an "Iron Spider" costume made specifically for Peter's heroic needs. Able to deflect bullets, camouflage itself, and pick up radio frequencies, the suit gave Spider-Man key advantages in his war against crime, including a few extra arm-like appendages that extended out of the suit's back. While Peter eventually rejected the suit when he and Tony fell out over the Super Hero Civil War, the technology was later adapted by a group of government agents called the Scarlet Spiders.

Though Spider-Man tends to focus on his hands and feet when climbing up a wall, every part of his body has the same clinging ability.

He has the proportionate strength of a spider, the ability to adhere to nearly any surface, and an almost supernatural sense of when danger is approaching. But that's just the beginning of Spider-Man's amazing arachnid powers. His enhanced reflexes, speed, agility, and quick-healing abilities all combine to mean that Spider-Man ranks right up there with the most powerful of all the Super Heroes.

# WITH GREAT POWER...

## STRENGTH

Although not as strong as the Hulk, the mighty Thor, or even the Thing, your friendly neighborhood web-slinger should not be underestimated. He can bend a solid iron bar with his bare hands, lift almost 10 tons, and shatter a concrete wall with a single punch. And in a single, spider-powered spring, he can leap the height of three stories or the width of a highway.

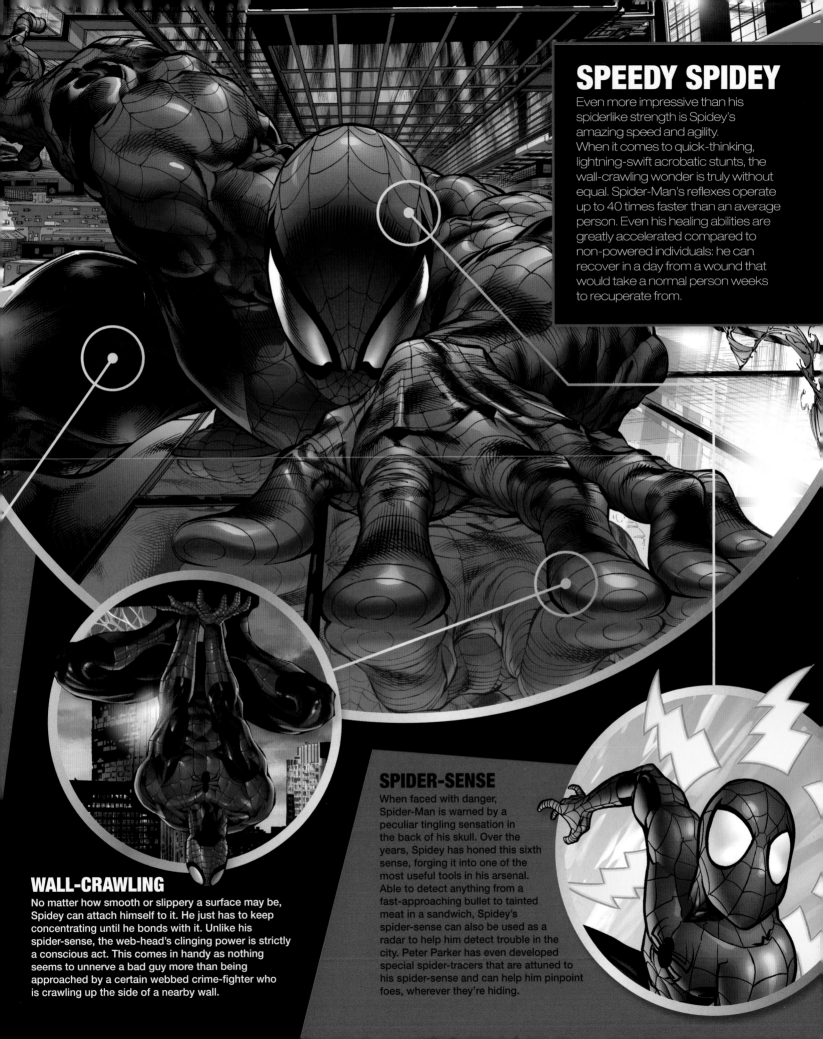

## SPEEDY SPIDEY

Even more impressive than his spiderlike strength is Spidey's amazing speed and agility. When it comes to quick-thinking, lightning-swift acrobatic stunts, the wall-crawling wonder is truly without equal. Spider-Man's reflexes operate up to 40 times faster than an average person. Even his healing abilities are greatly accelerated compared to non-powered individuals: he can recover in a day from a wound that would take a normal person weeks to recuperate from.

## SPIDER-SENSE

When faced with danger, Spider-Man is warned by a peculiar tingling sensation in the back of his skull. Over the years, Spidey has honed this sixth sense, forging it into one of the most useful tools in his arsenal. Able to detect anything from a fast-approaching bullet to tainted meat in a sandwich, Spidey's spider-sense can also be used as a radar to help him detect trouble in the city. Peter Parker has even developed special spider-tracers that are attuned to his spider-sense and can help him pinpoint foes, wherever they're hiding.

## WALL-CRAWLING

No matter how smooth or slippery a surface may be, Spidey can attach himself to it. He just has to keep concentrating until he bonds with it. Unlike his spider-sense, the web-head's clinging power is strictly a conscious act. This comes in handy as nothing seems to unnerve a bad guy more than being approached by a certain webbed crime-fighter who is crawling up the side of a nearby wall.

# THE WEB HE WEAVES

Every spider needs a web, and Spider-Man is no exception. Although the radioactive spider that bit Peter Parker granted the young man many of the natural skills and strength of arachnids, it didn't give him the ability to produce webbing. Peter had to do that the old-fashioned way, with hard work and incredible ingenuity.

## WEB FLUID

When Peter set out to create a web of his own, he used his high school's science laboratory after hours. Having studied multi-polymer compounds for a few years, he produced an adhesive fluid capable of imitating a spider's silk webbing. Extremely strong and durable, the web would dissolve after around one hour. While it would be no good as a practical adhesive to sell to chemical companies, the fluid was perfect for temporarily binding enemies of Spider-Man or swinging around the city.

## WEB-SHOOTERS

While his web fluid was revolutionary and a marvel of modern chemistry, Peter didn't stop there. Without a way to fire his webs, Spider-Man was back to square one. As a solution to this problem, Peter designed two web-shooters that snap onto his wrists and can be fired by pressing his fingers to his palms. But not wanting to accidentally fire them every time he made a fist, Peter rigged the trigger so that he must tap twice in rapid succession, like a PC's mouse, to release his webbing.

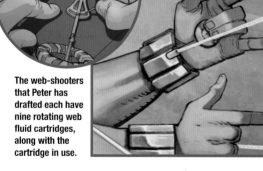

The web-shooters that Peter has drafted each have nine rotating web fluid cartridges, along with the cartridge in use.

Underneath Spidey's costume is a belt that he designed to not only hold his camera and spider-signal, but also 30 extra cartridges of web fluid.

Spider-Man's web hardens upon exposure to air. Given sufficient thickness, one strand could bind the incredible Hulk and hold him prisoner, so Spidey rarely worries about it snapping under his own weight.

## WEBMASTER

Always improving his technology, Spider-Man can now switch between different forms of webbing by the way he taps his trigger. With a short second tap he releases a thin cable-like strand that is perfect for web-swinging. A longer tap increases the strand's thickness for additional support, for example when binding a powerful foe like Norman Osborn. A series of brisk taps discharges many thin strands that form a fine spray, also good for blinding an opponent. If Spidey prolongs pressure on the trigger, web fluid squirts out in the form of an adhesive liquid.

## ORGANIC WEBS

After a battle with the mysterious Queen, Spider-Man found himself transformed into a giant spider. While he was eventually able to change back into his old self, his brief metamorphosis was not without consequence. For some unknown reason, Spider-Man was then able to produce webbing from his own body. While it relieved some of the stress in Peter's daily life due to the fact that he no longer had to save up money to purchase the expensive chemicals needed for his webbing supply, the change was a bit off-putting for the wall-crawler, making him feel a little less human. This ability has faded away recently, however, and the details of the power loss remain a mystery.

After many hours of practice, Spidey has trained himself to use his webbing without conscious thought.

## "SO, THEY LAUGHED AT ME FOR BEING A BOOKWORM, EH? WELL, ONLY A SCIENCE MAJOR COULD HAVE CREATED A DEVICE LIKE THIS!"

PETER PARKER

## A WEB FOR ALL SEASONS

Over the years, Spider-Man has developed quite a few other uses for his webbing. He can easily use the webbing to form shapes like web-balls, bats, and bolos. Spider-Man has also been known to create more complex articles such as rafts, hang gliders, and skis. In addition, Spidey's normal webbing is also fairly heat-resistant and can easily withstand temperatures of 1,000°F (550°C). As a result, he's been known to wrap his fists in webbing as insulation to combat some of his more "hot-headed" foes. For extreme cases, he's even developed a webbing that resists temperatures of up to 10,000°F (5500°C).

# PETER PARKER

The true face of Spider-Man, Peter Parker has seen more tragedy in his young life than most people three times his age. Racked with guilt and stress, Peter still often boasts a smile on his face, even though it's normally hidden by a skin-tight red mask.

## PETER'S CHILDHOOD

Peter Parker was only a young boy when his parents, Richard and Mary Parker, died in a plane crash. He immediately moved in with his father's older brother and wife. Ben and May Parker were an elderly couple with no children of their own, and they raised Peter as if he were their son, but they rarely spoke about Peter's real parents. Peter became convinced that his parents had left him because of something he had done. Afraid of being abandoned, Peter worked hard to win his aunt and uncle's approval—though he didn't have to worry. Ben and May truly loved their nephew and would have done anything to please him.

As he grew older, Peter showed little interest in the hobbies of his peers. Although he would attend the occasional Mets game with his Uncle Ben, he never displayed any athletic prowess of his own. In fact, before he gained his spider-powers, Peter Parker had considerably less than average strength for a boy of his age. He had a fear of heights, too—even getting a book from the top shelf in the library resulted in his suffering severe symptoms of vertigo. He seemed ill-equipped for the often-harsh reality of teenage life.

When Peter's parents, Richard and Mary, were reported dead, Ben and May welcomed the orphaned child into their lives. The couple were living on a low income and had to make many sacrifices for the boy.

Peter's Uncle Ben enjoyed sharing his extensive comic collection with his nephew. Peter spent hours reading about courageous heroes and dreamed of being a costumed adventurer like Captain America, striking terror into the hearts of criminals.

## MIDTOWN HIGH

In high school, Peter was an honor student, and his teachers thought very highly of him. The other students, however, had little time for a know-it-all like "Puny Parker." The girls thought he was quiet, and the boys considered him a wimp. Peter was painfully shy, and some of his fellow classmates misinterpreted his silence for snobbery. He had trouble making friends, but he never stopped trying. He often invited other students to join him at science exhibits or monster movies. But they usually responded with ridicule and almost never asked him to join them. But as he began his secret career as Spider-Man, Peter found a renewed sense of self-confidence, one his classmates slowly began to acknowledge.

**"I WISH I COULD BE A SUPER HERO. IT MUST FEEL SO GREAT TO BE ADMIRED BY THE POLICE AND THE PRESS..."**
PETER PARKER

## COLLEGE STUDENT

Peter Parker graduated from Midtown High with the highest scholastic average in the school's history. He was thrilled to discover that he had won a full scholarship to Empire State University. Now secure in who he was, Peter immersed himself in his scientific studies despite web-swinging and a hectic social life. After graduating, Peter even took a job as a teaching assistant on campus to continue his postgraduate studies. Peter has never stopped learning and innovating, something that has served him incredibly well in his other life as the amazing Spider-Man.

Spider-Man ruined Peter's university graduation. In the week before the ceremony, Spidey was battling the Green Goblin and the Rocket Racer. He couldn't graduate with the rest of his class since he'd missed a required gym class.

## THE MAN BEHIND THE MASK

Throughout his career as Spider-Man, Peter has always been torn between his sense of duty and the mixed feelings he has received from the public. This reception has varied from praise to outright condemnation. It has even driven him to the brink of despair, causing him to throw away his costume and renounce his alter ego. Nevertheless, his dedication to using his powers responsibly has always led to Peter donning his mask again in the hope that some day the world will learn to appreciate Spider-Man.

While Peter may have mastered the art of the quick change over the years, he finds it hard switching between his civilian and Super Hero identities, and often wishes he could just live a normal life.

# FRIENDS & FAMILY

While Spider-Man has many trusted allies in his life as a hero, Peter Parker's world wouldn't be one worth fighting for without his family and circle of friends. In addition to former girlfriends turned lifelong companions, such as Betty Brant and Mary Jane Watson, Peter has had many people in his life who truly care about him. And even through difficult times, Peter has stood by those people closest to him.

## UNCLE BEN PARKER

Born in Brooklyn, New York to a struggling working-class family, Ben Parker was a bright and happy boy who grew to never truly lose his inner child. He had a vivid imagination, collected comic books, and read science fiction—qualities and passions that he passed on to his nephew Peter, son of Ben's younger brother, Richard. After the tragic death of Peter's parents, Ben and his wife May took the young Peter in and raised him as their own. Loving and encouraging, Ben was Peter's best friend. It was Ben who instilled Peter with the knowledge that with great power, also comes great responsibility. And, ultimately, it was Ben's shocking death that inspired Spider-Man to become a hero.

## RICHARD & MARY PARKER

Secretly operatives for the C.I.A., Peter's parents Richard and Mary Parker tried their best to give their only son as normal an upbringing as possible. But having been recruited by super spy Nick Fury, Richard had to have known that a normal life was going to be nearly impossible to accomplish. With adventures that involved fighting alongside heroes, including the man who would become known as Wolverine, Richard and Mary lived a dangerous life. And it was a life that was cut dramatically short when they died in a plane crash when Peter was just a young boy.

## AUNT MAY JAMESON

May Parker didn't hesitate when she and her husband Ben were asked to take care of their nephew Peter for a few months while his parents were away on a business trip. And even more amazingly, she didn't balk at her new set of responsibilities when Peter's parents were killed and she and Ben became the boy's legal guardians. Instead she saw taking care of Peter as an opportunity to achieve her lifelong dream of becoming a parent.

But with so much death in her life, May couldn't help but be overprotective of Peter Parker. While she showered him with love every chance she had, she also worried constantly about his health and wellbeing, an almost obsessive behavior that grew even worse after Ben was murdered. These days, May has finally learned to relax, a quality she's picked up from her new husband, J. Jonah Jameson Sr.

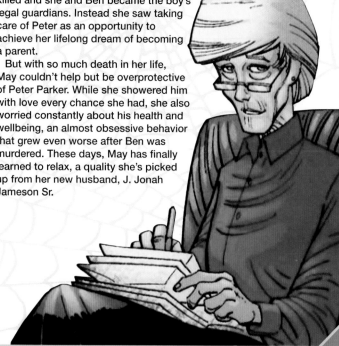

## RANDY ROBERTSON

Peter Parker met Randy Robertson during his days as a college student at Empire State University. Introduced by Randy's father and Peter's employer Joe Robertson of the *Daily Bugle*, Randy and Peter hit it off and began a friendship that continues to this day. Originally a political activist and avid protestor, Randy's personality has mellowed over the years, and he has gone from a career in social work to that of an actor. Lately, Randy has been dating one of Peter's friends at the *Daily Bugle*, Norah Winters.

## FLASH THOMPSON

Peter Parker didn't have many friends in high school, and one of the main reasons for that, was the work of his greatest adversary, Eugene "Flash" Thompson. An all-round athlete, gifted with good looks and popularity, high school bully Flash enjoyed making Peter's life miserable, ironically even as he was a staunch supporter of Spider-Man. While Peter and Flash clashed repeatedly, their animosity would blossom into friendship when they later found themselves attending the same college. While not above giving Peter a hard time on occasion, Flash is very aware of how loyal a friend Peter has become, sticking by him even through his troubles with alcohol and the terrible wartime injury that cost Flash his ability to walk.

## VIN GONZALES

Vin Gonzales, a tough New York City cop, was Peter Parker's roommate. But he is not a fan of Spider-Man. While Peter's and Vin's friendship was a bit rocky from the start due to Peter's secret escapades as Spider-Man, it got worse when Vin was discovered as part of a conspiracy to frame the wall-crawler. Vin was sentenced to jail time and Peter began dating the object of Vin's affection, Carlie Cooper. But despite their differences, Vin shares Peter's sense of responsibility, and willingly paid the price for his actions.

## HARRY OSBORN

When Harry Osborn first met Peter Parker at college, Peter snubbed him completely. Always lost in his own world of worry, at the time Peter was more concerned about the health of his sickly aunt than meeting classmates at his new college. But Harry gave him the benefit of the doubt and a second chance, and the two became fast friends. They later even became roommates when Harry's father, the wealthy mogul Norman Osborn, paid for the boys' luxury apartment. Peter has seen Harry through several serious problems, including a lingering drug addiction, as well as a life as the heir to the Super Villain legacy of the Green Goblin. While many people would have given up hope in their friend years ago, Peter has always done just the opposite, convinced that Harry Osborn is truly worth saving.

## J. JONAH JAMESON SR.

Peter first met J. Jonah Jameson Sr. as Spider-Man when the villainous Shocker trapped the two in a subway train alongside several other innocent bystanders. Peter was impressed by the man then, and continued to be impressed with him as he stayed in Peter's life and eventually married his aunt. Always approving of Jay and May's relationship, Peter has a hard time understanding how such an honorable man like Jay Jameson could sire a child as scheming and self-centered as J. Jonah Jameson Jr., publisher of the *Daily Bugle* and Spider-Man's worst critic.

March 1963

# THE AMAZING SPIDER-MAN #1

*"We cannot allow that masked menace to take the law into his own hands! He is a bad influence on our youngsters!"*

J. JONAH JAMESON

**MAIN CHARACTERS:** Spider-Man; Aunt May Parker; J. Jonah Jameson; John Jameson; the Chameleon; Mr. Fantastic; Invisible Girl; the Human Torch; the Thing

**MAIN SUPPORTING CHARACTERS:** The Burglar; Professor Newton

**MAIN LOCATIONS:** The Parker residence; unnamed rocket launch site; the Baxter Building; unnamed defence installation, New York City; the Chameleon's secret hideout; unnamed waterfront, New York City

**EDITOR-IN-CHIEF**
Stan Lee

**COVER ARTISTS**
Jack Kirby and Steve Ditko

**WRITER**
Stan Lee

**PENCILER**
Steve Ditko

**INKER**
Steve Ditko

**LETTERERS**
Johnny Dee
and John Duffi

## BACKGROUND

Picking up right where they left off in *Amazing Fantasy* #15 (August 1962), writer-editor Stan Lee and artist Steve Ditko took Spider-Man out for another web-spin in the debut issue of the character's ongoing comic book series, *The Amazing Spider-Man*. The debut issue featured two self-contained stories. The lead story was a fairly standard adventure, and while it boasted the first appearance of the recurring thorn in Peter Parker's side, J. Jonah Jameson, it wasn't the reason most readers were buying the issue.

That honor fell to the second story, featuring the first-ever meeting of Spider-Man and the famous Fantastic Four. Already a hit in Stan Lee's new era of Marvel Comics, the Fantastic Four were also featured on the cover as a clever marketing strategy. Not only did their appearance solidify the fact that Spider-Man operated in the shared Marvel Universe, but it also succeeded in coaxing some of the Fantastic Four's fans to give Spider-Man a try. And if the resultant success of *The Amazing Spider-Man* is any indication, most of those fans stuck around for the long haul.

"I came up here to join up with you! I wanna be a member of the **Fantastic Four!**"

**SPIDER-MAN**

## THE STORIES

**Spider-Man saves the life of astronaut John Jameson, despite the smear campaign against the hero, orchestrated by John's father, J. Jonah Jameson. In the second story, Spidey meets the Fantastic Four for the first time before battling the enigmatic Chameleon.**

Being Spider-Man was quickly proving more trouble than Peter Parker had imagined. Not only could Spider-Man not cash the checks he made for his TV appearances (he would need identification to do so), but also the publisher of the *Daily Bugle*, J. Jonah Jameson, was actively delivering lectures all over town about the supposed threat Spider-Man posed to the citizens of his city (**1**). While many believed Jameson's campaign was merely a publicity stunt to draw in new readers and promote his son, astronaut John Jameson, Spider-Man nevertheless saw his career in showbiz take a brutal nosedive.

However, while attending the launch of John Jameson's space shuttle (**2**), Peter stood by in witness as John lost control of the craft due to a technical malfunction. Realizing what had happened, the officials at ground control tried, unsuccessfully, to think of a way to save the space shuttle (**3**). But Peter Parker was no longer content to sit idly by when faced with the opportunity to help others in need. Peter changed swiftly into his Spider-Man costume (**4**), and commandeering a plane and its pilot from a nearby airfield, used a web-line to swing aboard the capsule (**5**). He attached a space guidance unit he'd been given by a military official to the capsule (**6**). With Spider-Man's help, John landed the craft safely, and Peter returned home, only to discover that J. Jonah Jameson had increased his anti-Spider-Man agenda, claiming the web-slinger had deliberately put John's mission in harm's way in order to rescue him in a public arena (**7**). It seemed Spider-Man had had his first run in with the all too infamous "Parker luck."

In the issue's second feature, Peter Parker was no closer to helping his poor aunt pay her bills. But there were other heroes who didn't seem to share Peter's financial woes. Spider-Man headed to the world-famous Baxter Building in an attempt to meet and join the fabled Fantastic Four.

Of course, one doesn't just waltz into the Fantastic Four's home and say "hello." In order to meet with the heroes, Spider-Man broke into their headquarters, bypassing their security safeguards (**8**). An alarm sounded and the Fantastic Four saw that it was Spider-Man who was breaking in (**9**). They weren't pleased that a "teenage show-off" thought he could take them by surprise. A violent clash ensued (**10**), until Spider-Man was able to plead his case. He had wanted to prove to them that he had what it takes to be a member of the Fantastic Four. Spidey's mission had been made in vain, however, as the team informed him that they didn't receive a salary for their heroics.

Meanwhile, the mysterious master of disguise and Super Villain known as the Chameleon (**11**) decided to capitalize on Spider-Man's outlaw status with the press. After devising his own artificial web-shooting gun, the Chameleon stole prized missile plans from a government installation, while wearing a replica of Spider-Man's costume (**12**). Despite the clever frame-up, Spider-Man managed to track the villain to the waterfront, and was just about to return him to the authorities (**13**) when the Chameleon disappeared. Spidey used his spider-sense to detect that the villain was disguised as one of the cops (**14**), but the real police officers refused to believe that Spider-Man wasn't the criminal. Spider-Man fled in anger, leaving the police officers to figure it out. Spider-Man may have saved the day, but he wished he had never got his superpowers. He was a loner with a tarnished reputation and a laughable bank balance.

# THE DAILY BUGLE

An always-crowded inbox

Joe "Robbie" Robertson

Paper filing system

Breaking news

The latest big stories

Research files

Although it's been through about as many changes as Spider-Man himself, the *Daily Bugle* is one of the world's most trusted tabloid newspapers. The newspaper has been a New York City institution since 1897, and is manned by an ever-changing staff that has included publisher J. Jonah Jameson and photographer Peter Parker.

## A NEW YORK ICON

In letters 30 feet high, the original *Daily Bugle* office proudly displayed its name with a lack of subtlety that could only be matched by the passion of its editorial page and the flamboyance of its publisher, J. Jonah Jameson. The paper itself is a picture-dominated tabloid that goes for the jugular. Its photos are often graphic and shocking, and its stories are powerful.

Recently, when Jameson suffered a near-fatal heart attack, his wife sold the *Daily Bugle* to publisher Dexter Bennett, who renamed the paper *The DB*. Many of the staff left to work at a new start-up venture, *Front Line*. While Bennett's *The DB* focused on exploitative, paparazzi-styled articles, *Front Line* continued to retain the integrity that the *Daily Bugle* had always been known for.

Spider-Man takes photographs by webbing up an automatic camera in strategic locations before his fights.

## PETER PARKER: ACE PHOTOGRAPHER

J. Jonah Jameson didn't hesitate to buy photos from the teenage Peter Parker, especially since Parker seemed to have a special talent for catching Spider-Man in action. Peter's first pictures appeared in Jameson's early venture, *Now Magazine*, but Jonah soon began to feature his work in the *Daily Bugle*, helping jumpstart the teen's career. Despite Peter's consistent success in getting photos of Spider-Man, Jonah has never discovered the young man's secret.

# THE STAFF

## J.J. JAMESON

He may appear to be a grouchy, self-centered old skinflint on the outside, but peel away his protective layers and you will discover that the real J. Jonah Jameson is actually even worse. The *Daily Bugle* publisher and staunch anti-Spider-Man activist never tires of hearing his own voice, and he'll gladly give you the opinions he thinks you ought to have. Although he no longer works at the *Daily Bugle*, Jameson will undoubtedly be back in the paper business before too long.

Jameson left the newspaper business behind when he became New York City's mayor.

### JOE ROBERTSON
Usually the voice of compassion and reason, Joe Robertson worked as Jameson's right-hand man and conscience, before graduating to become the paper's Editor-in-Chief.

### BETTY BRANT
Peter Parker's first real girlfriend and former *Bugle* secretary, Betty is a talented reporter whose dedication to her job has sometimes cost her her friends.

### NORAH WINTERS
Full of energy and determination, Norah Winters is quickly becoming one of the *Bugle*'s top reporters, and has often partnered Peter Parker.

### FREDERICK FOSWELL
Although a trusted *Daily Bugle* employee, Frederick Foswell led a double life as the criminal mastermind and ringleader known as the Big Man.

### THOMAS FIREHEART
Secretly the vigilante the Puma, Thomas Fireheart once purchased the *Bugle* and wrote pro-Spider-Man articles as a way of paying a perceived debt to the wall-crawler.

### BEN URICH
The *Bugle*'s star reporter and the founder of rival paper, *Front Line*, Urich is an ally of both Spider-Man and Daredevil, and known for his daring stance against corruption.

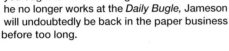

### NED LEEDS
One-time husband of Betty Brant, Ned Leeds served as a reporter for the *Daily Bugle* before being brainwashed into becoming Hobgoblin by the original Hobgoblin.

### DEXTER BENNETT
Purchasing the *Daily Bugle* and renaming it *The DB*, Dexter Bennett seemingly had none of the integrity of his predecessor, J. Jonah Jameson.

### GLORY GRANT
Formerly a secretary to J.J. Jameson and Joe Robertson at the *Daily Bugle*, Glory Grant has moved up in the world, and is now an assistant to Mayor Jameson.

### LANCE BANNON
A photographic rival of Peter Parker's, Lance Bannon had a healthy career under J.J. Jameson due to his unflattering photos of Spider-Man.

### PHIL URICH
Nephew of Ben Urich, Phil has been dabbling in some web reporting for the newest incarnation of the *Bugle*, while moonlighting as the villain Hobgoblin.

### JACOB CONOVER
Another in the long list of corrupt *Daily Bugle* employees, reporter Jacob Conover was known in criminal circles as a ringleader named the Rose.

## *THE DB* BUILDING

Under Dexter Bennett's watch, *The DB* building was attacked and razed by the Super Villain known as Electro. Losing all interest in the business and the expense it would take to get the paper back on its feet, Bennett sold the company back to J. Jonah Jameson. In a moment of almost uncharacteristic generosity, Jameson then gifted the name of the *Daily Bugle* to *Front Line*, instantly giving the underground paper the name recognition it needed.

Although Peter Parker is best known as a photographer, snapping pictures for the *Daily Bugle* was not really his dream profession. With a genius-level scientific intellect and a desire to pass that knowledge onto others, photography was not so much a life goal for Peter, but rather a way for him to earn money to care for his sickly Aunt May and to pay his many bills.

## MR. PARKER

It seems that Peter Parker had always held the idea of being a teacher in the back of his mind. So when the opportunity arose to teach science at his old school, Midtown High, Mr. Parker decided it was the perfect opportunity to make an impact on the lives of other promising students, just as his teachers had made such a difference in his life. Although his teaching career ended sooner than he'd have liked due to the attention he received at the time of the Super Hero Civil War, Spider-Man occasionally subs at the Avengers Academy when he finds himself missing the blackboard.

## THE RIGHT-HAND MAN

As a huge fan of science and its innovators, Peter had long been in awe of his fellow Super Hero and Avenger Tony Stark, also known as the Golden Avenger Iron Man. In the days preceding the controversial Super Hero Civil War, Peter served as Tony's aide of sorts, learning directly from Stark's genius as he accompanied him on trips and lived in Tony's plush Stark Tower.

Peter was shocked to learn that J.J. Jameson was able to release *Webs* without his permission, paying him a paltry $100 "gratitude fee."

## THE RELUCTANT AUTHOR

Peter's career as a photojournalist peaked when a collection of his Spider-Man photographs was released in a hardbound book entitled *Webs: Spider-Man in Action*. While the book was just another money-making stunt by the *Daily Bugle* publisher J. Jonah Jameson, and didn't land Peter any real money, it did give him the opportunity to get paid for a book-signing tour and to enjoy his very own 15 minutes of fame.

Spider-Man made a surprise appearance on the book tour after chasing the jewel thief, Black Fox.

## THE OVERACHIEVER

When Peter decided to continue his education, he became a teaching assistant at Empire State University. Although he often found himself extremely overworked due to juggling life as Spider-Man and also as a photographer, Peter met a lot of good friends through his co-workers and found his work with the undergrads particularly rewarding.

## GLOBE TROTTER

After years of being treated like he was on the lowest rung of the ladder by J.J. Jameson at the *Daily Bugle*, Peter found the respect he deserved for a time as Chief Photographer at the *Daily Globe*. The *Bugle's* biggest rival, the *Globe* is more balanced in its reporting of Spider-Man.

# HORIZON LABS

All through his life, Peter Parker was never able to live up to his full potential when not in costume as Spider-Man. But with the help of J. Jonah Jameson's wife Marla, Peter was given the opportunity to shine when she introduced him to Max Modell, the head of Horizon Labs, a research facility that creates revolutionary technology. After impressing Modell, Peter was offered a job at Horizon's coveted think tank.

Peter proved his merit on a tour of Horizon Labs and landed a job in the inner think tank.

## BEYOND THE HORIZON

Peter's current employer, Horizon Labs, is a state of the art research facility. Laid out in a way to inspire its designers and engineers, the workspace has a social atrium area where its staff can mingle and swap ideas. It also houses the labs of its inner think tank where Horizon's star staffers can indulge in their most bizarre experiments to help the company—and technology— advance. As a member of this inner circle, Peter is free to design new technology for Spider-Man, as well as for the world.

**MAX MODELL**
The man behind Horizon Labs, Max Modell believes Peter is designing Spider-Man's technology, but doesn't know that he is actually the wall-crawler.

**GRADY SCRAPS**
A fellow think tank member, Grady Scraps doesn't seem like the most serious student of the sciences, although his incredible work proves otherwise.

**BELLA FISHBACH**
With an environmentally friendly mind and an eye towards our planet's future, Bella Fishbach is Horizon's resident green specialist, working in the inner think tank.

**SAJANI JAFFREY**
Another member of Horizon Labs' inner think tank, Sajani Jaffrey is the resident xenologist, specializing in alien biology, chemistry, and technology.

**UATU JACKSON**
All-around wonderkid Uatu Jackson graduated from high school at the age of ten before becoming the youngest member of Horizon Labs' think tank.

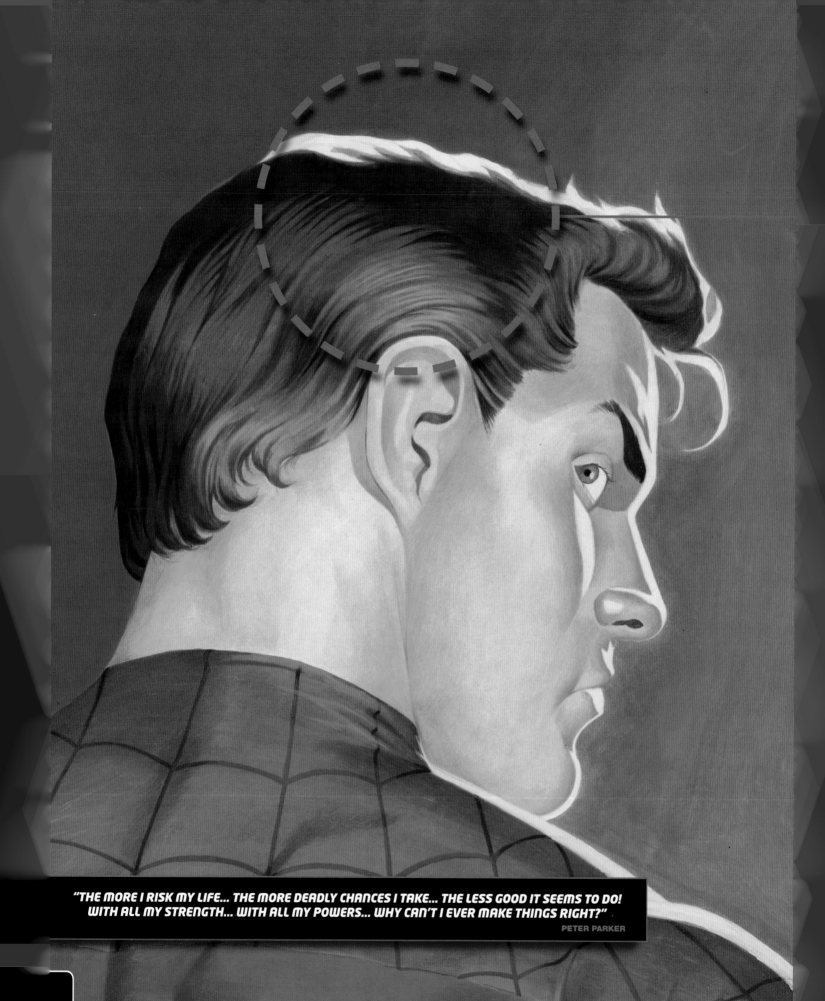

"THE MORE I RISK MY LIFE... THE MORE DEADLY CHANCES I TAKE... THE LESS GOOD IT SEEMS TO DO!
WITH ALL MY STRENGTH... WITH ALL MY POWERS... WHY CAN'T I EVER MAKE THINGS RIGHT?"

PETER PARKER

# PARKER'S PROBLEMS

Compared to fighting Super Villains and narrowly avoiding death as Spider-Man, you would think that life as Peter Parker would be a breeze. But, truth be told, Peter's daily struggles are every bit as challenging as those of his alter ego. It seems Peter is truly cursed with the infamous "Parker Luck."

## GUILT

Since the death of his parents, Peter Parker has been plagued with guilt. Despite having nothing to do with the death of Richard and Mary Parker, young Peter instinctively thought their absence was a result of his behavior. As time passed and Peter lost more of the people in his life, including his beloved Uncle Ben, to tragedies he believed he could have or should have prevented, those issues only intensified.

## GIRLS

Things never seem to be going smoothly in the romance department for Peter Parker. From his early experiences of being shunned by the objects of his affection in high school, to his near marriage to Mary Jane Watson, Peter has had his share of dating troubles. As long as he continues being Spider-Man and having to make up excuses to hide his secret identity, he can only expect more problems in the future.

## AUNT MAY

Having lost his parents and his Uncle Ben at such an early age, Peter has come to realize how much his Aunt May means to him. And unfortunately, May has been plagued with health problems for a good portion of Peter's life. With hospital bills often piled up alongside other accumulated debt, Peter was constantly worried about May's wellbeing, and was forced to take several jobs to help her as best he could.

## SPIDER-MAN

Strangely enough, Peter's biggest problem is probably Spider-Man himself. All Peter ever really wanted was to lead a normal life and be happy. Although he has managed to carve out a lot of happiness amidst the tragedy in his world, Peter has led anything but a normal existence. Compelled to be Spider-Man for the sake of the greater good, Peter is constantly skipping out on friends or loved ones to battle the latest Super Villain or save a family from a towering inferno. Although he loves web-swinging and helping others, Peter knows that his double life is a giant roadblock in his personal life.

February 1966

the AMAZING SPIDER-MAN

MARVEL COMICS GROUP 12¢

33 FEB

IND.

APPROVED BY THE COMICS CODE AUTHORITY

"The FINAL CHAPTER!"

# THE AMAZING SPIDER-MAN #33

"But, I can't give up! I must keep trying! I must!!"

SPIDER-MAN

**EDITOR-IN-CHIEF**
Stan Lee

**COVER ARTISTS**
Jack Kirby and
Steve Ditko

**WRITER**
Stan Lee

**PENCILER**
Steve Ditko

**INKER**
Steve Ditko

**LETTERER**
Art Simek

**MAIN CHARACTERS:** Spider-Man; Aunt May Parker; Dr. Curt Connors; Dr. Octopus; J. Jonah Jameson; Betty Brant
**MAIN SUPPORTING CHARACTERS:** Fredrick Foswell; Bennett Brant; Kraven (cameo)
**MAIN LOCATIONS:** A hospital, New York; Dr. Connor's lab; Dr. Octopus's underwater hideout; the *Daily Bugle* office; various New York City streets

## BACKGROUND

While it might not rival the cliffhangers of TV shows, such as the "Who shot J.R.?" conundrum in *Dallas*, or the mysteries surrounding the premise of the TV hit *Lost*, back in 1965, Spider-Man fans had their own ongoing mystery to ponder. Just who was the enigmatic Master Planner?

A seemingly new player trying his hand at the criminal underworld, the Master Planner emerged in *The Amazing Spider-Man* #31, stationed in an exotic underwater hideout that was staffed with hundreds of minions clad in purple uniforms. While Spidey fans only had to wait until issue #32 to find that the Master Planner was in fact Spider-Man's old foe, Dr. Octopus, by then, the readers were hooked in a multi-part storyline that held the life of Peter Parker's elderly Aunt May in the balance.

However, this wasn't the first time Lee and company had used a mystery to keep readers coming back month after month. Perhaps their most successful attempt had been the question of the secret identity of the recurring villain Green Goblin. The use of these tantalizing subplots only added to the enjoyment of the title, and created a more serialized feel for the issues than the stand-alone comics created by some of Marvel's competitors.

"I've done the best I could, Aunt May!" Now there's nothing left, but prayer–!"

**SPIDER-MAN**

## THE STORY

### Pinned by a seemingly impossible weight, and with his beloved Aunt May's life depending upon his escape, Spider-Man must find the strength to battle his way to safety.

They called the serum ISO-36. An experimental concoction developed on the West Coast, it was reported to help significantly in alleviating radiation poisoning. But to Peter Parker, it was more than just a scientific curiosity. To Peter Parker, ISO-36 was his Aunt May's last hope (**1**).

Weeks earlier, in an effort to help the ailing May, Peter had eagerly volunteered his own blood for a transfusion. At the time, May had recovered completely, but after a while, the radiation in Spider-Man's blood had weakened her, until she was once again hospitalized and at death's door. After visiting the lab of the sometime Lizard, Dr. Curt Connors, Spider-Man learned of ISO-36's existence, and pawned all of his science equipment in order to afford its high cost. Connors arranged for a shipment of the serum from the other side of the country, but neither he nor Peter had any idea that a familiar face from Spider-Man's past had his eye on the experimental formula.

Under the guise of the Master Planner, Dr. Octopus had his men pilfer the serum when it arrived in New York, and deliver it to his secret underwater headquarters. There, Doc Ock planned on continuing his research, hoping to master radiation in an effort to gain even more power. Spider-Man tracked the villain back to his headquarters, but in a violent scuffle, found himself trapped under a pile of heavy machinery, with the canister of ISO-36 just out of his reach, and water slowly leaking in from the damaged structure of the underwater lair (**2**).

Channeling all of his inner strength, and thinking of the life of his Aunt May, and that of his beloved Uncle Ben before her, Spider-Man managed the impossible. Little by little, he began to rise to his feet, lifting the wreckage higher and higher until he was finally free (**3**). Stumbling through the wet chamber with fairly severe injuries and the canister of ISO-36 clasped tightly to his chest (**4**), Spider-Man then fought his way through a flash flood in the underwater chamber, complete with a few of Dr. Octopus's men garbed in scuba gear. Finally emerging into a dry chamber of the headquarters, Spidey was then faced with a dozen more of the villainous henchmen (**5**), before he escaped to the laboratory of Dr. Curt Connors.

Spider-Man worked with Dr. Connors to test the serum (**6**). While Dr. Connors wasn't looking, Spider-Man took a sample of his own radioactive blood. He tested the serum on the sample (**7**), not telling the doctor where or whom it came from. Spider-Man knew that if the serum worked on his own radioactive blood, it should work on his aunt, too. All that remained was to deliver the serum to the hospital, and hope that it would be enough to cure his aunt.

The next two hours of anxious waiting went by in a hazy blur for Peter Parker. Spider-Man returned to the warehouse to discover the Master Planner's gang were still out cold (**8**). He alerted the police and snapped pictures of the arrest of the henchmen (**9**). He delivered them to the *Daily Bugle* and into the ecstatic hands of its publisher, J. Jonah Jameson (**10**).

But the time did indeed pass, and soon enough Peter was at the hospital by his aunt's side. The doctors told Peter that Spider-Man's serum had stopped the blood deterioration, and that his dear aunt was going to pull through. Aunt May woke briefly, squeezed Peter's hand, and even smiled (**11**). Spider-Man had won this battle. While baffled doctors pondered how Spider-Man fitted into this all, Peter Parker headed home to finally allow himself some much-needed rest.

# When a SPIDER-MAN *Loves* a Woman

To hear Peter Parker tell it, he's never had a lucky day in his life. But for someone who sees himself to be the victim of constant bad fortune, both Peter and his alias Spider-Man have certainly had more than their fair share of romantic encounters. With so many women vying for Peter's attention, it's hard not to see Spider-Man as one of the luckiest Super Heroes in the universe.

## MARCY KANE

Back when Peter Parker was a teaching assistant at Empire State University, he met and briefly dated Marcy Kane, a graduate student. What Peter wasn't aware of at the time was that Marcy was actually an alien from the planet Contraxia. She had been sent to Earth to try to find a method to save her star system.

## LIZ ALLAN

Liz Allan was one of the most popular and attractive girls at Peter's school, Midtown High. She developed a crush on Peter as the shy and bookish teen slowly grew out of his shell. However, their flirtation fizzled into friendship territory, and she later went on to date and marry Peter's friend Harry Osborn, with whom she had a son, Normie.

## DEBRA WHITMAN

Debra Whitman desperately wanted her relationship with her fellow graduate student Peter Parker to develop into something more than friendship, but Peter never realized how much she truly liked him. Although they went on several dates, their romance never reached the committed level that Debra was hoping for, partly due to Peter's hectic secret life as Spider-Man.

## Betty Brant

Peter's first steady girlfriend Betty Brant entered his life when he was viewed as just a shy bookworm by his fellow high school classmates. Forced to drop out of high school and become a secretary at the *Daily Bugle* to support her family, Betty understood and empathized with Peter's worries. They fell in love, but Peter's dual identity took its toll on their relationship. Unhappy with the risks Peter seemed to be taking for his job as a photographer, Betty began dating reporter Ned Leeds.

Although Peter's relationship with Betty Brant ended, the two remained dedicated friends.

The one-time fiancée of Peter Parker, Mary Jane Watson will forever be "the one that got away."

## Mary Jane Watson

Peter Parker certainly hit the jackpot when it came to Mary Jane Watson. The beautiful niece of Peter's neighbor and Aunt May's best friend Anna Watson, Mary Jane discovered Peter's dual identity even before they went on their first date. Hiding under the façade of a fun-loving party girl, MJ was more complicated than she'd ever let on, a fact adult Peter only discovered when they finally began their years-long romance.

## SARAH RUSHMAN

Sarah Rushman, a waitress and student at Empire State University, met Peter at a party, and the two decided to go out on a date. However, their affair quickly ended when Peter discovered that Rushman was actually the violent mutant known as Marrow. She had been brainwashed into her civilian identity of Sarah Rushman by the government intelligence agency S.H.I.E.L.D.

## Gwen Stacy

For a time, Gwen Stacy was the love of Peter Parker's life. Peter and Gwen began a college romance that was cut much too short when the Green Goblin hurled the innocent girl off the top of the Brooklyn Bridge. Gwen's death has affected Peter profoundly, and he has tortured himself on many a sleepless night, replaying the horror in his head. He still finds himself daydreaming about their life together and what could have been.

Peter was convinced he would spend the rest of his life with his dream girl, Gwen.

Spidey's on-off love interest Black Cat shares his sense of adventure.

## Black Cat

A cat burglar by heritage, Felicia Hardy always lived a dangerous life, and her relationship with Spider-Man wasn't that different. She felt a kinship with the lone hero, but quickly became obsessed with him. Not only did she wear the black cat costume to attract Spider-Man's attention, but she also kept a shrine to his honor, and even reformed her criminal ways to stay close to the hero. The two have had an on-off relationship for years, with neither truly getting what they need out of it. Felicia had difficulty understanding Spider-Man's need to live a civilian life.

While she loves the "spider," the Black Cat isn't really that keen on the "man."

### LILY HOLLISTER

Peter first met fun-loving socialite Lily Hollister through her boyfriend, Harry Osborn. Living a double life as the villain Menace, Lily once kissed Peter in order to hide her secret identity, but it was a gesture that caused Parker more grief—he felt terrible for kissing his good friend's girlfriend.

### MICHELE GONZALES

The sister of his former roommate Vin Gonzales, Peter Parker was caught off guard when Michele Gonzales moved in with him and became his roommate. The two had a few brief affairs before realizing that they weren't a good fit for each other.

### MS. MARVEL

Spider-Man's fellow Avenger Ms. Marvel was initially annoyed by team-ups with the wall-crawler. But the two became friends when Spider-Man helped her on missions, and as they've grown closer, Ms. Marvel has developed feelings for her teammate that either has yet to fully explore.

## Carlie Cooper

Peter's most recent love interest Carlie Cooper is a forensic officer for the New York Police Department and Lily Hollister's friend. While it took Peter some time to fully notice and appreciate Carlie, once they finally connected, the couple realized how much they had in common, including a mutual love for science.

# AMAZING FRIENDS

New York City is a crowded town, and no one knows that better than Spider-Man. In a city that is home to millions of people, it's no surprise that the web-spinner has met dozens of other heroes over the years. Through the course of his career, Spidey has teamed up with other Super Heroes, and he has even made a few friends from those he once considered enemies.

## SILVER SABLE

Silver Sable is one of the toughest mercenaries that Spider-Man has ever come across. Having adopted her father's profession as a bounty hunter and taken it to the next level of profitability and efficiency, Silver and her team of employees—the Wild Pack—will use their expertise in combat, gymnastics, and martial arts to take down any criminal for a hefty price. Silver is usually, but not always, an ally of Spider-Man.

## MORBIUS

When Dr. Michael Morbius discovered that he was dying from a rare blood disease, he attempted to treat his illness with electroshock therapy and substances found in the bodies of vampire bats. The radical treatment transformed Morbius into a living vampire of sorts with enhanced strength and bloodlust. After clashing with Spider-Man several times, the two eventually became allies.

## VENOM

Peter Parker's former school bully, Eugene "Flash" Thompson has always looked up to Spider-Man. The founder of a Spider-Man fan club, Flash has never wavered in his support of the world famous wall-crawler. So when he lost his legs while serving his country, Flash didn't hesitate when the government offered him not only a chance to regain his mobility, but also to possess superpowers, by donning a living alien symbiote suit as the new Venom.

## MADAME WEB

When Julia Carpenter was injected with a mysterious serum that gave her spider powers, she became known as Spider-Woman. A longtime crime fighter and ally of Spider-Man, Julia was also a member of several Super Hero teams, including the Avengers, Force Works, and Omega Flight. Having adopted many different monikers, including Arachne, she recently became known as Madame Web, after developing extra precognitive abilities.

## SCARLET SPIDER

The notorious clone of Peter Parker, Ben Reilly adopted a crime-fighting identity of his own when he realized that he could not escape the responsibility that came with possessing all of the same powers and memories as the real Peter Parker. Dubbed the Scarlet Spider by the press, Ben fought valiantly alongside his "brother" and even in place of him when Spider-Man retired briefly. But Ben nobly sacrificed his own life to his cause.

## PUMA

A master of martial arts with enhanced animalistic abilities, Thomas Firehart now uses his skills and powers as a contract mercenary, after conquering the world of corporate business. With his own strict moral code and a need to repay his own debts, the Puma has fought alongside Spider-Man at times. Although they often met as enemies in the past, the Puma has gained great respect for the wall-crawler.

## SPIDER-WOMAN

The original Spider-Woman, Jessica Drew, has appeared on and off in Spider-Man's life, although she and the wall-crawler have spent the majority of their careers pursuing very different paths. An agent of the government peacekeeping force S.H.I.E.L.D., and later a double agent for the terrorists Hydra, Drew also joined the Avengers where she and Spider-Man are now regular partners.

## TOXIN

When the serial-killing alien symbiote called Carnage gave birth to a spawn, the offspring took roost in the body of Patrick Mulligan, a New York City police officer. Although Mulligan is aware of his symbiote's corrupting influence, he has managed to keep control of the creature, and has even created an identity for himself as the crime-fighting Toxin—the first symbiote that Spider-Man considers an ally.

## JACKPOT

When Jackpot first appeared, Spider-Man thought it might be Mary Jane Watson lurking under the costume. However, he soon deduced that she was Alana Jobson, a regular civilian who used Mutant Growth Hormone to give herself enhanced abilities. When Alana died, Sara Ehret adopted the Super Hero role, reluctantly realizing that her own superhuman powers were a gift she could not squander. Like Alana before her, she became an ally of Spider-Man.

## ANTI-VENOM

Eddie Brock's brutal vigilante career as the villainous Venom landed him the reputation as one of Spider-Man's greatest foes. But after losing his alien symbiote suit and encountering the Super Villain Mister Negative, Eddie mysteriously manifested the rapid healing powers of Anti-Venom. Calling a truce with Spider-Man, he teamed up with the wall-crawler to battle mutual foes.

## BLACK CAT

Influenced by the career of her cat burglar father, Felicia Hardy adopted the identity of the thieving Black Cat. After her adventures led her into a few conflicts with the wall-crawler, Felicia eventually changed her ways, using her "bad luck" powers to aid Spider-Man, and even becoming his girlfriend. While they're no longer romantically entangled, Spider-Man and the Black Cat still partner occasionally, something Spidey struggles to keep strictly professional.

## SPIDER-GIRL

While she was reluctant to adopt the Super Hero name Spider-Girl, Anya Corazon wasn't so hesitant when it came to putting on a costume and fighting crime. The benefactor of powers from a mystical spider cult, Anya began her career as the hero Araña soon after she gained her abilities. But it wasn't until after the Kraven's Grim Hunt of spider heroes, where she had fought alongside Spider-Man, that she fully accepted the role and costume of Spider-Girl.

## PROWLER

Embarking on a criminal career to prove himself after he lost his job as a window washer, Hobie Brown donned the costume of the Prowler and soon crossed paths with Spider-Man. Later reforming his illegal ways, Hobie teamed up with Silver Sable as well as several other reformed villains. He and Spider-Man have partnered on several occasions, and the Prowler even designed some new technology for one of the wall-crawler's missions.

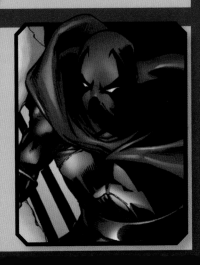

## THE FF

When the Human Torch, one of the founding members of the super-powered Fantastic Four, died, it seemed the Fantastic Four would be no more. However, one of the Human Torch's final requests was for Peter Parker to take his place on the team. Spider-Man accepted the role, only to learn that the team's patriarch, Mr. Fantastic, had decided to rebrand the team. Now called the FF (the Future Foundation), the team has become much more than a group of four crime fighters. It is a collective of young people dedicated to making the world a better place.

### KEY DATA

**TEAM'S FIRST APPEARANCE:**
*The Fantastic Four* #579
(July 2010)

**FOUNDER:** Mr. Fantastic

**ISSUE SPIDER-MAN JOINED:**
*FF* #1 (May 2011)

**BASE:** The Baxter Building,
New York City, New York

1. MR. FANTASTIC
2. SPIDER-MAN
3. INVISIBLE WOMAN
4. THE THING

THOR

SPIDER-MAN

HAWKEYE

# TEAM PLAYER

Although a loner for the majority of his career, Spider-Man has recently become a major believer in the power of teamwork. He currently serves as a member of three Super Hero groups at the same time: the FF, Avengers, and New Avengers.

1. GHOST RIDER
2. HULK
3. SPIDER-MAN
4. WOLVERINE

## THE NEW FANTASTIC FOUR

Early in Spider-Man's career, the wall-crawler helped to found a new, but short-lived incarnation of the Fantastic Four. The original members of the Fantastic Four had been taken captive by an alien shape-shifting Skrull named De'Lila, who then manipulated Spider-Man, Wolverine, the Hulk, and Ghost Rider into forming a new Super Hero team.

### KEY DATA

**TEAM'S FIRST APPEARANCE:**
*The Fantastic Four* #347
(December 1990)

**FOUNDING MEMBERS:**
Spider-Man, Hulk, Ghost Rider, Wolverine

**ISSUE SPIDER-MAN JOINED:**
*The Fantastic Four* #347

**BASE:** Mobile

IRON MAN

SPIDER-WOMAN

WOLVERINE

CAPTAIN AMERICA

# AVENGERS

They're the world's greatest heroes. The mightiest assembly of super beings that the planet has ever known. They're the Avengers, and finding a place on their roster is the crowning achievement in any hero's career. Although Spider-Man was made a reserve Avenger years ago, he didn't achieve full membership to the ever-changing team until much later. These days, the web-crawler serves on two branches of the team, both with the icons of the Avengers as well as the heroes in the New Avengers.

1. THE THING
2. LUKE CAGE
3. MS. MARVEL
4. WOLVERINE
5. SPIDER-MAN

# NEW AVENGERS

The New Avengers originally banded together after a prison breakout at the Vault, a New York maximum security penitentiary, and they were the first incarnation of the Avengers that Spider-Man joined on a full-time basis. The group faced clandestine organizations, alien threats, and mutant manifestations. But no threat tore at the team like the Super Hero Civil War, which split the New Avengers into two factions—the government-supported Mighty Avengers and the underground Secret Avengers. Spider-Man took his place with the underground faction, and has remained with the team since its rebirth under the leadership of Luke Cage.

# SPIDEY TEAM-UPS

While it took Spider-Man years before he was recruited to an actual Super Hero team, he was partnering with other heroes almost right from the beginning of his career. From the gruff Wolverine to the welcoming Firestar, Spidey found a way to earn each hero's trust and respect.

Spider-Man had grown up reading about Captain America, so partnering with the living legend was a bit surreal.

## CAPTAIN AMERICA

An icon in the world of Super Heroes, Spider-Man was more than a little intimidated by Captain America when they first teamed up. Even though Spider-Man's reputation was spotty with the police and the press, Captain America gave the fledgling hero the benefit of the doubt when they battled the Rogue Scholars, a group of time-traveling scientists, and a mutual respect was born.

## WOLVERINE

On paper, they seem like an unlikely pairing. One's a natural rebel who's bucked the system for over a century—a wandering mutant with a fight-first mentality. The other's a wise-cracking bookish type whose guilt complex causes him to do the right thing above even his own personal safety. But despite their differences, Wolverine and Spider-Man have found themselves partners on many occasions. From fighting through jungles off the coast of Japan, to local Manhattan bar brawls, these two make an excellent team, something even Wolverine would admit—when Spider-Man isn't around, of course.

## FIRESTAR & ICEMAN

Firestar, a former member of the Super Hero team dubbed the New Warriors, has partnered with Spidey on several occasions, most notably when she helped to curb the bloody massacre that was orchestrated by the Super Villain Carnage. Spidey and Iceman have also crossed paths a few times, both with and without Iceman's X-Men teammates. But the three found that they worked best as a trio, conquering threats like Videoman. Their teaming even led to a romance between Iceman and Firestar, but it was rather short-lived due to the two mutants' conflicting personalities.

## HUMAN TORCH

Spider-Man and Johnny Storm didn't really like each other at first. Spidey always thought that the Fantastic Four's young hotshot, the Human Torch, was too arrogant. But over the years, with dozens of team-ups under their belts, the two discovered that they were actually more like brothers. So much so, that when the Human Torch died, his last wish was for Spider-Man to take his place on the Fantastic Four.

## DAREDEVIL

Blind lawyer Matt Murdock, also known as Daredevil, first teamed up with Spider-Man when they took on the villainous Ringmaster and his Circus of Crime. With foes like the notorious Kingpin in common, the two crime fighters often found themselves joined in battle, and grew to become true friends. On one occasion, the pair even ended the partnership of two of their greatest respective villains: the Vulture and the Owl.

## CLOAK & DAGGER

When two teen runaways were kidnapped and experimented upon with a powerful drug, they manifested bizarre powers. Now young Super Heroes, Cloak absorbs criminals into the darkness that engulfs him, while Dagger strikes them down with daggers of light. The pair met Spider-Man early in their careers and have found themselves teaming up many times since. From helping Dagger with family issues, to teaming up to defeat the Super Villain Carnage, Spider-Man and Cloak and Dagger continue to work together, and they are slowly realizing that that might not be such a bad thing.

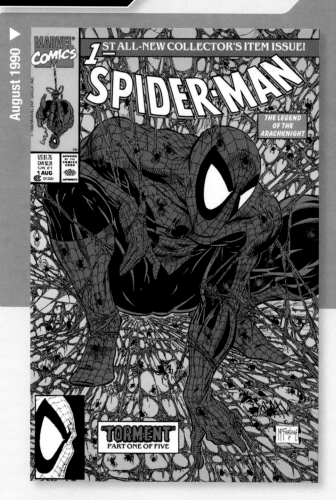

August 1990

# SPIDER-MAN #1

*"But I've got to tell you, when it comes right down to it, I can be pretty awesome if I want."*

**PETER PARKER**

**EDITOR-IN-CHIEF**
Tom DeFalco

**COVER ARTIST, WRITER, PENCILER, AND INKER**
Todd McFarlane

**LETTERER**
Rick Parker

**COLORIST**
Bob Sharen

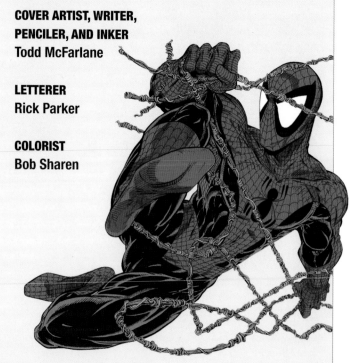

**MAIN CHARACTERS: Spider-Man; the Lizard; Mary Jane Watson-Parker; Calypso**
**MAIN SUPPORTING CHARACTER: Ralph Dill**
**MAIN LOCATIONS: Various streets of New York City; Calypso's mysterious Upper East Side sanctuary; Peter Parker's SoHo apartment**

## BACKGROUND

During the biggest comic book boom in the 1990s, you didn't get any bigger than Todd McFarlane. An artist who seemingly crept out of nowhere on titles like DC's *Infinity Inc.* and Marvel's *Incredible Hulk*, Todd McFarlane exploded onto the scene with *The Amazing Spider-Man* alongside writer David Michelinie. Todd's drawing style was noticeably dynamic, adding flair and energy to everything from Spider-Man's exaggerated swinging positions to the weblines he shot from his wrists. Suddenly, Spider-Man was flashy, exciting, and the hero to watch.

So it only made sense for Marvel's editorial team to give Todd McFarlane all the room he wanted to play. The result was *Spider-Man #1*, the first issue in a brand new ongoing series launched in 1990, which showcased McFarlane's talents. Not only was he the penciler and inker of the fledging title, but he was also named the writer as well. And as expected, the readers devoured the issue, causing it to sell a record-breaking two million copies, and to shoot to the top of every comic store's most demanded issue list.

While McFarlane would soon leave Marvel to found his own comic company, Image Comics, with a few fellow luminaries, Marvel was left with a popular mainstay title that lasted 98 issues before it came to its end in 1998.

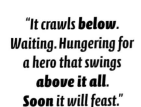

## THE STORY

**While Spider-Man busies himself in his home life with Mary Jane and with stopping an average mugger, a sinister force is building beneath his beloved city.**

There was something growing in the corners of New York City. Something evil was lurking just beyond the view of the thousands of citizens going about their daily lives. A veritable force of nature was preparing her bid for revenge—and now all the pieces were falling into place. But above the crowded streets, away from the growing tension, Spider-Man swung through the air on a thin webline, blissfully ignorant of what was brewing somewhere else in the dark.

Soon night arrived, and with it, came the things only found in the shadows. A woman frightened out of her mind, a man desperate for the contents of her purse, and a gun just inches from her face (**1**). They were the sorts of things Spider-Man was used to. Everyday horrors birthed in Manhattan's crevices. But as he dropped onto the scene, surrounded by his own makeshift web, it seemed Spider-Man himself might be the most terrifying thing that the night had to offer (**2**). The rescue was routine for the web-crawler. He saved the woman, captured the man, and shattered the gun. But what was happening across town was anything but commonplace. A woman named Calypso was concocting a potion (**3**), causing a ferocious creature called the Lizard to rise from the depths of the sewers (**4**).

Back in the safety of his SoHo apartment, relaxing in the arms of his wife Mary Jane, Spider-Man had shed his costume and returned to life as normal New York citizen, Peter Parker (**5**). But outside, in the humid air of the city, a primal sound was reverberating. Under its influence, the Lizard was feeding—first on a rat, and then on the human equivalent: criminals and thieves (**6**). Although mostly acting on animal instinct and at the will of the unseen Calypso, the human trapped inside the Lizard took the time to label his kill. In blood, on the wall behind his victims, he wrote the letters "CNNR", standing for Connors (**7**)—his human name. A name far removed from the raving beast he'd become. For Spider-Man, it would be the first clue to a murder mystery that would test his resolve, his endurance, and even his humanity.

As Spider-Man swung happily from rooftop to rooftop (**8**), he was oblivious to the creature that lurked below. Darkness loomed and the Lizard hid in the shadows. Dinner came in the form of poor Ralph Dill, who took an ill-fated shortcut to work (**9**). And the Lizard waited. His plan? To crush Spider-Man (**10**).

As the story continued in the following four issues, Spider-Man and the Lizard clashed in a bloody battle, as savage as any either had ever faced. Eventually, the trail of pain led to Calypso, the former ex-lover of Kraven the Hunter, and a master of the darkest voodoo arts. Having surrendered herself to the forces of evil years earlier, Calypso wanted nothing more than another soul to claim for her own. Spider-Man would go on to defeat the voodoo witch and her unwitting reptilian pet. However, when the smoke cleared, Peter Parker did not feel the return to normalcy that usually accompanied a job well done.

There was something still out there. And it was bad. And it was dark.

*"It crawls below. Waiting. Hungering for a hero that swings above it all. Soon it will feast."*

# MAIN ENEMIES

For a guy who is just trying to pay the bills and lead a modest life, Peter Parker has amassed one of the largest groups of enemies of any Super Hero. While Spider-Man is always trying to do the right thing, the criminals he comes into conflict with don't appreciate his actions, and tend to hold quite a grudge against the wall-crawler.

## GREEN GOBLIN

There is probably no foe in Spider-Man's life that has struck as close to home as Norman Osborn, the original Green Goblin. He was responsible for the death of Peter Parker's longtime girlfriend, Gwen Stacy, and also corrupted his own son Harry's mind through verbal abuse, forging him into his goblin successor. Certifiably insane, but with a seemingly inexhaustable bank account and a horde of fanatical followers, the Green Goblin is one of the most powerful and dangerous men on the planet. Unfortunately for Peter Parker, it is Norman Osborn's avowed intention to destroy his wall-crawling archenemy, Spider-Man.

## SANDMAN

One of the most powerful villains on Spidey's enemy list, the Sandman isn't quite as corrupt as many of the other rogues the wall-crawler battles against. Sandman has tried to reform himself, and he was even a reserve member of the Avengers at one point. Despite his attempts to change, he always falls back into his criminal ways in the end.

## VULTURE

An elderly engineer with a brilliant mind, Adrian Toomes turned to a life of crime when he created a flying suit that gave him superior strength to any man half his age. As the Vulture, Toomes is corrupt and untrustworthy, and he has been known to betray other villains foolish enough to ally themselves with him. The activities of this hardened old bird are a cautionary tale for the equally gifted Peter Parker.

## DOCTOR OCTOPUS

While there is certainly room for argument, Doctor Octopus just might be the greatest foe Spider-Man has ever faced. With a scientific mind that rivals that of Peter Parker, Doc Ock has challenged the web-slinger throughout Spidey's career. Between almost marrying Peter's Aunt May, carving out another criminal identity for himself as the "Master Planner," and attempting to take over all of the electronics in the entire city of Manhattan, Doctor Octopus is always brainstorming his next scheme. The thrill of the game seems to motivate Doc Ock just as much as the idea of a final victory over Spider-Man. He even saved Spider-Man's life on one occasion, just to ensure Spidey would live to fight him another day.

## ELECTRO

Maxwell Dillon—the criminal known to the world as Electro—has been many things in his life: an electrical lineman, a super-powered thief, a pawn in a greater game, a voice of a political movement, and a living thunderbolt able to solidify himself into human form. But despite where his life takes him, it seems Electro will always side with the corrupt, and oppose everything Spider-Man stands for.

## KRAVEN

A patient hunter who stalks his prey like a jungle cat, Kraven fought Spider-Man to prove he was the world's greatest hunter. Bested many times by Spidey, he shot and killed himself during his "last hunt." He has since reemerged by mystical means and remains in the shadows, preparing to hunt down his old foe.

## VENOM

The Venom name and legacy started with a man named Eddie Brock. An unethical individual from childhood, Eddie grew up to be a lazy and untrustworthy journalist. Brock put his desire for fame and fortune above the integrity of his profession, and his lack of effort in carrying out proper research led to the downfall of his career. Blaming Spider-Man for proving his articles inaccurate, Brock's hatred attracted Spidey's former symbiote suit, and the first Venom was born out of their merging. Currently, Spidey's former bully Flash Thompson wears the symbiote suit, trying valiantly to control it's primal anger as a heroic incarnation of Venom.

## MYSTERIO

Another of Spider-Man's foes to be personified by more than one criminal, Mysterio is far and away the most enigmatic of Spidey's enemies. With a vast knowledge of "movie magic" and special effects to craft a mysterious persona armed with bizarre weaponry, there is very little about Mysterio that is known for certain. Hiding behind smoke and mirrors in order to concoct elaborate traps for his prey, Mysterio has hunted Spider-Man many times, obsessed with seeking revenge for the numerous occasions that Spidey has foiled his plans.

## CHAMELEON

The Chameleon is an expert in the field of espionage, a master criminal, and one of the first Super Villains Spider-Man faced. Using realistic masks or holographic projections, he is able to change his appearance at the drop of a hat. The Chameleon can be anyone at anytime in order to achieve his nefarious goals. Just by studying his subject for a few minutes, the Chameleon can master his victim's mannerisms, voice, and subtleties to such a degree that he can even fool those closest to his target.

## CARNAGE

Already an unrepentant serial killer when he merged with a piece of Venom's symbiote suit, Cletus Kasady became a true monster as the Super Villain known as Carnage. Mentally imbalanced and with a sick bloodlust, Carnage has unleashed several campaigns against the innocents of New York City. He is so powerful that Spider-Man has barely been able to stop him. Even being ripped in two by the Avenger known as the Sentry wasn't enough to keep Kasady at bay, and he continues to return to Spider-Man's life to strike up his next campaign of terror.

## HOBGOBLIN

Although several men have adopted the role of Hobgoblin over the years, Roderick Kingsley was the first to don the bizarre costume. While his equipment was mostly pilfered from the original Green Goblin, Norman Osborn, Kingsley was much more than a cheap imitation. He represented the very real threat of a sane goblin, a cold and calculating danger in Spider-Man's life until he was dethroned and killed by the current Hobgoblin, Phil Urich.

## GREEN GOBLIN II

Harry Osborn followed in his father's destructive footsteps when he took up the role of the Green Goblin. One of the most tragic cases in Spider-Man's career, Harry is possibly Peter's best friend, despite being one of Spidey's greatest enemies. Struggling with a past drug addiction and a need to contain the inner mania that the goblin has caused him, Harry is constantly attempting to rebuild his life and be the father to his children that Norman Osborn never was to him.

## LIZARD

Dr. Curt Connors wanted nothing more than to regrow his missing limb and help countless others in a similar situation. Unfortunately, his experiments led to him becoming the blood-craving Lizard, a creature more animal than man. Instead of making his life and the world that much better, Curt's transformation led to the death of his son, as well as that of his own humanity and many a battle with Spidey.

## KINGPIN

He is the master of organized crime, and his name fits him well. Wilson Fisk is the notorious Kingpin, and he has had a hand in the corruption of New York City for many years now. A foe of both Spider-Man and the vigilante Daredevil, the Kingpin runs a tight ship and has earned the respect of even the most hardened criminals. While his reign of crime has been interrupted from time to time by other would-be crime lords and heroes seeking to bring him to justice, Fisk has always reemerged on top. A brilliant fighter despite his size, the Kingpin isn't afraid to deal with situations personally when required. However, he is smart enough to hire assassins and other immoral employees to carry out the majority of his dirty work, ensuring his place at the top of the heap.

## SCORPION

Private detective Mac Gargan got more than he bargained for when he allowed J. Jonah Jameson to use him as a guinea pig in his campaign against Spider-Man. Transformed into the monstrous Scorpion by scientist Dr. Farley Stillwell, Mac used his new powers to strike out against Spider-Man. While he hates the wall-crawler, Mac also developed an equal loathing for Jameson when the newspaper editor attempted to distance himself from the Scorpion's criminal ways. Although briefly interrupted by his short tenure as Venom, Gargan continues his corrupt Scorpion career to this day.

## HYDRO-MAN

Spider-Man made another enemy for life when he accidentally knocked Morris Bench off a cargo ship and into the ocean just as an experimental generator was being tested in the water. Transformed into a being capable of turning his body into a water-like liquid at will, Hydro-Man embarked on a criminal career and has even joined an anti-Spider-Man Super Villain group called the Sinister Syndicate.

## JACKAL

By all appearances, Professor Miles Warren was just another college professor at Empire State University. A closeted genius with an obsession for his former student Gwen Stacy, Warren eventually adopted the identity of the Jackal, and concocted a revolutionary cloning process. Blaming Peter Parker for the death of Gwen, the Jackal cloned Parker several times. He even convinced Peter that he wasn't the original Spider-Man, but just a genetic copy. His plan was to populate the Earth with his clones, all the while toying with Peter's life to avenge Gwen's death.

## SHOCKER

Convicted burglar Herman Schultz upped his game by inventing a sonic-projection suit using the tools available to him in a prison workshop. Sending out powerful sonic waves to break out of jail, Herman created the criminal persona of the Shocker, and has been repeatedly brought to justice by Spider-Man ever since.

## RHINO

Just like his animal namesake, it's nearly impossible to stop a charging Rhino, but Spider-Man has done his best to try. Stuck in a permanent suit that gives him superstrength and nearly unbreakable skin, the Rhino has often tried to deny his criminal nature. Despite volunteering for the experiment that gave him his bizarre appearance, the Rhino has sought a way to surgically remove his costume in order to return to a normal life. He recently attempted to retire from crime, but his heart is truly in the wrong place, and his corrupt nature surfaces when he's faced with tragedy or even simple desire. The Rhino is a lifelong criminal, even if he hasn't fully accepted that fact.

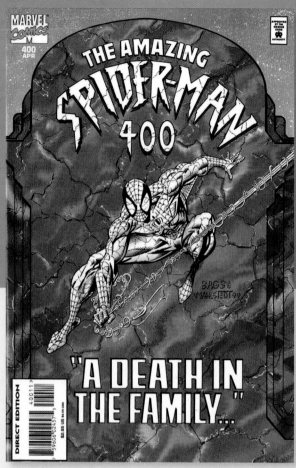

April 1995

## THE AMAZING SPIDER-MAN #400

"No doctors. No hospitals... This time is for **us**–to say our **good-byes**."

AUNT MAY PARKER

**EDITOR-IN-CHIEF**
Bob Budiansky

**COVER ARTISTS**
Mark Bagley and Larry Mahlstedt

**WRITER**
J.M. DeMatteis

**PENCILER**
Mark Bagley

**INKER**
Larry Mahlstedt with Randy Emberlin

**COLORIST**
Bob Sharen

**LETTERER**
Bill Oakley and NJQ

**MAIN CHARACTERS:** Spider-Man; Aunt May Parker; the Scarlet Spider; Mary Jane Watson-Parker
**MAIN SUPPORTING CHARACTERS:** Dr. Julia Caputo; Anna Watson; J. Jonah Jameson; Marla Jameson; Liz Osborn; Norman Osborn Jr.; Flash Thompson; Black Cat; Joe Robertson; Detective Connor Trevane; Lieutenant Jacob Raven
**MAIN LOCATIONS:** A hospital, New York; Ravencroft Institute; the Parker residence; the Empire State Building; undisclosed cemetery, New York

### BACKGROUND

Easily the most controversial storyline ever to shake up the so-called "Spiderverse," the Clone Saga, which was launched in *Web of Spider-Man* #117 (October 1994), had already turned the life of Peter Parker on its ear. It started as just another idea thrown out by writer Terry Kavanagh at a brainstorming summit about bringing back Spider-Man's clone. But when faced with the story potential that could spring out of that simple concept, the idea blossomed into an ambitious comic book event that strived to be something more than the means to nab increased sales.

The folks in the Spider-Man offices wanted a story with weight and long-lasting consequence. And while her death might not have lasted as long as originally intended, May Parker's final moments in *The Amazing Spider-Man* #400 were meant to be just the kind of weighty story the team set out to tell. Even though it is often hard for good characters to stay dead in the world of comic books, Aunt May's death can still be read as the end of an era it originally signified.

## THE STORY

**In "The Gift" story, Peter Parker spends his last treasured moments with Aunt May before she seemingly dies, while his clone watches on, unable to say goodbye.**

> "Let go. Fly. 'Second to the right—and straight on till morning.'"
>
> **PETER PARKER**

It must have felt like a dream for Spider-Man. His Aunt May had been in a coma for days, and the doctors feared she might never wake up. So when Peter got a call from the hospital, he naturally assumed the worst (**1**). Swinging across town at a breakneck speed, the wall-crawler switched into his civilian identity with a heavy heart and entered the room of the woman who had been like a mother to him. A woman he wasn't ready to say goodbye to.

And luckily for Peter, he wouldn't have to. Because the woman who waited behind the door was as full of life as she'd ever been (**2**). She'd awoken from her coma, and would soon be ready to head home and resume her life. While Peter cried happy tears, he saw something else out of the corner of his eye. Ben Reilly, the Scarlet Spider, was watching the scene from outside (**3**). Although Spider-Man's clone might have been an outcast from the life he'd once thought was his, he couldn't help the fact that he loved Aunt May as if she was his aunt.

May returned to her familiar Forest Hills home to the delightful news that Peter and Mary Jane were expecting a baby (**4**). But just as Peter should have been enjoying this happy family time, the Scarlet Spider appeared from the shadows, intent on having a word with him. As the two talked, the Scarlet Spider revealed his plan. Now that he knew May was going to be OK, the Spider was going to leave the lives of the Parkers forever (**5**).

For a while, life at the Parker residence returned to normal. There was a lot of happy reminiscing about the past, and Aunt May and Peter even took a trip to the top of the Empire State Building to spend a little alone time together. It was there that May revealed to Peter that she'd known about his secret for years (**6**). She'd known he was Spider-Man and although his other life frightened her, she was proud of him just the same. The revelation was a weight off Peter's shoulders, even though it seemed to exhaust the elderly May. The two decided to head home, a new understanding now existing between them in the space where an unmentionable secret used to live.

What Peter didn't know at the time was that May had done what she set out to do. Now her fever had returned, but she wasn't fighting any longer (**7**). It was her time, and she knew it. Even though Peter still wasn't ready, May was. So he held her hand, and talked to her softly about a book she'd read to him as a child. May fell asleep and Peter and Mary Jane mourned her passing (**8**).

Outside May's window, another man was feeling her loss. A man who had sworn to leave the Parkers alone. A man dressed in a red and blue spider costume who was affected by Aunt May's death just as deeply as any of those lucky enough to be standing by her side (**9**).

It was cold on the day they buried May Parker. Peter and Mary Jane stood among a crowd of some of their closest friends and tried to keep their emotions in check (**10**). May's casket was lowered into the ground, and soon enough, the crowd dispersed and people went back to their daily lives. Peter and MJ were the last to leave. No words were spoken. Only an unsaid understanding passed between the two before they too left the cemetery.

And then another silent mourner arrived. Ben Reilly wasn't able to say goodbye to his "aunt," but still needed to pay his respects to the woman who had so influenced his life. Placing a single rose on the fresh earth before her tombstone, Reilly let himself cry, mourning not just May, but the life that he had never truly known (**11**).

# OTHER ENEMIES

With years of crime-fighting under his belt, Spider-Man has amassed quite an impressive rogues gallery. Spidey's clashes with these repeat offenders have become such a part of his daily routine, that even he would be hard-pressed to list every villain that has ever attempted to end his career.

## BOOMERANG

Australian Fred Myers moved to the United States to became a professional baseball player. Suspended for supposedly accepting bribes, Myers turned to crime with help from the clandestine organization Secret Empire. The group equipped him with an array of weaponized boomerangs—landing him his codename. Later becoming a freelance assassin, Myers often clashed with Spider-Man and joined up with other rogues to form the Sinister Syndicate.

## GRAY GOBLIN

Norman Osborn and Gwen Stacy's illegitimate son, Gabriel Stacy suffered accelerated aging as Norman's newest project. With Norman's goblin formula flowing through his veins, Gabriel became the Gray Goblin, often attacking Spider-Man, and later took on the role of the American Son, all in an attempt to please his absent father.

## MOLTEN MAN

Mark Raxton was the step-brother of Peter's longtime friend Liz Allan. He became the gilded Molten Man after an accident in which he was coated in a liquid metal derived from a meteor and developed by Spencer Smythe. With a hard frictionless skin and the ability to increase his external temperatures to over 500°F (260°C), Raxton became a formidable foe of Spidey's after turning to crime.

## BEETLE

Abner Jenkins began his career in the world of Super Heroes as the Beetle, an enemy of the Human Torch. Using a technologically advanced flying suit of armor, the Beetle might have appeared cumbersome at first, but he was still a force to be reckoned with. Pursuing a life of crime led to him clashing with Spider-Man—giving the villain an arch foe that he would battle with many times as part of the Sinister Syndicate. These days, Jenkins has reformed and become a Super Hero going by the handle Mach-V.

## JACK O'LANTERN

Jason Macendale debuted as the villainous Jack O'Lantern before upgrading his identity to that of a new Hobgoblin. Employing deadly flying devices, Jack O'Lantern was a haunting presence in Spidey's life, and one that several other criminals have filled since Macendale's departure from the role.

## ENFORCERS

A trio of hired muscle available for the right price, the Enforcers have had a variety of employers over the years. However, it was when they were hired by the criminal known as the Big Man that they first encountered Spider-Man. Comprised of strong man Ox, the master of the lariat, Montana, and martial art expert and group leader Fancy Dan, the Enforcers often live up to their name.

## SWARM

One of Spider-Man's most bizarre foes, Swarm is the living skeleton of former Nazi scientist Fritz von Meyer. If that wasn't strange enough, Swarm's skeleton is covered in an active hive of bees that respond to his every command and are a part of his very being. Originally an enemy of the short-lived Super Hero team the Champions, a clash with Spider-Man led Swarm to adopt the wall-crawler as his arch foe.

## SPIDERCIDE

One of the Jackal's Peter Parker clones, Spidercide was corrupted from the start. After being released from a cloning chamber with no memories of who or what he was, the clone wandered the streets of New York before "realizing" that he was Peter Parker. With an obsessive sense of entitlement and complete control over his molecular structure, Spidercide was willing to kill anyone who would prevent him from taking his "rightful" place as Parker.

## BURGLAR

He was the first true villain in Peter Parker's life. The man known only as the Burglar first met Spider-Man when he was robbing a TV studio during Spidey's short-lived television career. At that time, Peter couldn't be bothered to stop the obvious thief—he was more concerned about his own life, and assumed that the Burglar was someone else's problem. However, when that same thief re-emerged to rob the Parker home and shoot and kill Peter's Uncle Ben, Spidey would live to regret his inaction. Although he eventually brought the Burglar to justice, Spider-Man would never forgive himself for the criminal's deeds.

## SPOT

Jonathan Ohnn was a scientist employed by the Kingpin—a thug who was attempting to recreate the powers of the Super Hero known as Cloak. Eventually succeeding in creating black disc-like portals to another dimension, Ohnn adopted the name of the Spot after his experiments caused his skin to be covered in those same black dots.

## FAKE MR. AND MRS. PARKER

Peter Parker's parents had lived a fantastic life as spies for the CIA before they were killed in a sabotaged plane flight. Since Peter was a child when his parents died, he didn't have very many memories of them, so when they suddenly reappeared in his life, Peter couldn't believe his eyes. Claiming to have been held as political prisoners all these years, Peter's recently returned parents were eventually revealed to be life-like androids created by the villain Chameleon.

## TINKERER

One of Spider-Man's earliest foes, Phineas Mason, aka the Tinkerer, is the modern equivalent of a mad scientist. Although he may not possess the most threatening of codenames, the Tinkerer is a brilliant inventor who has not only committed his own crimes, but has also built technology for many of Spidey's other foes.

## TOMBSTONE

Hardened by a childhood as Harlem's only albino resident, Lonnie Lincoln became the whispering gangster Tombstone—a recurring presence in Spider-Man's life and one who nearly ruined the career of *Daily Bugle* mainstay, Joe Robertson.

## TARANTULA

Armed with poisonous stingers built into his boots, Anton Miguel Rodriguez took his terrorist lifestyle as the Tarantula from South America to New York City. When his Super Villain career was initially cut short by a partnership between Spider-Man and the Punisher, the Tarantula's focus turned to revenge, as he now harbored a deep-seated hatred for the web-swinger.

## SLYDE

Disgruntled former chemical engineer Jalome Beacher was fired from his job after inventing a frictionless chemical coating that he thought would revolutionize the frying pan industry. With no career to speak of, Jalome turned to crime, using the coating to skate over surfaces with ease and repel Spider-Man's webbing. Recently, Jalome's career was apparently ended when he was shot and seemingly killed by the criminal Underworld.

## SILVERMANE

A Maggia crime lord obsessed with achieving immortality, Silvio Manfredi was dubbed Silvermane due to his prematurely white hair. Past his prime, Silvermane uses a cyborg body to stay mobile and increase his strength to superhuman proportions. He resents Spider-Man for trying to stop his quest.

## SPEED DEMON

James Sanders has led a rather amazing life. Chosen by the galactic gamesman known as the Grandmaster to be one of his pawns in a grand power contest, Sanders was given super speed and originally adopted the identity of the Whizzer. After fighting the Avengers and then later the Super Hero team called the Defenders, Sanders wisely changed his name to Speed Demon to avoid confusion with a World War II era Super Hero. He then became a recurring enemy of Spider-Man's, joining up with the nefarious Sinister Syndicate.

## SCORCHER

One of Norman Osborn's earliest operatives, the Scorcher—alias Steven Hudak—is an arsonist for hire, seeking revenge on Spidey for his time in prison. Using a sophisticated battle suit with built-in flamethrowers, Hudak commits crimes while remaining safely insulated.

## HAMMERHEAD

When a Maggia gunman was attacked beneath a movie poster for *The Al Capone Mob*, his life was saved by disgraced surgeon Jonah Harrow. With a repaired skull made of steel alloy, he adopted the name Hammerhead and the persona of a 1920s era gangster—influenced by that landmark poster. Now he will let no one, not even Spidey, stand in his way.

## SPIDER-SLAYER

Genius Inventor Spencer Smythe created the very first "Spider-Slayer," a device meant to end the career of Spider-Man. After Spencer's death, his mentally unbalanced son Alistair Smythe decided to carry on his father's legacy. Although his career got off to a rather rocky start, Alistair would later surpass the technology employed by the senior Smythe. He has since launched several campaigns against the wall-crawler, even upgrading his own body to that of a cyborg in order to become the so-called Ultimate Spider-Slayer.

## CARRION

Originally a failed clone project of the Jackal, Carrion sought revenge for the assumed death of his master by lashing out at Spider-Man. Armed with a death-touch and the ability to turn his body immaterial, Carrion could make himself lighter than air, giving him a ghost-like quality that created quite a challenge for the web-slinger.

## LOOTER

Experimentation on a meteorite caused would-be scientist Norton G. Fester to gain super-strength. Immediately turning to crime, Fester garbed himself in a purple and white costume and became the Looter. Reluctant to retire from his criminal ways, the Looter has battled both Peter Parker and Ben Reilly, always meeting with defeat in the end.

## GRIZZLY

Maxwell Markham was a professional wrestler until the *Daily Bugle* ruined his career. After nursing his anger for eleven years, circumstances led Markham to meet the Super Villain called the Jackal. The Jackal gave the disgruntled wrestler an exo-skeleton bear costume and set Markham on the path to becoming the criminal known as the Grizzly, a fierce foe of Spidey's.

## DEMOGOBLIN

When Jason Macendale made a deal with dark forces, he became a threatening presence as a demonic Hobgoblin. Later, when the demon half of his personality split off, it became Demogoblin, obsessed with killing perceived "sinners"—including Spidey.

## WHITE DRAGON

The White Dragon's bid to be crime lord of Chinatown's underworld ended when he attracted Spider-Man's attention. Although he has used his skills in martial arts and gadgets, such as steel claws and a flame-throwing mask, in several grabs for power, the White Dragon has always failed, and eventually he became a pawn of Mr. Negative.

June 2006

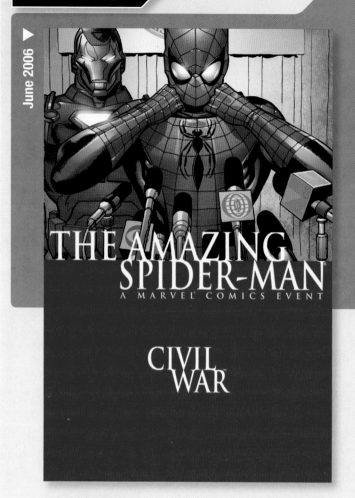

THE AMAZING
SPIDER-MAN
A MARVEL COMICS EVENT

CIVIL WAR

**EDITOR-IN-CHIEF**
Joe Quesada

**COVER ARTIST**
Ron Garney

**WRITER**
J. Michael Straczynski

**PENCILER**
Ron Garney

**INKER**
Bill Reinhold

**COLORIST**
Matt Milla

**LETTERER**
Cory Petit

# THE AMAZING SPIDER-MAN #533

> "My name is Peter Parker, and I've been Spider-Man since I was fifteen years old."
>
> PETER PARKER

**MAIN CHARACTERS:** Spider-Man; Iron Man; Mary Jane Watson-Parker; Aunt May Parker
**MAIN SUPPORTING CHARACTERS:** J. Jonah Jameson; Joe Robertson; Mr. Fantastic; Invisible Woman; Pierce McPherson; Flash Thompson; members of Spider-Man's rogues' gallery; various other Super Heroes
**MAIN LOCATIONS:** Press briefing room, Washington, D.C.; the *Daily Bugle* office; the Baxter Building; Stark Tower; unspecified airfield

## BACKGROUND

Writer J. Michael Straczynski had reinvented the Spider-Man franchise at a time when it needed it most. Falling stagnant a few years after John Byrne's revamp, *The Amazing Spider-Man* got a shot in the arm when Straczynski and legendary artist John Romita Jr. started on the title with the 30th issue of the second series. Spider-Man's origins were examined and a mystical layer was added to the mix.

Spidey met the offspring of his greatest enemy and also Gwen Stacy, he gained new powers as a result of The Other storyline, and he earned a new armored costume from Iron Man, Tony Stark. While fans argued about these controversial subjects, the result was just what Marvel had wanted. People were talking about Spider-Man again.

Then came the Civil War. As the greatest heroes split into two factions, Spider-Man had to make a decision that would cause even more controversy.

## THE STORY

**Spider-Man reveals his secret identity to the world, forcing his friends, family, enemies, and allies to react to the shocking news.**

The Super Hero community might have been divided, but Spider-Man had chosen his side. With the looming threat of the Superhuman Registration Act requiring every masked avenger and vigilante to register their powers and identity with the United States government, the heroes couldn't seem to stop arguing among themselves about the constitutionality of this proposed idea. But Peter Parker had to do what was best for his family. And at the time, that meant siding with the law, and his mentor Tony Stark, Iron Man.

Tony had taken Spider-Man under his wing a few months ago, helping the Parker family out when their house was destroyed by a malicious face from Peter's past. So when it came time to pay back Iron Man with his loyalty, Spider-Man stepped up to the plate and did what Tony Stark asked him to do. He went before the public at a highly touted press conference in Washington, D.C., and took off his mask. To show his support for the Registration Act, Peter Parker revealed his secret identity to the world (**1**).

And everything changed. Thirty million people searched the internet simultaneously for the name Peter Parker. In the *Daily Bugle* office, J. Jonah Jameson was shocked (**2**). He threw his coffee mug across his office, betrayed by a young man he'd always thought of as honest and forthright.

Meanwhile, Peter was having conflicted feelings almost rivaling those of the public. Always keeping the safety of Mary Jane and Aunt May in mind, Peter believed in his cause, but not at the cost of his family's wellbeing. So making his way through a mixed hoard of protestors and supporters (**3**), Peter headed to one of Stark's limos to be taken to the airport to return home to New York.

Of course, Peter's greatest supporter was, as always, Mary Jane. Calling her from the limo, Peter talked to MJ before being interrupted by a call on the limo's car phone from Reed Richards of the Fantastic Four (**4**). As Reed, his wife Sue, and even Aunt May chimed in on simultaneous conversations, Peter needed a moment to collect his thoughts, so he webbed the two phones together and continued the rest of the ride to the airport in solitude.

But Spider-Man's homecoming didn't go exactly as he had hoped. First he was greeted by a lawyer who let him know in no uncertain terms that the *Daily Bugle* was suing him for misrepresentation, fraud, and breach of contract (**5**). After that, he had to walk through the densely packed press on the sidewalk surrounding his home at Stark Tower. And the whole time, the world observed via constant TV coverage. Watching from his own home, Flash Thompson assumed the news was some sort of hoax (**6**). While in seedier areas of the city, villains like the Vulture and Dr. Octopus began to plot their revenge (**7**).

But Peter's worst surprise upon returning to New York was Tony Stark's own little twist that he sprung on Peter by way of another press conference. In his public address, Stark announced to the nation that the deadline for registration had come and gone (**8**). Those who chose not to comply would now be hunted down and arrested, with no exceptions. He then went on to announce that he had formed a strike force to combat these underground rebels, and that Spider-Man would be part of it. Shocked, Peter decided to leave the tower for some fresh air, but instead was greeted by another onslaught of the press (**9**), this time complete with an assassination attempt. Peter managed to stop the gunman (**10**), but the Captain America fanatic threatened to sue him for blowing up his hand (**11**). Like it or not, a war between Super Heroes was brewing, and Peter Parker had just been drafted (**12**).

*"... so it's best I introduce you to the others you'll be fighting with in this war–before the dying starts tomorrow."*

**IRON MAN**

# TIMELINE

- Peter Parker is born to parents Richard and Mary Parker.

- Mr. and Mrs. Parker die in a plane crash and are revealed to be spies for the CIA. Peter's Aunt May and Uncle Ben raise him as they would their own son.

- Peter attends Midtown High in Queens and excels at schoolwork, especially in the sciences. He fares much worse with his classmates, including Liz Allan and the bullly Flash Thompson.

- While attending a seminar about radiation, Peter is bitten by a spider that was accidentally doused with radioactive rays. He slowly realizes that he has somehow inherited the proportionate strength and other natural abilities of a spider.

- Experimenting with his chemistry set at home, Peter develops his trademark web fluid and web-shooters. He also sneaks into school to create his first material Spider-Man costume.

- Spider-Man stars in a TV special. Backstage after the show, he lets a burglar escape past him without trying to stop him.

- Peter's Uncle Ben is killed during a botched robbery at his home.

- Peter changes into his Spider-Man costume, unaware that his neighbor's niece, Mary Jane Watson, has secretly witnessed his impressive transformation.

- Spider-Man tracks the killer to an abandoned warehouse and discovers that the criminal is none other than the same burglar he let get away back at the TV studio. He then vows to use his powers to help others, having learned that with great power there must also come great responsibility.

- *Daily Bugle* Publisher J. Jonah Jameson begins his public crusade against Spider-Man.

- Spidey saves the life of J. Jonah's son, astronaut John Jameson.

- Spider-Man petitions the Fantastic Four for membership, but reconsiders when he discovers that they don't receive salaries.

- Spider-Man battles and defeats the Chameleon for the first time.

- The Vulture and Spider-Man have their first airborne encounter.

- Peter Parker sells his first photo to J. Jonah Jameson in an effort to help his Aunt May with her money problems.

- Spider-Man fights the Tinkerer for the first time, and also unknowingly meets Mysterio who is disguised as an alien.

- Spidey develops his spider-signal belt projector to help instill fear into the hearts of criminals.

- Otto Octavius becomes Doctor Octopus and clashes with Spider-Man on their first meeting.

- The Sandman debuts and is defeated by Spider-Man.

- Spider-Man confronts the Fantastic Four's most notorious enemy, Doctor Doom.

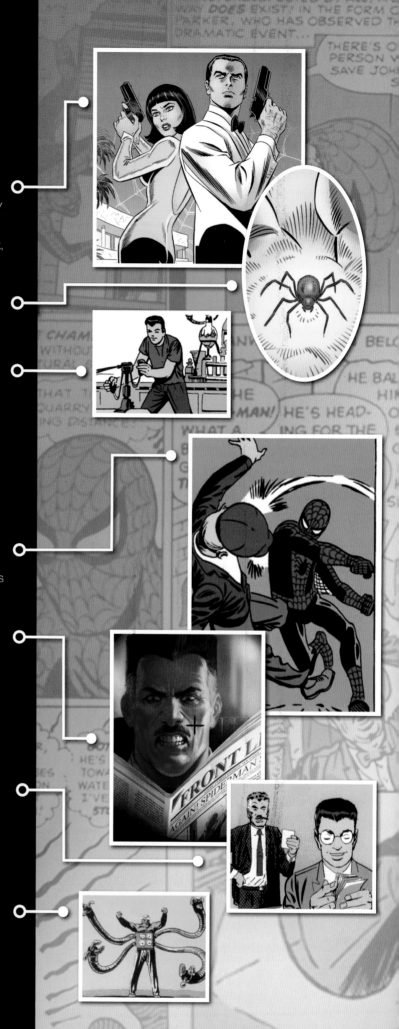

- Heading to Florida on an assignment for the *Daily Bugle*, Spider-Man fights and defeats the Lizard for the first time.

- Spider-Man meets the Scorcher, unaware that the villain is bankrolled by Norman Osborn.

- Spider-Man meets Captain George Stacy and attempts to apply to the police force.

- Spidey helps the misunderstood Batwing after their first meeting.

- Peter Parker and Betty Brant begin to date after the Vulture returns to attack the *Daily Bugle*.

- Electro and Spider-Man clash for the first time, with Spider-Man emerging the victor.

- Spidey faces down the Enforcers and their leader, the Big Man.

- Spider-Man takes on the Headsman for the first time, another criminal under the employ of Norman Osborn.

- Peter Parker develops his first spider-tracer.

- Mysterio battles Spider-Man, the villain now garbed in his signature costume.

- Spider-Man battles the Green Goblin for the first time, but the villain gets away after leading Spidey into a fight with the Hulk.

- The Chameleon sets Kraven the Hunter on Spider-Man's trail, jumpstarting Kraven's new obsession.

- Doc Ock joins forces with Electro, Mysterio, the Vulture, Sandman, and Kraven to form the first incarnation of the Sinister Six.

- Spider-Man and Daredevil team up for the first time when they take on the Ringmaster and his Circus of Crime.

- Betty Brant's relationship with Peter begins to fizzle when she meets and dates Ned Leeds.

- J. Jonah Jameson funds Spidey's newest foe, the Scorpion.

- The Human Torch teams up with Spider-Man to battle another new member of Spidey's rogues gallery, the Beetle.

- Spencer Smythe introduces his first Spider-Slayer to J. Jonah Jameson.

- Spider-Man first crosses paths with the Crime-Master.

- Spider-Man witnesses the birth of the Molten Man, and is then forced to fight him.

- Peter graduates high school and learns of Liz Allan's crush on him.

- Peter enrolls at Empire State University alongside former bully Flash Thompson. There the two meet fellow classmates Harry Osborn and Gwen Stacy, as well as Professor Miles Warren.

- The Looter debuts and challenges Spider-Man.

- Spider-Man is faced with the robot menaces of Norman Osborn's old business partner, Mendel Stromm.

- The Green Goblin discovers Peter's dual identity and reveals himself as Norman Osborn. However, an electric charge grants Osborn with selective amnesia, and he forgets about their double lives for a time.

- The Rhino charges Spider-Man's way in their earliest encounter.

- After weeks of stalling, Peter Parker finally lets his Aunt May set him up with her friend's niece. Peter is floored when he meets the beautiful Mary Jane Watson and is instantly taken with her.

- The Avengers attempt to recruit Spider-Man, but a misunderstanding leads to Spidey sticking to his solo act.

- The Shocker sets his sights on Spidey for the first time, as does a new Vulture, Blackie Drago.

- The Kingpin makes his first play for control of New York's mobs.

- Spider-Man retires briefly before remembering the true inspiration behind his career: his Uncle Ben.

- Peter Parker meets the *Daily Bugle*'s voice of reason, Joe "Robbie" Robertson.

- Peter Parker and Gwen Stacy start dating more seriously.

- Peter meets Joe Robertson's politically active son, Randy.

- Silvermane crosses paths with both Spider-Man and the Lizard for the first time on his quest to regain his youth.

- The Prowler begins to haunt the New York night, originally clashing with Spider-Man.

- The villainous Kangaroo leaps into Spider-Man's life.

- Captain George Stacy is killed during Spider-Man's rooftop battle with Doc Ock. Spider-Man is mistaken for the killer.

- Gwen Stacy travels to Europe to deal with her loss and has a fling with Norman Osborn that results in the birth of illegitimate twins—a boy and a girl.

- Norman Osborn adopts the role of the Green Goblin again.

- Peter discovers Harry Osborn's drug addiction was due in part to Harry's failed relationship with Mary Jane Watson.

- Spider-Man grows two extra sets of arms for a time, truly appearing like his namesake. He then crosses paths with Morbius for the first time before being cured of his condition with the help of Dr. Curt Connors.

- The villainous Gibbon swings into Spider-Man's life, as does the would-be mafioso Hammerhead.

- The Green Goblin hurls Gwen Stacy, newly returned from London, from the top of the George Washington Bridge. She does not survive the fall.

- In a violent fight with Spider-Man, the Green Goblin accidentally impales himself with his glider in an incident Harry Osborn witnesses. Norman is believed to be dead.

- Peter seeks out Mary Jane Watson for comfort and sees another side to the so-called "party girl."

- John Jameson becomes the lycanthropic Man-Wolf, much to Spidey's chagrin.

- The third Vulture, Clifton Shallot, takes up the nefarious role.

- Professor Miles Warren emerges as the Jackal for the first time and hires the Punisher to fire his first shots into Spider-Man's life.

- Spider-Man takes the Spider-Mobile out for its maiden voyage.

- Spidey teams up with Ka-Zar to take on Stegron the Dinosaur Man for the first time.

- Doctor Octopus nearly marries Aunt May Parker.

- The Tarantula debuts and is instantly caught in Spidey's web.

- Harry Osborn adopts his father's identity as a new Green Goblin.

- The Grizzly rears his ugly head for the first time.

- Spider-Man moves into a new apartment and meets his neighbor Glory Grant, establishing a longtime friendship with her.

- Spider-Man not only meets the Jackal's clone of Gwen Stacy, but also his own clone doppelgänger. His clone escapes death only to leave Manhattan and adopt the identity of Ben Reilly.

- A new Mysterio, Danny Berkhart, attempts to play tricks on the wall-crawler's mind.

- Spider-Woman Jessica Drew makes a rather unorthodox debut.

- Will-O'-the-Wisp shines into Spider-Man's life.

- The heroic White Tiger and Spider-Man clash for the first time over a simple misunderstanding.

- Rocket Racer and Spider-Man meet for their initial fight.

- Harry Osborn's psychiatrist, Dr. Bart Hamilton, briefly takes over as the third Green Goblin until his untimely death.

- The White Dragon takes his first swipe at Spider-Man.

- Peter Parker graduates from Empire State University.

- Spider-Man meets the Jackal's just-as-evil clone, Carrion, as well as the sinister Fly.

- The Black Cat first crosses the wall-crawler's path.

- Peter enrolls in graduate schools at ESU and begins working as a teaching assistant for the science department.

- Spider-Man encounters a familiar new foe, the Iguana , as well as the former Champions' enemy, Swarm.

- Spider-Man has his first encounter with the mysterious and precognitive Madame Web.

- Hydro-Man wades into Spider-Man's life, followed swiftly by villains Jack O'Lantern, the Ringer, and Speed Demon.

- Spider-Man battles Cloak and Dagger, unaware that the two new vigilantes would soon become his uneasy allies.

- The killer-for-hire Boomerang focuses his attention on Spider-Man, becoming a longtime foe of the wall-crawler.

- Spidey discovers the hard way that nothing can stop the X-Men foe known as the Juggernaut—except for drying cement.

- Spidey teams up with the Frog-Man during the "hero's" debut.

- The villainous Vermin develops a new hatred for spiders after he battles the wall-crawler and Captain America.

- Spider-Man meets the criminal known as the White Rabbit during another embarrassing team-up with Frog-Man.

- The mysterious Hobgoblin begins his career by picking up where the Green Goblin left off.

- Peter Parker decides to drop out of graduate school.

- The Answer questions Spider-Man's abilities for the first time.

- Julia Carpenter adopts the role of the second Spider-Woman.

- Spider-Man returns from the Secret Wars on the alien planet Battleworld, wearing a new black symbiote alien costume.

- Spidey encounters several new rogues, including crime boss the Rose, the burglar Black Fox, and the bestial Puma.

- Spider-Man abandons his new black costume when he realizes it's alive.

- The Spot first dots the landscape of Spider-Man's life.

- Some time after marrying Harry Osborn, Liz Allan gives birth to Harry's first child, Norman Harry Osborn.

- Spider-Man meets bounty hunter Silver Sable for the first time when she is contracted to capture the Black Fox.

- The Sin-Eater viciously murders police Captain and Spider-Man ally, Jean DeWolff.

- Alistair Smythe, scientist Spencer Smythe's son and the future Ultimate Spider-Slayer, makes his less-than-impressive criminal debut, mistaking Mary Jane Watson for Spider-Man.

- A host of new criminals appear in the wall-crawler's life, including the slippery Slyde, and the deadly Chance and Foreigner.

- The Sinister Syndicate form to attempt to destroy their wall-crawling archenemy.

- Solo begins his war on terrorism, crossing paths with Spidey.

- Jason Macendale picks up the reigns as the new Hobgoblin after Ned Leeds is outed as the villain and killed.

- Long after Peter Parker realizes his true feelings for Mary Jane Watson, she finally accepts his marriage proposal.

- Peter is late to his wedding due to his adventures as Spider-Man and Mary Jane calls off the ceremony. The two soon rekindle their relationship, but marriage is now seemingly off the table forever.

- Kraven defeats Spider-Man during his "last hunt" and then commits suicide.

- Tombstone takes on the web-slinger for the first time.

- Eddie Brock becomes Venom and takes his anger out on Spidey.

- The hitmen team of Styx and Stone manifest in Spidey's life, as does the horrific Demogoblin.

- Spider-Man gains the cosmic powers and abilities of Captain Universe, as a cadre of villains stage their "Acts of Vengeance," employing the robotic Tri-Sentinel.

- Spidey is finally granted Avengers status as a reserve member.

- The Sinister Six reunite years after their original formation.

- Cardiac suits up for the first time and meets Spider-Man.

- Serial killer Cletus Kasady bonds with a part of Venom's symbiote and first unleashes Carnage.

- Spider-Man meets his ferocious six-armed Doppelgänger during the Infinity War.

- Peter Parker discovers his parents are still alive, only to later find out they were robots created in a twisted game by the Chameleon.

- Spider-Man adopts his Spider-Armor to better deal with the threat of the New Enforcers.

- Harry Osborn seemingly dies due to complications with the Goblin Formula.

- Carnage meets the disturbed Shriek, and then instigates a killing spree in Manhattan.

- Spidey faces Kraven's son, the Grim Hunter, for the first time.

- Ben Reilly returns to New York when Aunt May slips into a coma. There he accidentally confronts a confused Peter Parker.

- Judas Traveller journeys to the Ravencroft Institute for the first of his bizarre experiments on Spider-Man's mind. He is accompanied by the Scrier.

- Ben Reilly adopts the persona of the Scarlet Spider.

- Kaine rears his ugly cloned head into Peter Parker's life.

- Mary Jane reveals to Peter that she is pregnant.

- The first female Scorpion, the villainous Scorpia, debuts.

- The Jackal returns from the seeming dead, and releases another Peter Parker clone, Spidercide.

- Aunt May revives from her coma only to seemingly die a week later.

- Phil Urich debuts as a heroic Green Goblin.

- A new female Doctor Octopus challenges the Scarlet Spider.

- Peter Parker officially retires from his career as Spider-Man, allowing Ben Reilly to fill the role. Ben changes Spidey's familiar costume to better suit his style, and even dyes his hair blond.

- Mary Jane gives birth to a daughter, only to have the baby stolen from her and presumed dead.

- A very much alive original Green Goblin is revealed to be the manipulator behind the Jackal and the entire Clone Saga.

- Ben Reilly makes the ultimate sacrifice to save Peter Parker from the Green Goblin. In dying, Reilly is truly confirmed to be the clone, and Parker the original.

- Peter Parker returns in full to the role of Spider-Man.

- Spider-Man meets Kraven's other son and inheritor of his moniker, Alyosha.

- Spider-Man suffers an "identity crisis" of sorts, creating four new Super Hero personas for himself.

- Aunt May is revealed to be alive—her death a masquerade orchestrated by the Green Goblin.

- Mattie Franklin, foster daughter of J. Jonah Jameson, takes on the role of the new Spider-Woman.

- Spider-Man meets Ezekiel and begins a long journey into a possible new theory behind his spider powers.

- Peter Parker embarks on a new career as a high school teacher at his old alma mater.

- Spider-Man meets the mysterious Morlun and is nearly killed in the process.

- Aunt May discovers Peter's double life, and is surprisingly accepting.

- The illegitimate children of Gwen Stacy and Norman Osborn appear in Spidey's life, as does the threat of the Gray Goblin.

- The spider-themed young heroine Araña debuts.

- Spider-Man gains organic web-shooters as a result of a confrontation with a giant spider creature called the Queen.

- Mac Gargan, formerly known as the Scorpion, becomes the new Venom after Eddie Brock auctions the symbiote off.

- Carnage gives birth to a symbiote offspring that bonds with police officer Patrick Mulligan and becomes the heroic Toxin.

- Captain America recruits Spider-Man for the New Avengers.

- The young Carmilla Black becomes the new Scorpion and goes to work for S.H.I.E.L.D.

- In a final battle with Morlun, Spider-Man is killed and reborn with enhanced powers and spike-like stingers housed in his forearms.

- Fellow Avenger Iron Man, billionaire Tony Stark, becomes Peter's mentor and designs him a hi-tech Iron Spider costume.

- Peter reveals his true identity to the world in support of Tony Stark and the Superhuman Registration Act: a law requiring all costumed heroes to register their identities with the government.

- The Super Hero Civil War breaks out over the Registration Act. Spider-Man originally sides with Iron Man and the law. However, he soon changes his allegiances after witnessing the horrors of war, and joins Captain America's group of underground rebels.

- Norman Osborn is promoted to head of the government operatives group called the Thunderbolts.

- Aunt May is shot and lies on her deathbed, forcing Spider-Man to make a deal with the devil Mephisto, costing the hero his relationship with Mary Jane Watson.

- As a favor to Spider-Man, Doctor Strange arranges it so no one remembers the wall-crawler's secret identity, save for Mary Jane.

- A Brand New Day begins in Spider-Man's life as he meets a new circle of friends including Vin Gonzales, Carlie Cooper, Lily Hollister, and a newly returned Harry Osborn.

- The mysterious heroine Jackpot debuts in New York City, as do villains Overdrive and Mr. Negative.

- The *Bugle* is bought out by Dexter Bennett, and renamed the *DB*.

- Lily Hollister secretly dons the identity of the goblin-like Menace to aid in her father, William Hollister's, mayoral campaign.

- Spider-Man meets new villains Freak, Screwball, Paper Doll, and Kraven's daughter Ana.

- Eddie Brock becomes Anti-Venom after an encounter with Mr. Negative and Venom.

- Peter meets energetic reporter Norah Winters when working at the recently established newspaper *Front Line*.

- Norman Osborn helps stop the "Secret Invasion" by the alien race known as the Skrulls. He is promoted to head of the organization formerly called S.H.I.E.L.D., renaming it H.A.M.M.E.R.

- Spider-Man meets J. Jonah Jameson Sr., and the elder Jameson soon begins to court Aunt May.

- Jackpot Alana Jobson dies of an overdose, leading to her friend Sara Ehret reclaiming the heroine's mantle.

- J. Jonah Jameson is elected Mayor of New York City.

- Spider-Man faces a new Vulture who preys on weak criminals.

- Norman Osborn takes on the public persona of the Iron Patriot, and creates his own Dark Avengers, convincing the public that Venom Mac Gargan is Spider-Man. He then attempts to get his son to take on the Super Hero role of the American Son.

- Spider-Man makes a few new enemies: the Raptor, a second Rhino, and a new Rose.

- Spider-Man joins two different branches of the Avengers after Norman Osborn is dethroned and the Superhuman Registration Act is repealed.

- The Gray Goblin assumes the role of the new American Son.

- Kraven is resurrected by his surviving family during their Grim Hunt for Spider-Man—a game that causes the death of the original Madame Web and Mattie Franklin, as well as Kraven's two sons.

- Arachne takes on the role of the new Madame Web and Araña reluctantly adopts the name of Spider-Girl.

- Lily Hollister gives birth to Harry Osborn's second son, Stanley.

- After toying with the idea, Peter Parker and Carlie Cooper finally commit to a serious relationship with one another.

- Peter takes a lucrative job as a member of the inner think tank of the innovative Horizon Labs.

- Spider-Man designs a new stealth suit to take on the newest incarnation of the Hobgoblin—a corrupted Phil Urich.

- J. Jonah Jameson's wife Marla is murdered by the Spider-Slayer.

- After a war injury leaves him a paraplegic, Flash Thompson accepts the role as the new heroic Venom.

- Spider-Man loses his spider-sense and adopts a bulletproof costume to compensate for the power downgrade.

- After the Human Torch dies, Spider-Man accepts an invitation to join the Future Foundation and dons a new costume.

- Carnage's symbiote gives birth to another spawn, which bonds with Dr. Tanis Nieves and names itself Scorn.

- The new Madame Web warns of the coming of Spider-Island.

February 2011

# THE AMAZING SPIDER-MAN #655

*"I swear to you... from now on... whenever I'm around, wherever I am, no-one dies!"*

**SPIDER-MAN**

**EDITOR-IN-CHIEF**
Axel Alonso

**COVER ARTIST**
Marcos Martin

**WRITER**
Dan Slott

**PENCILER**
Marcos Martin

**INKER**
Marcos Martin

**COLORIST**
Muntsa Vicente

**LETTERER**
VC's Joe Caramagna

**MAIN CHARACTERS:** Spider-Man; J. Jonah Jameson; Marla Jameson

**MAIN SUPPORTING CHARACTERS:** Joe Robertson; Martha Robertson; Ben Urich; Randy Robertson; Carlie Cooper; Max Modell; Jay Jameson; Aunt May Jameson; Glory Grant; Betty Brant; various deceased people from Spider-Man's past; Captain Yuri Watanabe

**MAIN LOCATIONS:** J. Jonah Jameson's home; Peter Parker's apartment; the *Daily Bugle* office; St. Patrick's Cathedral, New York City; unnamed cemetery; a New York City bank

## BACKGROUND

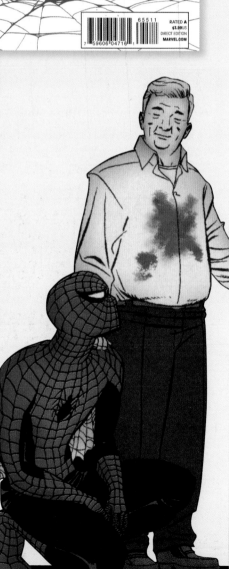

The Brand New Day in Spider-Man's life had come and gone, but its themes and concepts had formed the foundation of Spider-Man's revised and slightly reinvented universe. Among the changes was an emphasis on story over event. This new approach was in good hands with talented big-name writers such as Joe Kelly and Mark Waid. Meanwhile, the Spider-Man editorial offices were taking chances with the artistic approach by hiring artists who were previously rarely used on mainstream projects due to their original styles, to give each story a unique and imaginative feel.

Chief among those artists was Marcos Martin. With a simplistic yet intricate style, Martin seemed tailor-made for Spider-Man. And nowhere was that more apparent than in *The Amazing Spider-Man* #655, in which Martin got the chance to shine with a sequence of somber silent panels and a surreal dream world. Combined with Dan Slott's script, the issue was powerful, moving, and a perfect example of placing story above all else.

## THE STORY
### After attending the funeral of J. Jonah Jameson's wife, Peter Parker experiences a harrowing dream populated by all those who Spider-Man had been unable to save.

J. Jonah Jameson's alarm went off at 7:00 a.m., but he didn't need it. The former publisher of the *Daily Bugle* was finding it hard to get any sleep (**1**). He just lay there in his now all-too-empty bed, next to where his wife used to rest. But Marla Jameson was gone now, and Jonah had to get on with his day. So he got up, showered and shaved—and headed to his wife's funeral.

Peter Parker wasn't doing much better, and neither was the staff at the *Bugle* for that matter. But nevertheless they all made their way to St. Patrick's Cathedral in Manhattan, and sat through the terribly sad proceedings (**2**). Later at the cemetery, Jameson looked on as his wife's coffin was lowered into the ground (**3**). Peter watched his former boss walk away from his wife's fresh plot. But Peter's mind wasn't just on Marla Jameson and Jonah's loss. And when he went to sleep in his lonely apartment that night, Peter's true thoughts began to emerge (**4**).

He didn't stop the Burglar. Peter was living it all again as if it were yesterday. In a haunting dream, Peter was confronted by his Uncle Ben and then by his faceless, dead parents (**5**). To make matters worse, Ben's murderer was sitting down with all of them at the kitchen table in Peter's childhood home (**6**). And then suddenly, Marla Jameson greeted him.

Peter followed Marla through the dream and into a bizarre cityscape populated by the dead faces from his past (**7**). There were dozens of them, all people Spider-Man just couldn't save. From Aunt May's former love Nathan Lubensky, to the Scarlet Spider, to Gwen Stacy. From police detective Jean DeWolff to *Bugle* reporter Fredrick Foswell to businessman Ezekiel. It was a haunting laundry list of ghosts and phantoms from times past. And it brought Peter Parker to his knees.

All of a sudden he was back on a twisted version of the George Washington Bridge, staring down the Green Goblin with the lifeless Gwen hanging limply in the monster's arms (**8**). And then he was being pulled down into the hard split earth by Kraven's dead hand (**9**). Suddenly he was in a pub watching Scourge and the Punisher callously murder a few forgettable Super Villains. Then before he knew it, he was watching helplessly as the Sentry ripped Carnage in half while flying through outer space. And then he was backstage at that TV studio again as the Burglar ran past him.

But this time, Spider-Man wasn't going to let him get away. This time, the hero raised his fist and beat the soon-to-be killer into a pulp. But it wasn't the Burglar he'd beaten—it was his Uncle Ben.

Looking down at the bloody body of the man who raised him, Spider-Man swore that it would never come to this. That he wouldn't be responsible for the death of everything Ben had taught him. And from behind him, a woman's voice sounded. Marla Jameson was asking Spider-Man what he would do now (**10**).

Peter woke up in a cold sweat (**11**). He put on his Spider-Man costume and headed to greet the dawn from a nearby rooftop (**12**). He knew what he had to do. He made his city a promise that whenever he was around, no one else would die.

At a bank across town, a villain called Massacre had different ideas. Holding innocent people hostage, he proved that he had no regard for human life. With the simple squeeze of a trigger, he made a mockery of Spider-Man's new oath in an instant.

> "If that's so, then tell **us**...
> what will you do now?"
>
> **MARLA JAMESON**

# AMAZING ARTWORK

There is perhaps no image of Spider-Man more famous than artist Jack Kirby's iconic cover of Spider-Man's first appearance in *Amazing Fantasy* #15 (August 1962). In fact, the cover is so well known that many artists have chosen to pay homage to it by creating a similar image with their own personal twist. The cover has been rendered in media ranging from paint to a computer-generated hologram, and has featured subjects as diverse as zombies, villains, and Comedy Central TV star Stephen Colbert (in *The Amazing Spider-Man* #573). In fact, as a celebration of the cover, Marvel even offered comic book retailers an opportunity to be immortalized on a variant edition of *The Amazing Spider-Man* #669. Also of note is Steve Ditko's original unpublished cover for *Amazing Fantasy* #15 (second row, third from left), which didn't have quite the dynamic appeal that editor Stan Lee was looking for.

# INTRODUCING
# IRON MAN

Iron Man has always looked towards the future. From his debut in the pages of *Tales of Suspense #39*, to the most recent issue of his fifth ongoing comic series, his billionaire alter ego Tony Stark has been in a constant state of reinvention. Stark's goal? To stay one step ahead of the competition, and to lead by heroic example.

When he first appeared on the scene, Tony clad himself in a bulky gray armor with all the style and panache of an fire hydrant. His evolution into a hero was just beginning. His look soon transformed into that of an atomic knight in golden shining armor and then to the robotic equivalent of a hot rod. Flash with substance. The idea of piloting their own Iron Man armor became a daydream for thousands of readers. But Tony Stark was just getting warmed up.

Over the years, Iron Man has remained on the cutting edge of technology, adapting to the future almost before its arrival. Tony Stark has been a war profiteer, a playboy, a Super Hero financier, an electronics pioneer, a humanitarian, a business consultant, a computer technician, a super-spy and even the US Secretary of Defense. But always at his core, Tony Stark has been Iron Man, a visual symbol of heroism, change and faith in science to shape a better world.

He's Iron Man. The Golden Avenger. Shellhead. But most importantly, he's Tony Stark, one of the greatest minds of his generation.

# THE BIRTH OF IRON MAN

**The brainchild of some of the most creative individuals ever to work in the comic book medium, Iron Man made his dramatic debut on the cover to *Tales of Suspense #39*.**

By March of 1963, comic book writer and editor Stan Lee was getting pretty sure of himself. And by all accounts, he had every right to be. Working alongside already legendary artists like Jack Kirby and Steve Ditko, Lee had ushered in what was to be known as the Marvel Age of comics. Just a few short months earlier, in November of 1961, Lee and Kirby had introduced the world to the Fantastic Four, in their title's premier issue. They followed up that hit with the debut of the Hulk in May of the following year. Then, teaming with Ditko, Lee introduced Spider-Man that September in the pages of *Amazing Fantasy*'s 15th and final issue. With the introduction of Thor and Ant-Man soon to follow, Lee had a string of runaway successes on his hands, and he felt that practically anything he touched would turn to gold.

So he set out to test that theory. In an increasingly idealistic, anti-establishment age of Civil Rights and anti-Vietnam War protest, Lee decided to create a character that the readership wouldn't readily identify with. He created a weapons designer who worked for the government, rather than rebelling against it. Instead of an everyman character like Spider-Man, who gained instant sympathy from his readers due to his identifiable problems and inner conflicts, Lee created a millionaire playboy, aloof from society's ills and immune to any financial concerns. Despite all these apparent handicaps, Iron Man was a hit with the public—just as Lee had suspected all along.

Lee understood that like all great characters, Tony Stark just needed a touch of tragedy to humanize him. By making Tony injured in a wartime attack and forced to wear a metal chest plate in order to survive, Lee created sympathy for an otherwise detached character. In an unprecedented occurrence in Lee's experience, Iron Man began to receive more mail from female readers than any of his other popular titles, a fact Lee attributed to an inborn maternal instinct to take care of this romantically tragic figure.

Stan Lee had once more created a hero with a lasting fan base and media legacy. Iron Man first appeared sporting a gray suit of armor; as if to reflect Lee's own Midas touch, by Iron Man's second appearance, the color of his armor had turned to gold.

At the time, keeping a consistent shade of gray was a troublesome challenge for a newsprint press. To remedy the situation, Stan Lee decided to have Iron Man paint his armor gold (which conveniently printed as yellow) in his second appearance.

**"Here you have this character, who on the outside is invulnerable, I mean, just can't be touched, but inside is this wounded figure. Stan made it very much an in-your-face wound, you know, his heart was broken,**

## literally broken."

Iron Man writer Gerry Conway

# THE CREATORS

## STAN LEE

The creator behind hundreds of Marvel characters, Stan "The Man" Lee not only helped to usher in Marvel's rise to fame in the 1960s, but also served as a guiding force behind the company for years in a myriad of forms, including writer, editor, president, and chairman. Lee wrote nearly all of Iron Man's original adventures, inventing a gallery of villains for the hero, including the Mandarin and the Crimson Dynamo, as well as many supporting characters, such as Tony's longtime allies Pepper Potts and Happy Hogan. Legendary for his enthusiasm as a spokesman for all things Marvel, Stan even made a cameo in the 2008 Iron Man feature film, playing a Hugh Hefner-like playboy bachelor.

## LARRY LIEBER

Stan Lee's younger brother, writer Larry Lieber opted not to alter the family name as his brother had done. A newspaper cartoonist as well as a scribe, Lieber's main claim to fame was his scripting Iron Man's first appearance in *Tales of Suspense # 39*. With Stan only providing the plot of Iron Man's legendary origin, Larry provided the dialog over Don Heck's pencils. It was Larry who conceived the name Tony Stark, as Stan was in the habit of giving characters first and last names that began with the same letter, just to make them more memorable in his own mind.

## DON HECK

Although he didn't design the Iron Man armor itself, Don Heck did just about everything else to bring Tony Stark's adventures to life. The interior artist for *Tales of Suspense #39*, as well as most of Iron Man's other early exploits, Don Heck created the dramatic pacing that kept readers coming back for more. Designing the look of millionaire Tony Stark based on Stan Lee's suggestion of a Howard Hughes-type personality, Heck gave the character a trademark mustache, adding a dash of famous swashbuckling actor Errol Flynn to Tony's appearance. Over the years, Heck would design many other characters in Shellhead's life, including Pepper Potts and Happy Hogan.

## JACK KIRBY

The guiding force behind Marvel Comics' trademark look in the 1960s, Jack "the King" Kirby's work is as popular today as it was 40 years ago. Always experimenting with his craft and pushing the boundaries of forced perspective and dynamic storytelling, Kirby had already co-created dozens of Marvel icons, from Captain America to the Fantastic Four. Knowing Kirby's flair for creating characters that resonated with readers, Lee tasked Jack with designing Iron Man for the cover of the all-important *Tales of Suspense #39*. While Iron Man's look has evolved and changed many times over the years, Kirby's vision of a robotic suit of armor is still fondly remembered by fans as a symbol of the classic Marvel Age.

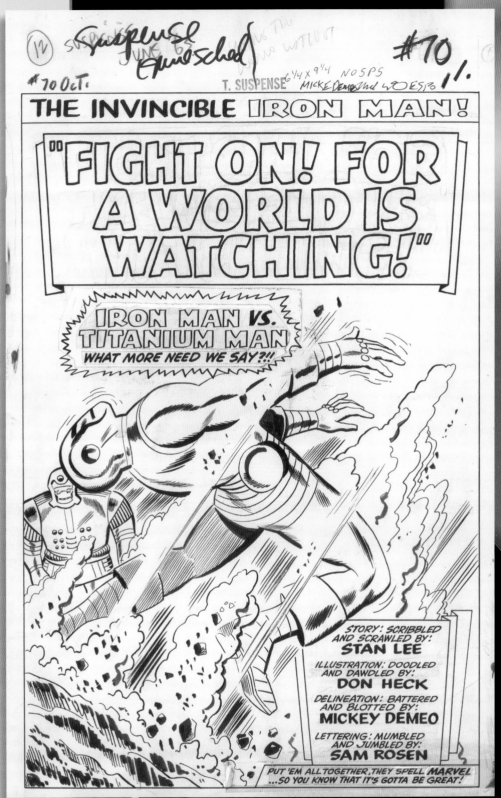

This original art for the splash page for *Tales of Suspense #70* showcases Stan Lee's lighthearted credit box, which was one of his trademarks. Lee always made sure his staff were acknowledged for their work, something rarely seen at the time.

# TALES OF #39 SUSPENSE

# TALES OF SUSPENSE

"**You are not facing a wounded, dying man now... or an aged, gentle professor! This is Iron Man who opposes you, and all you stand for!**"

IRON MAN

**MAIN CHARACTERS:** Iron Man; Wong-Chu; Professor Yinsen
**SUPPORTING CHARACTERS:** An unnamed general and US government employees; female socialites; prisoners and soldiers of Wong-Chu's camp
**LOCATIONS:** Stark Industries; Wong-Chu's South Vietnam camp; US military camp in South Vietnam

**PUBLICATION DATE**
March 1963

**EDITOR-IN-CHIEF**
Stan Lee

**COVER ARTIST**
Jack Kirby and Don Heck

**PLOTTER**
Stan Lee

**SCRIPTER**
Larry Lieber

**PENCILER/INKER**
Don Heck

**LETTERER**
Art Simek

## BACKGROUND

It was all told in a mere 13 pages. Despite having his landmark debut crammed into an anthology comic with a few other science fiction stories, there was no question that Iron Man was the true star of *Tales of Suspense* #39. Not only was this fledgling hero given the lead story feature, his top billing was also touted on the cover, with a blurb proclaiming that Iron Man had sprung from the same creative well as Spider-Man and the Fantastic Four. And for the most part, he did. Iron Man was Stan Lee's brainchild, but when the time came to actually pen his initial tale, Lee's busy schedule didn't permit him to script the hero's first outing. Lee plotted the adventure and handed the story summary to artist Don Heck. The dialog chores found their way to the desk of Larry Lieber, Stan's younger brother, and co-conspirator on another Marvel icon, the mighty Thor. The result was another certified success for Marvel, and Iron Man remained at the helm of *Tales of Suspense* for the rest of the title's lifespan.

# The Story...

**Millionaire Tony Stark suffers a debilitating injury and is taken captive by communist forces, only to escape by creating a new identity as Iron Man.**

Tony Stark was always a bit of a showboat. A millionaire munitions manufacturer, well regarded for his brilliant technological innovations that were often employed by the US military, Tony lived a life of luxury and acclaim. He had a girl hanging on his arm at every party, and a prospective client hanging on his every word at any business meeting. He had just wowed one of his military associates with a demonstration of his newest invention: high-powered miniature transistors **(1)**. By attaching one of these small devices to a normal everyday magnet, Stark was able to rip a thick, steel door right off its hinges **(2)**. The demonstration was more than enough to impress the general in charge, and Tony was given a contract to help aid US forces in Vietnam.

Meanwhile, in the heart of the jungles of that war-torn country, communist leader Wong-Chu **(3)** was enjoying his own exhibition. The unscrupulous commander of a band of guerrillas, Wong-Chu had just added another conquered village to his fiefdom and, as was his custom, had issued a challenge to the male inhabitants. If one of them could best him in a wrestling match, he would set the entire village free. Several villagers accepted Wong-Chu's challenge, but the tyrant dispatched each one with ease. Once again, Wong-Chu was victorious.

Tony Stark's arrival in Vietnam threatened to change that. Unable to transport heavy artillery through the jungle, the heads of a US military base near Wong-Chu's latest camp were testing Stark's new miniature transistors in hand-held mortars. Tony wanted to see the action firsthand **(4)**. But when he accidentally set off a booby-trapped trip wire **(5)**, he was knocked unconscious by the resulting explosion, with a piece of shrapnel lodged dangerously near his heart. To make matters worse, the helpless businessman was soon captured by the communist forces and brought back to Wong-Chu's camp.

Fortunately, like most of the civilized world, Wong-Chu had heard of Tony Stark. So rather than kill the brilliant inventor outright, the communist leader instead instructed Tony to build a weapon that would help in combating the American forces **(6)**. In exchange, Wong-Chu promised to have his finest surgeon see to Tony's heart and cure him of his condition. Knowing that Wong-Chu had no intention of giving him any medical treatment, Tony agreed to the terrorist's terms, and set out with his own agenda. He would build a suit of armor that would not only help sustain his life, but would also be his means of escape.

With the aid of Professor Yinsen **(7)**, a fellow prisoner and brilliant physicist whom the world at large believed dead, Stark constructed an iron suit of armor, powered by his experimental transistors. Donning the armor just as his heart began to fail, Stark lay down on a table, waiting for the suit to fully charge and for its electronic transistors to save his life **(8)**. In order to stall Wong-Chu's approaching troops, Professor Yinsen ran madly into the hallway only to be gunned down by the tyrant's men. The momentary diversion was all Stark needed, and as Iron Man, he made his escape from his living quarters.

Later, as Wong-Chu dispatched yet another hopeful in a wrestling match, a new challenger called to him from the crowd. While Wong-Chu gawked in disbelief at the metal marvel standing before him, Iron Man attacked his foe, and easily bested him **(9)**. Fighting through a hail of bullets, Iron Man took down Chu's entire camp, before defeating the fleeing tyrant himself by trapping him in an explosion of a nearby ammunition shed **(10)**. Trapped inside his iron shell and alone in the Vietnamese jungle, Iron Man disappeared into the wilderness, pondering where this new life of his would take him next **(11)**.

"I know I've only days to live, but my last act will be to defeat this grinning, smirking, red terrorist!"

# THE SUIT'S POWERS

They say the clothes make the man, and Tony Stark would have no reason to argue. Iron Man's actions make him a hero, but his armor is what gets the job done.

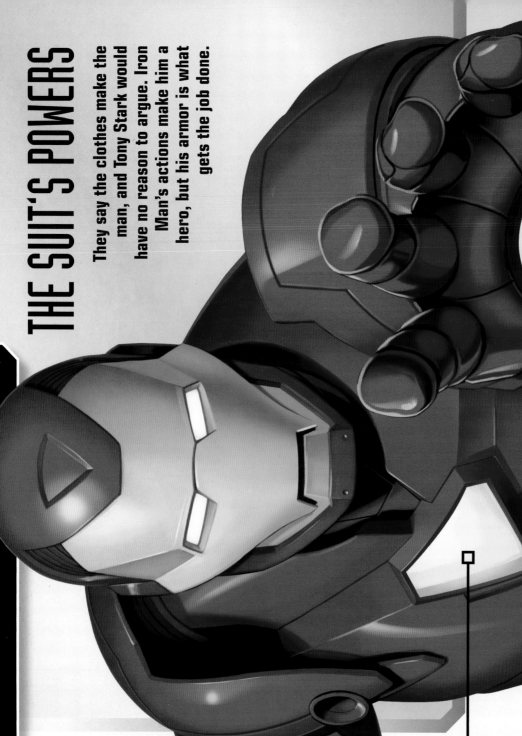

## CHEST PLATE

The Iron Man chest plate has been of special importance to Tony Stark ever since he first donned his armor. Originally structured to keep his injured heart beating through the use of a magnetic-field generator, the chest piece was soon adapted to serve as one of the many offensive tools in Iron Man's arsenal. While he no longer needs the armor to keep himself alive, Iron Man frequently relies on his chest plate's powerful unibeam in battle.

Capable of firing a blast similar to that of his repulsors, the unibeam can also function as a searchlight able to project in nearly every spectrum, even infrared and ultraviolet. The unibeam can also produce a local electro-magnetic pulse, a laser beam, holographic images, and a wavelength scanner.

# REPULSORS

Tony's magnetic repulsor beams have always been the cornerstones of his Iron Man technology. Originally utilizing high-powered transistorized magnets capable of localized repelling force, Stark soon refined the tech into his modern-day repulsor blasts. Essentially a powerful particle beam, the ray can be focused to a narrow area, or be dispersed to cover a wider range. When fired from his gauntlets at an enemy target, the repulsors have the ability to repel energy and physical attacks alike.

In addition, the Iron Man armor allows Tony to switch to pulse bolts, which are also focused through his palm apertures. Segmented flashes of energy, the pulse bolts actually grow stronger and more powerful the longer the distance they travel, giving Iron Man the perfect weapon for long-range attacks against particularly daunting foes.

# JET BOOTS

Also utilizing repulsor technology, Iron Man's jet boots have often played a vital part in his adventures. Powered by scramjet and air-jet propulsion systems as well as afterburner thrust, the jet boots are the armor's main utility for transportation and can fly at speeds of up to Mach 8. In addition, when Iron Man wants to take things a bit slower, perhaps to survey an enemy installation, the boots take advantage of a localized gravity field, granting the armor hovering capabilities. Combining the boots' raw power with the usage of Tony's in-flight computer and built-in gyroscope, Iron Man is able to maintain his balance and follow any trajectory of his choosing. In earlier models, Tony installed magnetic suction cups in his boots to allow him to do his best impression of Spider-Man and adhere to flat surfaces.

# THE SUIT

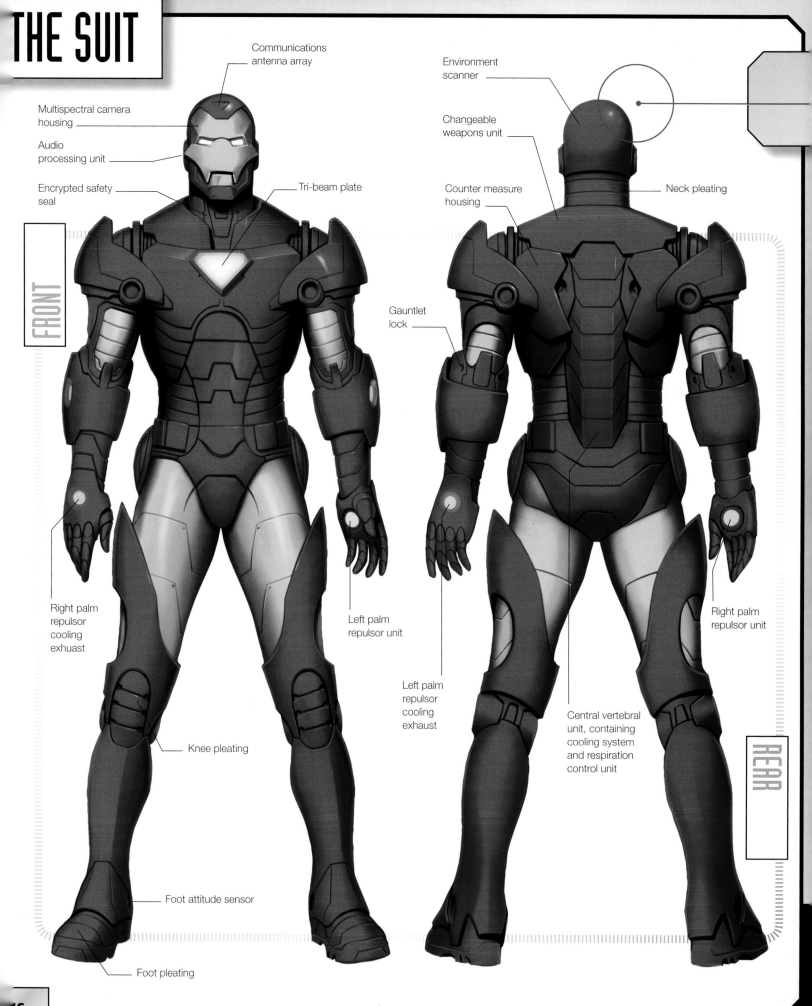

Communications
antenna array

Multispectral camera
housing

Audio
processing unit

Encrypted safety
seal

Tri-beam plate

FRONT

Right palm
repulsor
cooling
exhuast

Left palm
repulsor unit

Knee pleating

Left palm
repulsor
cooling
exhaust

Foot attitude sensor

Foot pleating

Environment
scanner

Changeable
weapons unit

Counter measure
housing

Neck pleating

Gauntlet
lock

Right palm
repulsor unit

Central vertebral
unit, containing
cooling system
and respiration
control unit

REAR

# HEADPIECE DETAILING

**Originally constructed in three separate pieces, Tony Stark upgraded his helmet so that it could slip on over his head in a single motion.**

Everything about the Iron Man suit has been streamlined for efficiency in battle situations, as well as for quick and easy assembly. When Tony upgraded to the Extremis technology, his wardrobe changes became almost instantaneous.

Starboard top outer casing

Flat mesh-type neural net processor with storage

Parietal padding

Cybernetic antenna array

Sub-routine processor

Rear headpiece

Front orbital padding

Occipito mastoid padding

Optical cluster

Electronic transpiration control layer

Super orbicularis oris padding

Temporo-mandibular padding

Vocal harmonizer/changer

Transducer array

Audio processing

External case and audio pick up

Face piece

Using a combination of magnets and vectored repulsor fields, the Extremis Iron Man armor could assemble itself at Tony's mental command, forming around his thin undersheath. Keeping the bulk of his collapsible equipment in an everyday briefcase, Iron Man stored his undersheath in tiny sections inside his hollowed-out bones.

## NECKPIECE

Monolithic neck assembly

Front closure piece

Collar stress attenuation area

Suit safety seal

Neck cowl assembly

*Schematics based on the work of Eliot R. Brown*

## 1963 to 1988

Tony Stark has gone through dozens of Iron Man suits since his first explosive heroic debut, improving and refining his armor each and every time.

Stark spray-paints his gray armor gold.

### GOLDEN AVENGER
### 1963

While rescuing a circus crowd from an assortment of escaped big cats, Tony realized the frightening effect his gray Iron Man armor had on the public. In order to make his appearance less threatening, Stark coated his armor in shiny, untarnishable gold paint, literally turning himself into a modern-day knight in shining armor. Tony continued to add new gadgets to his suit, including wheels, a heat ray, and a force field.

### THE GRAY ARMOR
### 1963

Utilizing Tony Stark's innovation of miniaturized transistors, his original gray armor was hastily constructed out of spare parts while Tony was held captive in Wong-Chu's camp. Although primitive by today's standards, Iron Man's original suit was equipped with powerful magnets that became the basis for his revolutionary repulsor system. Streamlining the armor after returning home, Tony altered the metal to make it thinner and more pliable.

### THE RED/GOLD ARMOR
### 1963

Tony still wasn't satisfied with his armor's bulky nature, despite many tweaks and upgrades. During a conflict with the voodoo expert, Mr. Doll, Tony created a brand-new suit, featuring a red and gold color scheme. Unlike its predecessors, this new armor was much easier to get on and off, as its individual, collapsible sections partially assembled themselves with the help of magnetic devices. The red and gold armor was equipped with a chest repeller ray, a light beam, a wrist calculator and energy monitor, and a radio receiver.

Iron Man's red and gold armor was much more compact than the original.

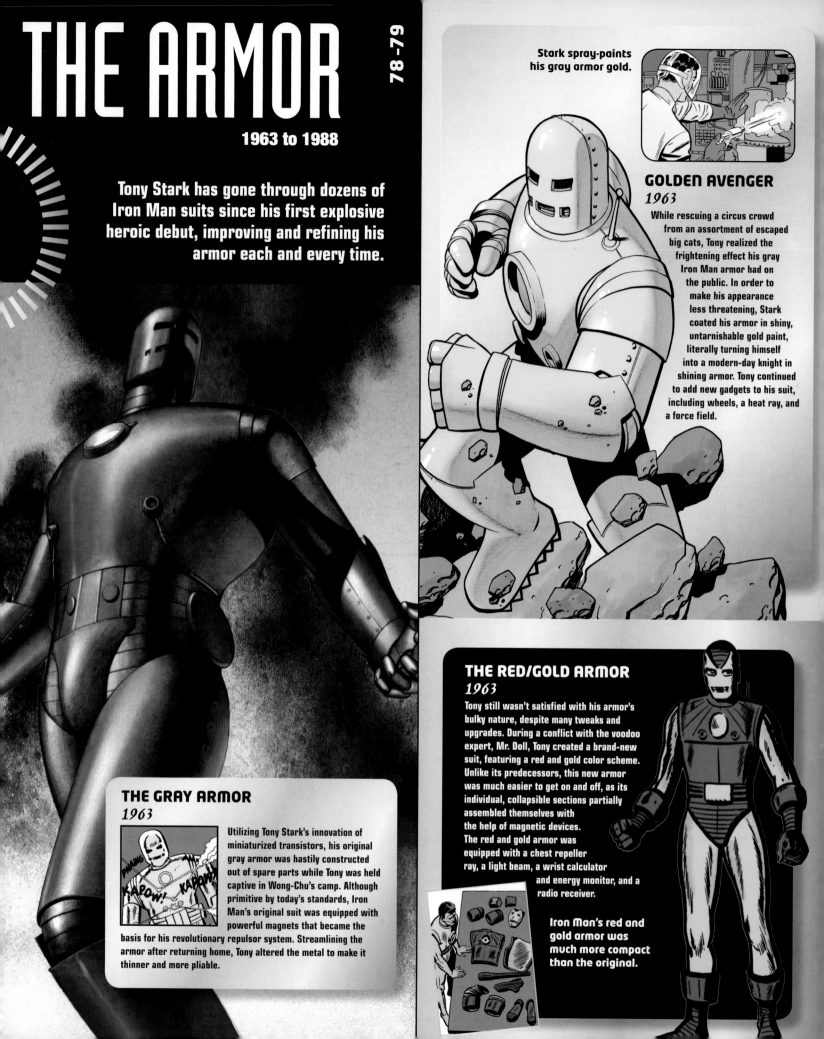

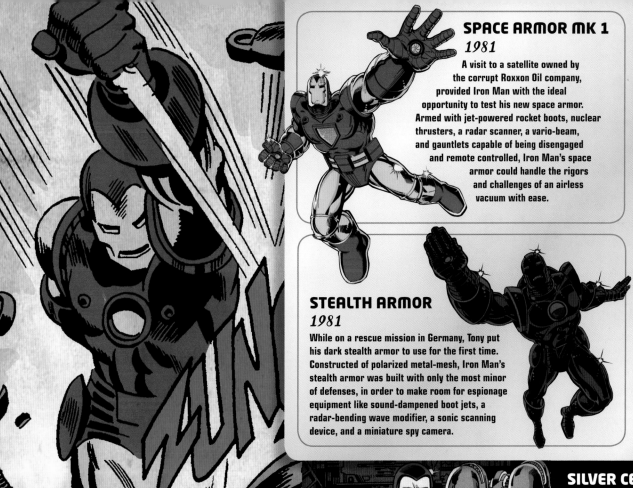

## SPACE ARMOR MK 1
### 1981

A visit to a satellite owned by the corrupt Roxxon Oil company, provided Iron Man with the ideal opportunity to test his new space armor. Armed with jet-powered rocket boots, nuclear thrusters, a radar scanner, a vario-beam, and gauntlets capable of being disengaged and remote controlled, Iron Man's space armor could handle the rigors and challenges of an airless vacuum with ease.

## RECOVERY ARMOR
### 1985

After Tony had temporarily handed his heroic Iron Man duties over to Jim Rhodes, he still found himself tinkering with armor designs. As a result, Tony created his recovery armor, a close replica to his original gray design, but with a few improvements here and there.

## STEALTH ARMOR
### 1981

While on a rescue mission in Germany, Tony put his dark stealth armor to use for the first time. Constructed of polarized metal-mesh, Iron Man's stealth armor was built with only the most minor of defenses, in order to make room for espionage equipment like sound-dampened boot jets, a radar-bending wave modifier, a sonic scanning device, and a miniature spy camera.

## SILVER CENTURION
### 1985

To finally overcome the machinations of the villainous Obadiah Stane, Iron Man unleashed a new, more powerful version of his armor. With a built-in navigational computer, radar invisibility, holographic camouflage, energy absorption and redistribution capabilities, powerful pulse bolts, a protection field, and the ability to fly into Earth's upper atmosphere, the Silver Centurion armor truly made Iron Man a force to be reckoned with.

## THE ICONIC ARMOR
### 1964

It's in Tony Stark's nature to constantly design and redesign. Thus Iron Man's most memorable look was more the result of a series of improvements than one dramatic overhaul. After streamlining his mask during a battle with the Mandarin, Tony continued to experiment with design and function, improving every aspect of his armor's performance, from its repulsor rays to its roller wheels. Iron Man's suit soon possessed numerous gadgets, such as a reverser ray, a black-light tracer, a built-in generator, a chemical spray, explosive darts, and a diamond-tipped blade. In addition, Iron Man was able to seal his armor for brief under-water travel, utilizing a back-up air supply.

## NEO CLASSIC
### 1988

While waging his infamous Armor Wars, Tony constructed a new suit of armor that improved on all his past designs. Built to trick the world into thinking a new man was piloting the Iron Man suit, his new red and gold design was armed with a gauntlet-projected energy shield, a more powerful pulse bolt, enhanced speed, rapid-fire sequencing, and an electromagnetic pulse beam.

## HYDRO ARMOR MK 1
### 1987

Built for long expeditions under water, Iron Man's first attempt at deep-sea armor was equipped with several hours worth of oxygen, enabling the wearer to travel miles while submerged. Able to withstand even the strongest pressures found at the ocean floor, Iron Man's hydro armor also had a searchlight and a sonar system.

# THE ARMOR

### 1993–2000

## NEUROMIMETIC TELEPRESENCE UNIT
### 1993

Tony Stark had been experimenting with encephalo-circuits in his helmet that could control a suit of Iron Man armor by remote control. He was soon forced to put this new technology to practical use. Experimental surgery to equip his body with an artificial nervous system had just saved his life, but Tony awoke from the operation to find that he was completely paralyzed. With the help of his old friend Abe Zimmer and a neural interface headpiece, Tony was able to create a new and improved remote-controlled armor operated by his brainwaves and voice commands.

Early remote-controlled armor.

VR Mask

## WAR MACHINE ARMOR
### 1992

Tony Stark secretly designed the War Machine armor with his friend Jim Rhodes' combat skills in mind. Iron Man first wore the War Machine suit into battle when facing the ninjas known as the Masters of Silence. Later, when circumstances forced Tony to fake his own death, he bequeathed this silver suit of armor to Rhodey, asking him to carry on his legacy as Iron Man in his absence. Rhodey agreed, but later changed his name to War Machine in a bid for independence when he discovered that Tony's death was a sham.

## MODULAR ARMOR
### 1994

Once Tony Stark regained full control over his muscles, it didn't take him long to jump back into battle as Iron Man. With the help of his computer program HOMER, Tony manufactured an innovative new design that re-examined the basic construction of Iron Man. Instead of a single integrated unit, Tony created a modular component system that could be reconfigured by swapping out various sub-systems such as boots, gloves, or helmets. This allowed Iron Man to "dress for the occasion," bringing only the equipment each adventure called for.

## HULKBUSTER MK 1
### 1994

As part of his modular armor system, Tony created the Hulkbuster suit, with impact-resistant carbon-composites and a magno-hydraulic pseudomusculature rated at 175 tons. This armor was tough enough to handle even the fiercest battle with the green goliath known as the Incredible Hulk.

## THE CROSSING
### 1995

Corrupted by the power of the time-spanning villain Immortus, Iron Man slowly began to lose control of his faculties. Under Immortus' thrall, Tony Stark set up shop in a remote Arctic fortress, and designed a blue and white snowsuit to aid his travel to and from his new base. Soon Tony designed another new look to fit his personality shift; this new, highly sophisticated armor possessed prototype teleportation abilities.

## YOUNG TONY MK 1
### 1996

After being recruited from the past to fight the Iron Man he was destined to become, a younger version of Tony Stark was forced to don an unused Iron Man suit in order to do battle with his older counterpart. With the Avengers by his side, young Tony's new armor stood up against Iron Man's every attack, until the older Tony unleashed a near-fatal blow that crippled the young boy's fragile heart.

## PROMETHEUM ARMOR
### 1996

Stranded in a pocket universe with no memory of his past, Tony found himself once again reinventing the wheel as he created his prometheum Iron Man armor. Equipped with a wide array of sensory input, repulsor housings, a chest laser, tractor beam, and advanced life-support technology, the prometheum armor withstood the ferocity of a rampaging Hulk.

## SENTIENT ARMOR
### 2000

Once in a while, Tony Stark's scientific genius threatened to make his armor too advanced. Constantly adding to the capabilities of his new armor, he finally went too far. Compact enough to be transformed into a small, metal backpack-like case, Tony's latest Iron Man costume was brought to life in a Frankensteinesque manner by a stray bolt of lightning. Tony's suit proceeded to battle its inventor for control. It possessed both sentience and a desire for independent life as strong as that of any animal. However, the man finally overcame the machine.

Sentient foldaway mode.

## YOUNG TONY MK 2
### 1996

Built from a variety of spare parts found around Avengers Mansion, including an everyday kitchen blender and toaster, young Tony invented his own Iron Man suit. He used the notes of his now-deceased elder to guide him along the way. A work in progress, just like many other versions of the armor, young Tony's suit included hyper-thrust boot propulsion, therma-screen shielding, built-in gyro-stabilizers, and a variety of lasers.

## RETRO ARMOR
### 1998

Back in his proper dimension, Iron Man began a new era in his life. Accordingly, he unveiled a new suit of armor. This version showcased various favorite battle-tested inventions, including boot jets, radio and police bands, and balancing gyros. Iron Man's new retro armor also offered a number of improved features, such as computerized target locking and firing, inertia dampening fields, advanced scanners, nightvision capabilities, and miniature explosive charges.

### SPACE ARMOR
*2000*

Iron Man got the chance to test his newest suit outfitted for an outer space environment when he was forced to confront Justin Hammer onboard the criminal's satellite base. With a thin layer of compression gel protecting his body from the elements, the newly improved space armor was much slimmer than previous models. It also offered detachable solid fuel boosters, compressed gas maneuvering pods, and a solar sail capable of automatic piloting during reentry.

### SKIN ARMOR
*2001*

Acquiring new technology from Manhattan's Askew Labs, Iron Man constructed his SKIN armor using revolutionary liquid metal circuitry that shaped around Iron Man's body in a nearly unbreakable shell. Yet when not in use, the substance could be compacted to the size of a baseball. To augment this impressive armor, Tony added smart bomb probes, an energy blade that could extend into a shield, chameleon-like capabilities, and a holographic projector.

### TIN MAN ARMOR
*2002*

Signifying a return to basics, Iron Man's tin man armor resembled older tried and tested armor models with less of an emphasis on cutting-edge tech. Still containing a wide variety of weapons and surveillance gear, the tin man armor incorporated Tony's own personal secretary of sorts into its circuitry. Called Friday, this computer program was capable of doing everything from analyzing rare poisons to holding unwanted telephone calls.

### STEALTH ARMOR MK 3
*2002*

When tracking down the seemingly renegade Black Panther, Iron Man utilized his latest-model stealth armor. Composed of advanced composite ceramics, the armor was capable of projecting holograms onto its surface and making the wearer virtually invisible. Ideal for espionage missions, the suit also had an innovative noise-reduction engine, but only possessed the ability to fire three repulsor shots. The armor contained absolutely no metal, and instead was built with experimental bio-neural gel-pack circuitry.

### THORBUSTER ARMOR
*2003*

When Iron Man was forced to battle Thor, he adapted magical armor powered by the same enchantment that gives Thor's famous magic hammer Mjölnir its strength. Combining the strength of Thor with his own power, Iron Man gave the thunder god a run for his money.

### ABLATIVE ARMOR
*2003*

When facing an alien entity that had the ability to adhere to electronics and animate them with artificial life, Tony decided to give his ablative armor a test run. Layered with thousands of high-impact polymer tiles, this suit was designed to shed tiles in the event of damage. When an enemy missile hit the armor, the damaged tiles would simply pop off. Meanwhile, a polymer kiln on the back of the suit produced more tiles, which the armor's force field locked in place.

## EXTREMIS ARMOR
### 2005

The Extremis armor is Iron Man's most advanced to date. Tony utilized Extremis virus technology to literally rewrite his body's own functions into a superior fusion of man and machine. With Extremis tech in his system, Tony could link with satellites or any other technological device, simply with the power of thought.

## HYPERVELOCITY ARMOR
### 2007

With awe-inspiring computing capabilities and storage—enough to house the entire catalog of Tony Stark's memories—the Hypervelocity armor also contained superior firepower. Possessing long arms with waldo extensions, multiple-mode boot jets, and a telescoping supercavitation induction spike with a compressed-air bubblefeed that allowed for near-supersonic speeds of underwater travel, the armor was aptly nicknamed Tony 2.0.

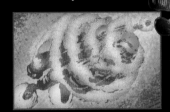

The Tony 2.0 armor had amazing underwater capabilities.

## HIGH-G ARMOR
### 2006

Bulky and heavy, similar to his three previous outer space suits, Tony's High-G (high-gravity) armor was constructed with stability very much in mind. With magnetic and jet compensators and advanced health readings at his fingertips, the High-G suit allowed Iron Man to survive and stay oriented while being rocketed through space, and even withstand an impromptu battle with Titanium Man.

## HULKBUSTER MK 2 ARMOR
### 2007

When Tony Stark helped exile the Hulk into outer space, he had planned for the contingency that the Green Goliath might somehow return to Earth. Wearing his largest, most protective suit of armor, Iron Man challenged the Hulk to a physical confrontation above Manhattan, while simultaneously broadcasting an inspiring address to the nation. Despite the Hulkbuster armor's remarkable durability and firepower, the Hulk made short work of Iron Man's impressive new toy.

## HYDRO ARMOR MK2
### 2006

When pursuing a convict to the undersea kingdom of Atlantis, X-Men member Wolverine recruited help from his fellow New Avenger Iron Man. Using one of Tony Stark's new deep-sea diving suits, Wolverine was able to stand the untold pressure extremes of the ocean's floor and continue to hunt down his prey.

# TALES OF #48 SUSPENSE

**PUBLICATION DATE**
December 1963

**EDITOR-IN-CHIEF**
Stan Lee

**COVER ARTIST**
Jack Kirby and Sol Brodsky

**WRITER**
Stan Lee

**PENCILER**
Steve Ditko

**INKER**
Dick Ayers

**Letterer**
Sam Rosen

"And now, though Mr. Doll won the first round in his battle with the old Iron Man... he's liable to find the new Iron Man a far more difficult foe to beat!"

IRON MAN

**MAIN CHARACTERS: Iron Man; Mr. Doll**
**SUPPORTING CHARACTERS: Pepper Potts; Happy Hogan; Charleton Carter; a Stark Industries security guard; New York City police officers**
**LOCATIONS: Stark Industries, Long Island, New York; Charleton Carter's mansion**

## BACKGROUND

As Iron Man's popularity grew, so did the length of his stories. By the end of his debut year, Iron Man's comics had grown from 13 pages to 18-paged "feature length" tales. A few guest artists helped with the increased workload, including Steve Ditko, who stopped by for a three-issue visit. Ditko was famous for co-creating and drawing Peter Parker, the amazing Spider-Man, so it made sense that, just a year after the debut of Mr. Parker's impressive duds, he was asked to pencil the first Iron Man issue featuring Tony Stark's new look.

This wasn't Iron Man's first costume change. As early as his second appearance, in *Tales of Suspense* #40, Iron Man had realized that his armor needed to appear less threatening to the public. He coated his suit in gold paint, turning himself into a modern-day knight in shining armor. Later, the red and gold look that Steve Ditko ushered in with *Tales* #48 slimmed down the previously bulky suit, creating perhaps the most iconic version of the Iron Man armor to date.

# The Story...

**When his first clash with the villainous Mr. Doll leaves him at death's door, Iron Man decides to upgrade his armor to better battle his mysterious new enemy.**

Mr. Doll's first strike hit Tony Stark right where it counted: his wallet. When wealthy steel man Charleton Carter backed out of a mutually lucrative business deal at the last moment, Stark decided to drop by Carter's mansion in order to talk some sense into his business associate. But as he pulled into the old tycoon's lane, Tony noticed an odd figure cloaked in what seemed like a masquerade costume **(1)** approaching Carter's home. Changing into his golden Iron Man armor to investigate **(2)**, Tony observed the costumed man blackmailing Carter out of his fortune by manipulating a small clay doll. It seemed the uniquely garbed individual was calling himself Mr. Doll, and his oddly shaped toy was a modern day voodoo doll, able to force the helpless Charleton Carter into obeying his every command.

Iron Man had seen enough, even if he didn't quite understand what was going on. He charged in through Carter's window, and lifted Mr. Doll into the air **(3)**, unfortunately giving the villain time to alter his doll's likeness to that of Iron Man himself. By squeezing the clay figure in his hand **(4)**, Mr. Doll made Iron Man feel as if his very bones were being crushed inside his armor. And if that wasn't bad enough, the power in Iron Man's suit was nearly depleted. If he didn't recharge his chest plate soon, he would suffer a fatal heart attack. Tony had no choice. He had to escape.

Reeling in pain, Tony sped back to his Long Island factory and stumbled into his private laboratory. There he managed to plug his chest plate into a special outlet even as he collapsed onto the floor, unconscious. Waking later thanks only to the miraculous device, Tony realized that it was his heavy, cumbersome armor that was slowing him down. If he was going to defeat Mr. Doll, he'd need a complete overhaul. He'd have to redesign Iron Man.

Hours passed as Tony toiled alone in his private workshop **(5)**. Meanwhile, across town, Mr. Carter was signing away his entire fortune. Mr. Doll's plan had succeeded, and it was time for the villain to pick a new target. He slowly reshaped his voodoo doll. Holding the totem to the light, Doll smiled as he looked down at a familiar face. The face of Tony Stark.

Back in his lab, Tony was finally completing work on his new armor **(6, 7, 8)**. Not only was his new Iron Man suit sleeker and more powerful than his last model, but it was slimmer and more compact as well. In fact, the arms and legs of the suit conveniently retracted into the glove and boot housings when not in use, making for much easier storage.

While the police grew wise to Mr. Doll's plans and set up a guard at Tony's office, Iron Man slipped out a secret passageway in order to surprise Mr. Doll when the villain finally reared his head at Stark Industries. After briefly being controlled again by Doll's clay figurine, Iron Man escaped to a nearby chamber. Locked safely away from his adversary, the hero then recharged his armor and began to construct his own little surprise for his unwanted trespasser. Attacking Mr. Doll once more **(9)**, Iron Man aimed his newly created pocket-sized device **(10)** at the clay voodoo doll before Mr. Doll could take hold of his faculties. And slowly, the clay figure began to shift its shape until it began to resemble Mr. Doll himself. In a moment of pure surprise, Mr. Doll dropped his prized totem, and as the doll hit the ground, the villain had no choice but to follow suit, collapsing to the floor, unconscious and thoroughly defeated **(11)**.

"I've got a little gadget here which is going to change all your evil plans... "

Tony Stark was a dreamer. Unfortunately, that was a quality he and his father didn't share. While young Tony built model iron men out of erector sets and fantasized about the ancient tales of King Arthur and knights in shining armor, his father Howard found his escape from the stress of running weapons manufacturer Stark Industries at the bottom of a whisky bottle. Tony had a genius-level IQ and an imaginative mind but as a boy never seemed to take life seriously enough for his overbearing father. When Tony turned seven years old, despite the protests of his wife Maria, Howard shipped Tony off to boarding school in an attempt to instill him with discipline. There, Tony excelled at his studies, and eventually grew to be a well-rounded young man, despite his shy nature. Graduating from college at an extremely young age, Tony became his father's right-hand man. Although he could knock off a radical innovative weapons design in less time than it took him to get ready for a night on the town, Tony's heart was never truly in his work. He preferred the life of a young playboy—which only served to distance the two Stark men even further.

# TONY STARK

**At age 15, he enrolled in MIT. By 21, he was running one of the largest companies in North America. Anthony "Tony" Stark has always been ahead of the pack, the curve, and his time.**

When Howard and Maria Stark were killed in a car accident, Tony found himself at the head of their multibillion-dollar company. After learning that his parents had died owing to a construction fault in their automobile, Tony's first act as head of Stark Industries was to purchase the car company responsible and overhaul their entire approach to brake design. To this day, Tony is still unaware that the "accident" was actually engineered by a group of industry competitors who would later found the corrupt organization Roxxon Oil.

After a year or two spent grappling with the complexities of running a massive business such as Stark Industries, Tony grew into the man his father had always wanted him to be. Working tirelessly to expand the company into a multi-national corporation, Tony's drive to succeed only increased following his injury in an explosion in Afghanistan and the commencement of his double life as the armored avenger Iron Man. Witnessing the terrible destructive power of his weapons firsthand, and realizing that the tide of public opinion was turning against those seen as war profiteers, Tony altered Stark Industries' focus from weapons manufacturing to a variety of other technological innovations, establishing his father's company as a true leader of the industrial world.

Growing up in the family mansion near New York's Central Park, Tony has a penchant for prime real estate. His luxury homes include a plush penthouse at Stark International's Long Island headquarters, and apartments in Manhattan's Stark Tower skyscraper, as well as atop Stark Enterprises in California.

Tony's social exploits have run a close race with his adventures as Iron Man. Perhaps he has been overcompensating for school days spent alone with his head buried in various scientific journals and works of fiction. Tony, for years one of the world's most sought-after bachelors, is often spotted at exclusive parties and events with a new girl on his arm—much to the annoyance of his longtime personal assistant Pepper Potts.

Much like the modern computer, the Iron Man armor is a work in progress. Tony is constantly adding innovations and streamlining aspects of his suit in order to remain at the forefront of cutting-edge technology. As a result, he manages to keep one step ahead of the corrupt men and women that his life of crime-fighting pits him against. Though Tony is more at home in his lab tinkering with new ideas than at the end of a boardroom table at a business meeting, he still finds time to juggle both, only allowing a select few trusted friends, such as James Rhodes and Pepper Potts, to aid him on either front.

## KEY DATA

**FULL NAME** Anthony Edward "Tony" Stark

**ALIASES** Iron Man; also known as Shellhead and the Golden Avenger

**HIGHT** 6 ft 1 in **WEIGHT** 225 lbs
**EYES** Blue **HAIR** Black

**KNOWN RELATIVES** Maria Collins Carbonell Stark and Howard Anthony Stark (parents, deceased), Morgan Stark (cousin), Edward Stark (uncle, deceased), Isaac Stark, Sr., Isaac Stark, Jr. (ancestors, deceased)

**OCCUPATION** Adventurer, CEO of Stark Industries, former Director of SHIELD, former head of the Initiative, founder of the Maria Stark Foundation, former CEO of Stark International, Stark Solutions, Stark Enterprises, Circuits Maximus, former US Secretary of Defense, former technician for Askew Electronics

Despite his ridiculously busy schedule, Tony still manages regular exercise, realizing that his brain isn't the only muscle he needs to flex daily. Whether training with his fellow Avengers or just starting his day with a morning jog, physical fitness is a key part of Tony's everyday routine.

# The Wit and Wisdom of Tony Stark

All of those who've wondered why **Iron Man** risks his life time and time again... if they could feel the indescribable **exhilaration** of flying in an armored suit, they'd wonder **no more!**

Two can play the game of gadgets, rabbit ears! On the other hand, there's a classic **simplicity** to a good **right hand jab** that's not to be denied!

All right, Doom, you've won that round. But that's only *check*... not check-*mate!*

If you want to *remain* saved, get back out of the line of fire.

Head butting like this could get me thrown out of most wrestling bouts—but I'm not fighting for trophies here! I'm fighting for my *life!*

No one has the right to defy the wishes of his government... not even Iron Man!

My appearance terrifies women and children as if I were a **monster!** I'm a frightening sight to the very people I want to aid and protect!

But could I have married Janice? Would it have been fair with a heart like mine?

Firebrand, you've come up with a *costume* that has powers and protection nearly *equal* to mine... How can you so insanely *misuse* it?!

What about **my** cause? What is it **I'm** fighting for? Whatever it **is**, I must **live** for it... and **die** for it.

I went from being a man trapped in an iron suit to being a man freed by it.

There is a pollution crisis in the world, but it can't be solved by taking the first **hysterical action!**

I don't deal in weapons any more... I'm more interested in creating the future than blowing it up.

Being a man in a metal suit doesn't solve any problems... It just gives you a whole lot of new ones to think about.

**You can't let somebody else do your suffering for you.**

Can I have a personal relationship with anyone and continue to function as Iron Man should?

I won't waste time defending the *past* or arguing about the present while a man's in *danger!*

I guess, in the final *reckoning,* it does add up... the life of a Super Hero has *meaning...* and *purpose.*

**Hiding?** Is that what it's **come** to? Hiding my feelings, my **life**—behind an iron **mask?**

This is the most **sophisticated**, most astonishing invention I've ever constructed! But that's the precise reason... why it has to be **destroyed**!

**With all the pain and sorrow my other armor caused, I shudder to think what could happen if this fell into evil hands.**

I've learned that free will isn't a gift—it's a muscle which needs to be exercised—and only when it's in peak condition—is a man truly awake.

# CAPTAIN AMERICA

He's a living symbol of freedom, and America's sentinel of Liberty. Captain America is a man Tony Stark has always wanted as a friend, but all too often faced as an enemy.

## ARMOR WARS

Everyone Captain America ever knew was either extremely old, or buried in the ground. So naturally, the Avengers became his closest friends. Both sharing strong moral values, Cap and Iron Man instantly hit it off, but their friendship would be called into question time and time again. One of the most testing times in their relationship occurred during Iron Man's so-called "Armor Wars." Tony broke laws and betrayed other heroes attempting to destroy all of his technology that had fallen into other people's hands. Captain America took issue with the extreme methods his friend was employing. After trying to persuade Stark to give up his crusade, Cap felt he had no choice but to stop his old friend when Iron Man broke into a government installation, the Vault prison.

Anticipating Tony's attack on the Vault prison, Steve tried to talk some sense into Stark.

While searching for Namor the Sub Mariner, the Avengers stumbled upon the thawing body of Captain America.

## MEETING THE AVENGERS

The phrase "man out of time" means more to Steve Rogers than most people realize. A shining example of what the common man could strive for during World War II, Rogers volunteered for a super-soldier program and became Captain America. An icon known the world over, Captain America was caught in an explosion and plunged into the ocean. While the world presumed their hero dead, Cap was actually frozen in a chunk of ice. When the Avengers stumbled upon his perfectly preserved body, they were as surprised as the public when the hero not only revived, but seemed to still be in top physical condition. Soon Cap joined the Avengers ranks, fighting for freedom in a new world.

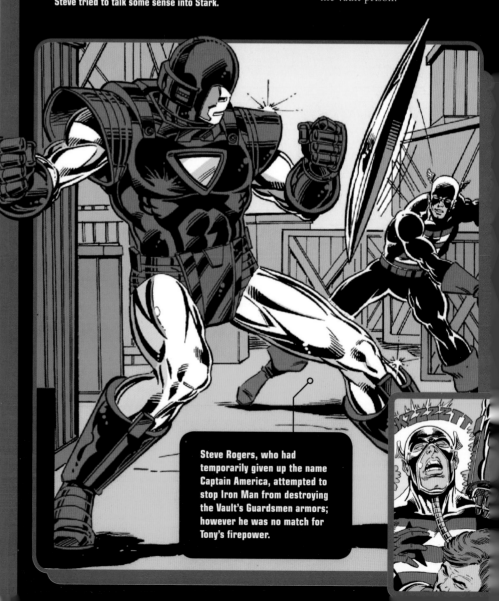

Steve Rogers, who had temporarily given up the name Captain America, attempted to stop Iron Man from destroying the Vault's Guardsmen armors; however he was no match for Tony's firepower.

## A LOYAL FRIEND

Back when Tony Stark was suffering from his worst bout of alcoholism, he dropped out from society, lost in his world of booze and pain. Captain America went to visit Tony in his squalid surroundings, but Stark refused his help even after Rogers rescued him from a burning building.

Captain America was forced to rely on dirty tricks to defeat Iron Man.

## CIVIL WAR

Iron Man and Captain America had violently disagreed on many issues over the years—the "Armor Wars" incident at the Vault, Tony dating the Wasp, the extermination of the alien Kree leader the Supreme Intelligence, to name just a few. But when the government passed the Superhuman Registration Act, Steve and Tony faced an insurmountable obstacle to their friendship when they realized that they were on diametrically opposed sides. It was a fight that neither wanted to lose, and neither could afford to win.

Iron Man never had the chance or the courage to tell Captain America why he had chosen to take a stand in favor of the Superhuman Registration Act.

## DEATH OF A HERO

The Civil War was over and Iron Man's forces had been victorious. Left with no acceptable alternative, Captain America surrendered himself to the government. While walking up the steps of the courthouse to face his arraignment, Cap was shot—an assassination planned by his longtime enemy, the Red Skull. Captain America was dead, and Tony Stark never got the chance to say goodbye to his former friend and ally.

## "Am I an arms dealer? No. Did I start out as a weapons designer? Yes. Do I intend to die as one? No." Tony Stark

### A Family Business

The brainchild of Isaac Stark Sr., Stark Industries was an engineering manufacturing business formed in the 19th century. The company continued to be a family-run organization, with the position of president and CEO being passed down through generations of Stark men. In modern times, Stark Industries began to focus on weapons manufacturing, relying on government contracts for the bulk of its income. When owned by Howard Stark, the corporation flourished until Howard and his wife Maria died in a car crash. Control of the company then passed to the couple's reluctant son, Tony. Despite being responsible for designing many of Stark Industries' technological innovations, Tony wasn't sure he was ready for the responsibility of running such a large business. However, with the help of his executive assistant Pepper Potts, Tony grew into the role, and soon learned to embrace his family's legacy, raising Stark profits to an all-time high. Since then, Tony has continued to put his own stamp on the company and led it through many varied incarnations.

Stark Industries has undergone many changes over the years—different names, different policies, different locations—its fluctuating fortunes mirroring those of its presiding genius, the endlessly inventive Tony Stark.

### STARK INDUSTRIES

When Tony first inherited the company, Stark Industries was primarily a weapons manufacturer. After his injury and his subsequent transformation into Iron Man, Tony began to have serious ethical misgivings about his deadly creations, and led the company away from weapons and into technologies more likely to benefit humanity.

### STARK INTERNATIONAL

A futurist at heart, Tony decided to alter the name of his company to reflect its presence on the global market. With subsidiaries in all parts of the world, and a growing interest in research, Stark decided that the new moniker Stark International better signified the changing times.

### CIRCUITS MAXIMUS

During Tony's relapse into alcoholism, Obadiah Stane staged an extremely hostile takeover of Stark's company, changing the name to Stane International and returning to weapons manufacturing. After getting clean once more, Tony decided to move to California and start from scratch with a new electronics firm.

### STARK ENTERPRISES

Not satisfied with chasing Stark out of his own business, Obadiah Stane began to sabotage Circuits Maximus, destroying the fledgling company in an explosion. After confronting Stane in a battle that led to Obadiah's death, Tony distanced himself from Stane's corrupt life by forming the Los Angeles-based Stark Enterprises.

### STARK-FUJIKAWA

After later reacquiring Stane International and eradicating its illegal practices, Tony seemingly perished while fighting Immortus as Iron Man. During the time of his absence, the foreign conglomerate Fujikawa staged a takeover of Stark Enterprises, one they maintained even after Tony's miraculous resurrection and return.

### STARK SOLUTIONS

Instead of attempting to fight to regain his old company, Tony created the consulting firm, Stark Solutions. Offering his services to anyone willing to pay his high price tag, Tony put Stark Solutions in place largely to donate much of the profits to his charitable Maria Stark Foundation.

### STARK INDUSTRIES 2

After becoming romantically involved with Rumiko Fujikawa, Tony Stark was able to regain controlling stock in his own company. He decided to return full circle and rename the corporation Stark Industries. The company has since been hit hard by a technological virus introduced by the Skrull aliens, and by destruction caused by Ezekiel Stane. Despite Stark's best intentions, his family's legacy is now on the brink of bankruptcy.

# STAFF

Besides his friends Pepper Potts, Happy Hogan, and Jim Rhodes, Tony has gone to great lengths to hire the best of the best.

### MRS. BAMBI ARBOGAST

Tony's sassy executive assistant for many years, Mrs. Arbogast proved time and time again that she could handle herself in a crisis, even standing up to the Melter on one occasion.

### MARCY PEARSON

Public Relations head of Stark Enterprises, Marcy took over briefly as CEO when Stark was shot and on his deathbed. Her ambitions later got the best of her, forcing Jim Rhodes to terminate her employment.

### KEVIN O'BRIEN

A researcher at the first incarnation of Stark Industries, O'Brien helped Tony develop the sophisticated Guardsman armor. Driven insane by a flaw in the equipment design, Kevin battled Iron Man and died in the melee.

### ABRAHAM KLEIN

A former engineering professor of Tony's, Abe petitioned for a job from his former student. Working undercover for the villain Mordecai Midas, Abe sabotaged the company from the inside for his notorious boss.

### ARTEMUS PITHINS

Former PR head of Stark International, Pithins resigned from his position during Stane's takeover. He and Tony were later reunited when Pithins served as the White House press secretary to Tony's Secretary of Defense.

### MORLEY ERWIN

Becoming Rhodey's trusted confidant and technical assistant when Jim first became Iron Man, Morley soon made the move to Circuits Maximus along with his sister and Tony, until his untimely death in an explosion.

### CLYTEMNESTRA ERWIN

Morley's sister, and a technological genius in her own right, Clytemnestra was one of the founders of Circuits Maximus. Blaming Tony for her brother's death, she betrayed him to AIM, and was killed in the resulting battle.

### ABE ZIMMER

Tony first met Abe when purchasing the company Accutech. Zimmer soon earned his place in Tony's trusted inner circle, and used his computer wizardry to help Tony several times, even sacrificing his life for his boss.

### JOCASTA

An artificial intelligence and former Avenger, Jocasta downloaded herself into Iron Man's armor in order to maintain her survival during a battle. She served for a time as a trusted component of Stark's computer systems.

# INVENTIONS

Tony Stark's ever-evolving Iron Man armor is just one of his amazing inventions.

### S.H.I.E.L.D. HELICARRIER

As one of the brilliant minds behind the international peacekeeping force SHIELD, Tony Stark designed weapons systems and technology for the agency for years, before he changed his company's focus to less lethal innovations. Working with director Nick Fury, Mr. Fantastic of the Fantastic Four, and X-Men member Forge, Tony created one of the SHIELD's most lauded innovations, the helicarrier, a flying aircraft carrier. With room for up to 1,000 crewmen, and utilizing revolutionary vortex-beam technology, the helicarrier served as the mobile headquarters for SHIELD's operations.

### MANDROIDS

Built by Tony Stark to protect SHIELD soldiers from superhuman attacks, the armored Mandroids were first employed against the Avengers.

### HAWKEYE'S ARROWS

Although most of Avenger Hawkeye's trick arrows are designed by the archer himself, some of his more technological arrows were devised by Tony Stark.

### CAP'S SHIELD

When the government stripped him of his title, Steve Rogers asked Tony to build him a replacement shield.

### THE QUINJET

The Quinjet, the Avengers' efficient shuttle, was originally designed by T'Challa, the Black Panther, and has since been redesigned by Tony Stark for use by the New Avengers and the Mighty Avengers. The jet is capable of vertical takeoff and can reach speeds of more than Mach 2.

## MISCELLANEOUS INVENTIONS

- Particle beam torpedo
- Evader personal protection unit
- Friday: a virtual personal assistant
- HOMER (Heuristically Operative Matrix Emulation Rostrum) computer system
- The Works: State-of-the-art "smart building"
- Guardsmen armor
- Plato (Piezo-Electrical Logistic Analytic Tactical Operator) artificial intelligence
- Flying Prowler (and other flying automobiles)
- Vroom Room: Virtual reality training center
- Sentinel landmine
- Uranus II rocket
- Jupiter Landing Vehicle
- Anti-missile Missile Gun
- SK-1 stealth jet
- Experimental Sea Tank
- Hex Ships *Pegasus* and *Chimera*
- SHIELD satellite
- Life Model Decoys
- Armor negator packs
- Transistorized blast gun
- Iron Spider armor
- Holo-Communicator
- Encephalo-circuitry
- Transistor-powered roller skates
- Warwagon tank

Behind his playboy persona and his charming, carefree wit, Tony Stark is a man tortured by past mistakes and future concerns. He lives a life of extremes, a life that has led him to battle potentially crippling health problems and a chronic addiction to alcohol.

# A TROUBLED HERO

**94-95**

## CRISIS OF CONSCIENCE

Tony Stark's entire fortune was founded on death. Although he has tried to see it from some other perspective, there's no avoiding the facts. His father was a weapons manufacturer, selling brilliant and efficient killing machines to the US government to aid their various war efforts. When Tony took over his father's business, he too became little more than a glorified arms dealer. Tony improved upon his father's ideas and Stark Industries reaped the benefits.

It wasn't until Tony witnessed firsthand the destructive might of his terrible creations that he began to have serious misgivings about his life's work. After a near-fatal injury caused by one of his own Stark landmines, Tony began to appreciate the consequences of his creations. It took time, paperwork, and wading through miles of red tape, before Tony was able to cease all Stark weapons manufacturing once and for all. He now fights as Iron Man trying to make amends for his past by protecting the people of the present. But the fact that he can never bring back the many thousands of lives destroyed by his company's inventions weighs heavily upon him.

## THE CONSTANT DEMON

Tony Stark's greatest fear is that he'll lose control again. Struggling with alcoholism nearly his entire adult life, Tony has hit rock bottom on more than one occasion. Alcohol is a persistent threat looming in the darkest recessses of his mind—a threat that some of Tony's enemies have ruthlessly exploited. Hardly a day goes by that Tony doesn't do battle with the demon in the bottle.

## UNLUCKY IN LOVE

High-octane exotic beauties, female teammates with excess personal baggage, charismatic but fatally flawed Super Villains: Tony hasn't had the best of luck when it comes to romance. Bad choices combined with his own guilt complex and secretive ways, has resulted in one unworkable relationship after another. To Tony, true love seems an elusive prize indeed. But there are some that feel that what he's looking for has been right under his nose all the while.

## BROKEN BODY

While the armor he's created seems to be nearly invulnerable, the man who wears it has proven to be anything but. From the very beginning of Iron Man's career, Tony has struggled with a near-fatal heart condition, brought on by shrapnel lodged close to his heart. Originally Tony was forced to wear his life-saving Iron Man chest plate at all times, just to keep his frail heart beating. He has undergone a heart transplant to cure this condition, but over the years has fallen victim to other ills, such as a shattered spine and a bout of total paralysis.

# FRIENDS & ALLIES

If a man can be judged by his friends alone, Iron Man certainly has nothing to worry about. Earning allies both in the boardroom and the battlefield, Tony Stark always has someone to call on in a crisis.

## Nick Fury

As one of the backers of the peacekeeping force SHIELD, Tony Stark helped appoint Nick Fury as the organization's director. Stark has continued to aid SHIELD in both of his identities, even after Fury tried to stage a hostile takeover of Stark International back when Tony pledged to end its weapon production. In fact, immediately after Tony foiled Fury's attempt, the two fought side by side against the towering automaton Dreadnought.

## Dum Dum Dugan

Nick Fury's right-hand man, and a fine leader in his own right, Timothy "Dum Dum" Dugan began working for Stark when Tony was named the Director of SHIELD. However, during the events of the Secret Invasion (see pp.180–181) by the alien, shapeshifting Skrulls, it was revealed that Tony had not been working with Dugan at all, but a Skrull impersonating the loyal soldier.

## Eddie March

A boxer inspired by Iron Man's crime-busting adventures, Eddie March was groomed by Tony Stark to replace him as Iron Man. Worried about his failing health, Tony enthusiastically trained Eddie to take over for him, only to discover that March's life was secretly threatened by a blood clot. However, after Tony reclaimed his role as a Super Hero, he and Eddie continued their friendship, and March subsequently joined Stark's charitable Iron Man Foundation.

## Scott Lang

The second hero to call himself Ant-Man (the first was scientist and original Avenger Henry Pym), Scott Lang worked for Stark International for years. Often trusted to help his employer out in a pinch, Lang was willing to go the extra mile for Tony, on one occasion even breaking into prison on his behalf to interrogate an inmate. Lang was tragically killed during the rampage of the unbalanced Avenger Scarlet Witch.

## Pepper Potts

Although perhaps the most loyal friend Tony Stark has ever had, his executive assistant Pepper Potts hasn't always got on well with her eccentric boss. When she first met Tony, she found him to be a bit sexist. And years later, when she married Happy Hogan, Pepper wanted little to do with Tony Stark, knowing the trouble he always brought into their lives. Regardless, Pepper is always drawn back to Tony, and probably always will be.

## Abe Zimmer

Tony first met computer technician Abe when Stark Enterprises was looking to purchase the research firm Accutech. After hearing Zimmer's informative account of the Ghost saboteur, the two started a working relationship that budded into a true friendship. Zimmer helped Stark hack into foreign computers during his "Armor Wars." He proved his loyalty to Tony when he died at the hand of the villainous Stockpile to keep Tony's secrets safe.

## Jim Rhodes

Their friendship forged in the heat of battle, Rhodey and Stark have seen the best and the worst in each other's nature, but still managed to maintain their original bond. Treating him him like his own brother, Tony even gave Jim a set of armor, a gesture reserved only for a chosen few.

## Bethany Cabe

One of Tony's former lovers, and the main reason he first overcame his alcohol dependency, the charismatic Bethany Cabe keeps appearing and reappearing in Stark's life. From working as his head of security, to taking over as commander of his War Machine project, Bethany has remained loyal to her old flame.

## Happy Hogan

Many people have claimed they would be willing to take a bullet for Tony, but Happy Hogan actually proved it. On more than one occasion, Happy saved his employer's life. But it was the last instance that proved fatal for him, when he stopped the Spymaster from assassinating Iron Man.

## Maria Hill

Nick Fury's original replacement as director of SHIELD, Maria Hill stepped down to allow Stark to lead the organization, and proved fiercely loyal to him. Fired alongside Tony when SHIELD merged with the HAMMER organization led by the villainous Norman Osborn, Maria and Tony shared a fling while on the run.

## Guardsman

After his mind was skewed by the circuitry in Tony's Guardsman armor, his former ally Kevin O'Brien became Iron Man's newest enemy. Long after Kevin tragically died in battle, Stark International usurper Obadiah Stane sold the Guardsman armor design to the prison known as the Vault, to better arm its security staff.

## Edwin Jarvis

Tony's childhood butler and a staunch friend of the Stark family, Edwin Jarvis had the opportunity to watch Tony grow up into the man he is today. He then became the Avengers' butler. Jarvis was replaced by a Skrull during the Secret Invasion.

## Ho Yinsen

A brilliant pioneer of medical science, and a futurist just like Tony Stark himself, Ho Yinsen was taken captive by the warmonger Wong-Chu. After being forced to examine alien rings at the behest of the Mandarin, Yinsen later sacrificed his life to ensure Tony's freedom.

## Sal Kennedy

A modern-day hippy and proponent of casual drug use, Sal Kennedy's unorthodox thinking led Tony to make Sal his SHIELD advisor and unofficial mentor. He challenged Tony's ethics on a few occasions, but grew to hate his SHIELD position. Sal was killed during a viral attack on the SHIELD helicarrier orchestrated by the Mandarin.

## Jack of Hearts

When his scientist father was murdered before his eyes, young Jack Hart was exposed to zero-fluid, which endowed him with superpowers. Hart became the crime-fighter Jack of Hearts. He was a protegé of Iron Man, before graduating to full Avengers membership.

## Guardsman II

Michael O'Brien was the second man to don the Guardsman armor, and the second to be corrupted by its circuitry into fighting Iron Man. He later became a friend of Iron Man and filled in for him on occasion, even pitting his skills against the Mandarin.

## Force

Laboratory assistant Clayton Wilson stole a force-field projector and embarked on a life of crime as Force. After having second thoughts about this career move, with the help of Tony Stark, Clay turned his life around and started over. To conceal his past, he changed his name to Carl Walker.

## Henry Hellrung

He's not a hero, he just plays one on TV. Famous for his role as television's Iron Man, Henry Hellrung became drinking buddies with the real Tony Stark. Years later, when they had both beaten their drinking problems, he was Tony's sponsor at Alcoholics Anonymous, before accepting a role as the hero Anthem in the Order.

# IRON MAN #182

**PUBLICATION DATE**
May 1984

**EDITOR-IN-CHIEF**
Jim Shooter

**COVER ARTIST**
Luke McDonnell and Steve Mitchell

**WRITER**
Denny O'Neil

**PENCILER**
Luke McDonnell

**INKER**
Steve Mitchell

**COLORIST**
Bob Sharen

"**What *am* I celebrating? A very, very good question. If I had to give an answer, I'd say... I'd say I'm celebrating the end. The living end. The end of living.**"
TONY STARK

**MAIN CHARACTERS: Tony Stark; Gretl Anders; Timothy Anders; Iron Man (Jim Rhodes)**
**SUPPORTING CHARACTERS: New York City police; Thor; Captain America; Hawkeye; Captain Marvel; Morely Erwin**
**LOCATIONS: A pawnshop, St. Vincent's Hospital; a graveyard, Central Park; Morely Erwins' apartment (all New York City)**

## BACKGROUND

By the mid-1980s, Dennis O'Neil was a prominent figure in the comic writing world. He had helped bring DC Comics' Batman back to his dark roots in the 1970s, and had achieved great acclaim for his mature storytelling and subject matter in a medium still primarily targeted towards youth.

When O'Neil took over writing *Iron Man* for a lengthy run of nearly 50 issues, it came as no surprise to readers that he threw Tony Stark's world on its end. Through the machinations of a new villain, Obadiah Stane, O'Neil reduced Stark once again to a desperate alcoholic, showcasing the gritty reality behind his disease. And this time there would be no easy out for Tony Stark...

After O'Neil's groundbreaking story, which culminated in issue #182, Stark would find it impossible to shelve his lingering addiction, and would live out his life haunted by his past weaknesses and failures.

# The Story...

**Reduced to little more than a homeless derelict, Tony Stark trudges through the streets of New York City in a snowstorm, forced to either succumb to his inner demons or rise above them.**

It was one of the worst blizzards New York City had ever seen, and Tony Stark was caught right in the middle of it. With only a thin coat and a swig of alcohol in his belly to keep him warm, Tony's life had been reduced to a pathetic mantra: find Gretl. She was his drinking partner and his only friend since he had begun to live on the streets. Plus she was nine months pregnant and probably caught in the same storm he was. He had to find her. But as he drained the last drop from his bottle **(1)**, Tony realized that he also had to find another drink.

Wandering into a rather unwelcoming pawnshop, Tony traded his coat for a mere ten dollars **(2)**. He went back out into the snow, walking past a cheap hotel in favor of ducking into the nearest liquor store **(3)**. There he spent his last few dollars and headed out into the cold, content to lean up against a nearby building and die. And that's when Gretl found him. And she was ready to have her baby.

Tony's first thought was to get his friend to a hospital. But it was too far away, and the storm was too fierce. Instead the two ducked into a nearby doorway, and huddled together for warmth **(4)**. As Tony continued to drink, Gretl began to go into labor, finally giving birth to a baby boy **(5)**. But the pain and the cold proved too much for the frail woman. As Tony warmed her child inside his suit jacket, Gretl died in his arms.

Tony probably would have died too if the police hadn't wandered by the next morning, finding him still huddled in the doorway, holding the still-breathing child **(6)**. Both Tony and the infant were taken to nearby St. Vincent's hospital. Gretl was buried, just another forgotten casualty of the New York City streets.

A few hours later in Central Park, a strange structure seemingly appeared out of nowhere. Suddenly, from inside it, a parade of costumed heroes emptied out onto the earth below **(7)**, happy to be touching familiar soil once more. From Captain America to Hawkeye to Iron Man himself, the heroes departed the strange vessel and went their separate ways, their adventure on the planet known as Battleworld finally at a close. As Iron Man, in the person of Jim Rhodes, was still fairly new to the Super Hero game, he had brought back a souvenir: a newly augmented suit of advanced armor. Testing his new suit's firepower on a nearby hill **(8)**, Rhodey realized that the armor was much too powerful, and decided to pay a visit to his technical advisor, Morley Erwin.

After learning from Erwin that Tony Stark was hospitalized earlier that day, Rhodey flew to St. Vincent's to pay his old friend a visit. As the new Iron Man loomed over the injured body of his predecessor **(9)**, Tony awoke, telling Rhodey that he had come to an epiphany, and he was finally ready to straighten out his situation. Seeing firsthand how precious life truly was, Tony was determined to end his nightmare. He was ready to start his life over, even if he wasn't quite prepared to don the Iron Man armor again.

A day passed, and then a week. Tony Stark was released from the hospital. He walked down the city streets with a new outlook on life, at a crossroads that could take him virtually anywhere he wished to go **(10)**.

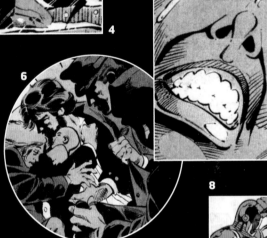

**"I'd say I'm celebrating the end. The living end. The end of living."**

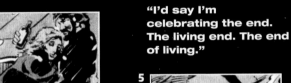

# Pepper Potts

Pepper Potts is the one reason Stark Industries didn't crash and burn ages ago. She's been Tony's right-hand woman for more years than either of them would like to admit. Infatuated with her boss almost from the first, Pepper has been flirting with Tony for as long as Iron Man has been flirting with disaster.

## Pepper in Peril

Unfortunately for Pepper, being Tony Stark's Girl Friday means she is constantly put in harm's way. Tony rescued her from the secretarial pool after Pepper caught and corrected an error that would have cost his company hundreds of thousands of dollars. However, Pepper's promotion to his executive assistant has made her the target of every Super Villain with a grudge against the Golden Avenger.

## In Good Hands

When Pepper first took over as Tony's assistant, she saw her workload increase tenfold. But soon Tony started to realize the importance of his job as head of Stark Industries, and the two became a solid team, even as their romantic tensions grew. Pepper helped Stark on all fronts and even saved Iron Man's life on more than one occasion.

## KEY DATA

**FULL NAME** Virginia "Pepper" Potts

**ALIASES** Rescue, Hera, formerly Pepper Hogan

**RELATIVES** Harold "Happy" Hogan (husband, deceased), unidentified foster son and daughter, Clay Hogan (brother-in-law), unidentified grandfather-in-law

**OCCUPATION** Executive assistant, former coordinator of the Order

**AFFILIATIONS** The Order, Stark Industries

## Bomb Victim

Despite their frequent flirtations, Pepper and Tony were never quite able to spark up a full-fledged romance. Tony worried about the state of his injured heart, while Pepper worried about Tony's reluctance to settle down with any one woman. It wasn't until Pepper was caught in a deadly blast while attending a gala with Tony that he truly realized how important she was to him. With shrapnel imbedded in her chest near her heart, Tony was forced to equip Pepper with repulsor technology to keep her alive.

Despite her quick recovery and miraculous new lease on life, Pepper was wary of having one of Tony's weapons inside her body.

However, the mag-field in Pepper's chest was created as a battery, not a weapon. The good news left Pepper literally walking on air.

## Goodbye Kiss

When Tony was fired from his position as head of SHIELD and replaced by the current media darling, Norman Osborn, he refused to share classified information with the supposedly reformed Green Goblin. As a wanted man for his principled stand, Tony gave Pepper a parting kiss before going on the run.

## Rescue

But the kiss wasn't Tony's last gift to his loyal assistant. While finishing up some final paperwork for the now bankrupt Stark Industries, Pepper stumbled upon a secret chamber that housed a suit of armor designed specifically for her. Equipped only with life-saving technology and run by a familiar computer program called JARVIS (Just Another Rather Very Intelligent System), the armor was a perfect fit for Pepper, who eagerly adopted it, renaming herself Rescue.

# HAPPY HOGAN

"He needs a chauffeur like a hole in the head! What does he keep me around for, anyway?"

More worried about injuring his opponents than winning a title, boxer Harold "Happy" Hogan never found much success in the ring. Retiring from the fight game and taking a job at Stark Industries as Tony Stark's personal chauffeur, Happy thought he'd put his days of violence behind him. Instead, his life became a powder keg, where any workday could be his last.

### The Rescue
When Tony was racing a custom stock car at the Indianapolis Speedway, he forgot to recharge his Iron Man chest plate that, at that time, kept his injured heart beating. Losing control of his car, Tony crashed into an embankment, and was pulled out of the flames by spectator Happy Hogan.

### Happy-Go-Lucky
Even after Tony Stark offered him a cushy job as his chauffeur as reward for his valiant act on the racetrack, Happy rarely dropped his trademark scowl—hence his "Happy" nickname.

## KEY DATA

**FULL NAME** Harold Joseph "Happy" Hogan

**ALIASES** formerly the Freak, Iron Man

**RELATIVES** Virginia "Pepper" Potts Hogan (wife), unidentified father, grandfather and siblings, unidentified foster daughter and son, Clay Hogan (brother)

**OCCUPATION** Personal assistant and chauffeur, former liaison for local affairs of the Maria Stark Foundation, CEO of Stark Enterprises, fight manager, rancher, security chief, bodyguard, boxer

**AFFILIATIONS** Iron Legion

### Mr. and Mrs. Hogan
Although Happy and Tony Stark's personal assistant Pepper Potts did not hit it off at first, they soon became friends. Happy's attempts to be *more* than just a friend to Pepper were unsuccessful at first— she seemed to have eyes only for Tony. However, his persistence finally paid off when Pepper gave up pining over the seemingly unreceptive Stark, and married the devoted former boxer.

### Love Triangle
From virtually the first time they met, Tony had feelings for Pepper. But because of his heart condition and his desire to keep his Iron Man identity secret, Tony distanced himself from her. However, the two still experienced the occasional romantic spark.

### Secret Itentitty
When he was severely injured during Iron Man's televised fight with the Titanium Man, Happy revealed to Tony that he had figured out his secret identity as Iron Man some time ago.

## Happy Becomes the Freak

In an attempt to heal the wounds Happy acquired at the hands of the Titanium Man, Tony subjected his friend to his experimental Enervation Intensifier, a device that could channel energy into its subject. Although Happy's injuries were healed, he was transformed for a time into a hulking shell of his former self called the Freak. He ran amok and terrified Pepper Potts. When transformed back, Happy retained no memory of becoming a monster.

BUT... HE'S SO GROTESQUE... SO HORRIBLE !! AND... THERE'S NO PLACE TO RUN... I... I'M TRAPPED...!

> "You know something, Hap? You're the only guy I ever met who can make me feel like a moron."
> Tony Stark

fine Let's go

Soon's I finish my drink

## Breaking Up, Making Up...

Pepper Potts was all Happy ever wanted. When the two eloped and decided to quit their jobs at Stark Industries to pursue their dreams, Happy thought everything was finally going his way. But when their relationship became strained due to the loss of their adopted foster children, their marriage ended in divorce. However, fate would bring them back together under Stark's employ, and the two eventually reconciled and remarried.

But the truth is, there's no cure for the one thing that's wrong with our marriage.

which is?

The couple would still have their share of problems. A rift again grew between them when Pepper had a miscarriage.

BLAM!

## Taking a Bullet

Instead of telling her husband about her miscarriage, Pepper confided in Tony Stark. When Tony revealed the news to a drunken Happy, the shock was overshadowed by an even bigger surprise: a sniper's bullet meant for Tony. Tony got Happy to a hospital, and with all their secrets out in the open, Pepper and Happy reunited once more.

## A Hero's Death

Despite his slow demeanor, it was never a good idea to underestimate Happy Hogan. The Spymaster made the mistake of doing just that when he attempted to use Happy as bait to lure Iron Man into a trap. Happy struggled valiantly, knocking the Spymaster and himself off of a catwalk to stop the attack. Happy's injuries left him in a coma. With no hope of his recovery, Pepper begged Tony to use his Extremis link to pull the plug on her husband's life-support machine and end his suffering.

# JAMES RHODES

# "RHODEY"

He's Iron Man's right-hand man and the first person Tony Stark turns to for help. Despite the occasional difference of opinion, Jim "Rhodey" Rhodes has never let Iron Man down.

## APOCALYPSE THEN...

It's surprising James Rhodes and Tony Stark ever became friends at all (1). After all, the first time Rhodes ever laid eyes on Tony Stark he shot at him with a machine gun. Few close friendships begin in a hail of gunfire, but it was somehow appropriate for Tony and Jim.

James Rhodes was born in a poor neighborhood in South Philadelphia. Seeking to make a name for himself and rise above his background, Rhodes enlisted in the US Marines and was assigned to a tour of duty overseas. A superb helicopter pilot, Rhodes was nevertheless shot down, crash-landing his prized bird right in the middle of enemy territory. To make matters worse, as he was repairing his craft, a strange armored man came out of the surrounding jungle and approached him. Jim opened fire on this mysterious threat (2), but his bullets couldn't penetrate his target's metal hide. The armored man was, of course, Tony Stark in his very first Iron Man suit. Tony had just escaped from Wong-Chu's prison camp and was seeking Rhodey's help.

After jumpstarting Jim's helicopter (3), and routing another camp of enemy soldiers (4), Tony and Rhodey flew back to a nearby US military outpost. This shared combat experience helped form a lasting bond (5).

## KEY DATA

**FULL NAME** James Rupert "Jim" Rhodes

**ALIASES** "Rhodey," War Machine, formerly Iron Man

**OCCUPATION** Adventurer, former Commander of Camp Hammond Initiative forces, ONE drill sergeant, marine salvager, political activist, CEO of Stark Enterprises, pilot, aviation engineer, soldier

**AFFILIATIONS** formerly the 50 State Initiative, ONE, the Crew, "Iron Legion," West Coast Avengers, Secret Defenders, Worldwatch, US Marines

**POWERS/WEAPONS** Stark-developed cyborg armor with advanced firepower

# Always there...

After changing out of his secret Iron Man identity, Tony offered Rhodey a job as his personal pilot right after their first adventure. Not wishing to pass up such a tremendous opportunity, Rhodey accepted, as soon as his tour of duty came to a close. As Stark's pilot, Rhodey now traveled the world with his jet-setting boss, and the two formed a close friendship that rivaled any in either of their lives. On several occasions, Rhodey went above and beyond the call of duty and saved Tony's life—a debt Tony repaid as Iron Man at every available opportunity.

When Tony's alcoholism made it impossible for him to handle his duties as a Super Hero, Rhodey nervously stepped up to the proverbial plate and took his piloting skills to the next level as the new Iron Man for a while. Even though the armor caused him pain and mental torment, Rhodey wore it proudly. He also donned the Iron Man armor on a few subsequent occasions to save his friend's life.

When Tony Stark seemingly lay on his deathbed, and asked Rhodey to resume Iron Man duties full time and also take over as Stark Industries' CEO, Jim didn't back down from the challenge. Only when Rhodes discovered that Tony had faked his death without telling him, did the two have a falling out, one that time and a bit of good old-fashioned armored combat finally mended.

**Since Rhodey first donned the Iron Man armor in an emergency, it was never tuned to his particular brainwaves, causing him headaches and even shifts in his personality.**

*"I'm handlin' the hero chores these days... you might want to write that down somewhere—so you remember it."*

## RHODEY IN LOVE

Marcy Pearson

Like Tony, Jim Rhodes never shied away from a pretty face. No stranger to romance ever since he first kissed his childhood sweetheart, Glenda Sandoval, Rhodey has been known to flirt with attractive women even while in a committed relationship. While in his Iron Man identity, Rhodes even tried to hit on the female Captain Marvel, but had no luck winning her affections.

One of Rhodes's most serious relationships was with former Stark public relations representative, Marcy Pearson. But when her ruthless career ambitions began to overshadow her romantic feelings, he ended their relationship and fired her at the same time. Rhodey also dated Tony's ex-fling Rae LaCoste for a time. Despite being more serious about each other than she and Stark ever were, Rae and Rhodey could never really make it work.

# War Machine

When Tony faked his death (see pp. 124–125), he bequeathed an Iron Man suit to Rhodey that was tailor-made for his combat strengths. When Tony revealed his deception, Rhodey renamed the suit War Machine and, furious with Tony for not letting him in on the secret earlier, briefly cut all ties with him. Joining the West Coast Avengers, and then the human-rights organization Worldwatch, Rhodey carved out his own place in the world. He later lost his original War Machine suit during a time-travel mission, but gained new alien armor to continue his war against crime.

Through it all, Rhodey never forgot the man he owed his career to, and when Tony truly needed him, he was always there. He later sacrificed his alien armor, all the power he had in the world, to protect the secrets of Tony's armory when the Fujikawa company staged a hostile takeover of Stark Enterprises.

**Rhodey had no desire to reclaim his role as Iron Man, but his loyalty to his friend compelled him.**

## INTO THE FUTURE

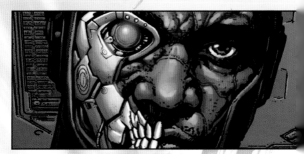

**"HOLD BACK AND WAIT FOR THE BLEED OUT..."**

**"SORRY SOLDIER... BUT RHODEY DON'T BLEED!"**

Jim Rhodes was always destined to be a soldier. Bouncing around careers such as working for the government by manning their giant robotic Sentinels, to commanding the training facility for Super Heroes at the 50 State Initiative's Camp Hammond, Rhodey seemed only happy when fighting the good fight. But when his body was horrifically injured during an attack on a military base in Dubai, it seemed like Jim had finally seen his last bit of action. A quadriplegic with half his face missing, Rhodey was rebuilt by Stark's War Machine facility and given a new lease on life. Now a true living weapon, Rhodey walks his own path, yet is still always only a phone call away if Tony needs his help.

# GIRLS, GIRLS, GIRLS!

Tony Stark's social activities have given new meaning to the term "playboy." A favorite hobby of his, equal to tinkering in his workshop, Tony has spent countless hours romancing society's most beautiful women.

### Marion
One of the many gorgeous socialites Tony has dated, Marion retained a special place in his heart, even if he couldn't quite remember her last name. After all, it was Marion who suggested that Iron Man paint his armor gold, in order to appear less threatening.

### Meredith McCall
His high-school sweetheart and first love, Meredith was forbidden by her father from seeing Tony, the son of a hated business competitor. Meredith became a college professor and later married Dr. Sloane Alden, the future villain Frostbite. She then encountered a younger Tony Stark from an alternate timeline.

### Natalia Romanova
One of the many beautiful women that helped occupy Tony's evenings during Iron Man's early days, Natalia Romanova was secretly a Soviet secret agent known as the Black Widow. Now a hero and an Avenger, on rare occasions Natalia and Tony have rekindled the passions of those former nights.

### Marianne Rodgers
The possessor of latent telepathic abilities, Marianne Rodgers was plagued with visions while she dated Tony. Although the two became serious about each other and even got engaged, Marianne's disturbing premonitions led to her keeping her distance, inducing Tony to call off their wedding.

### Janet Van Dyne
Years ago, when Janet Van Dyne, alias the Avenger Wasp, didn't know that Tony Stark was also her teammate Iron Man, she and Tony had a brief fling. Although they began to develop serious feelings for one another, the relationship ended when Tony revealed his double identity to Janet. No matter how she felt about Tony, the Wasp couldn't continue to be in a relationship with someone who was good friends with her ex-husband, Hank Pym.

### Joanna Nivena
Before his life-changing imprisonment by Wong-Chu, Tony had decided to settle down and marry his girlfriend Joanna. But when he returned from captivity reborn as the crime-fighter Iron Man, Joanna knew she could never be a part of his life.

### Janice Cord

The daughter of one of Tony's business rivals and the object of the affections of Crimson Dynamo Alex Nevsky, Janice Cord still attempted to date Tony despite the odds stacked against them. Unfortunately, during a battle between Iron Man, Titanium Man, and the Crimson Dynamo, she was accidentally killed.

### Whitney Frost
Born Countess Giulietta Nefaria, Whitney Frost didn't gain Tony's affections until her face was scarred in a horrible accident. Hiding behind a golden mask and renaming herself Madame Masque, Whitney fell for Tony when he showed her kindness despite her appearance. Though their romance died when Whitney chose crime over love, she remains obsessed with Tony to this day.

### Bethany Cabe
A complex woman with a life scarred by tragedy, Bethany nursed Tony back to health when she first realized that he was an alcoholic. But as quickly as she built Tony up, she tore him back down again when she left him in order to attempt a reconciliation with her husband, whom she had believed was dead.

### Indries Moomji
When Obadiah Stane set out to destroy Tony's life, he employed the services of the exotic Indries Moomji. Meeting Tony by seeming happenstance, Moomji instantly won the playboy's affections. She broke Tony's heart when he was at his lowest and needed her the most in a calculated and successful effort to drive him back to alcoholism.

### Roxanne Gilbert
A political activist and the sister of the volatile extremist Gary Gilbert (better known as the original criminal Firebrand), Roxanne dated Tony briefly before their relationship cooled.

### Sunset Bain
Dating Tony while he was still in college, Sunset Bain turned out to be more interested in acquiring Stark Industries' secrets than Tony's love. At the helm of the Baintronics company, sly Sunset later attempted to use stolen War Machine technology to sabotage a Stark Solutions deal in order to gain Tony's aid for her own corporation.

### Heather Glenn
She was the wrong woman at the wrong time. Heather was an alcoholic and party girl, a terrible influence on Tony when, owing to Obadiah Stane's manipulations, he relapsed into his old drinking habits.

### Brie Daniels

An actress dying to break into the business any way she could, Brie gatecrashed a party held at Tony's Los Angeles home hoping to hobnob with the rich and famous. Her scheme was discovered, but Tony was taken by her beauty and the two began dating.

### Rumiko Fujikawa

The image of a spoiled party girl concealed a highly intelligent woman. Rumiko met Tony on the island of Isla Suerte, and the two began to date, despite a few rough patches caused by Tony's double life as Iron Man. Tony was sure Rumiko was the one for him and bought her an engagement ring. Tragically, Rumiko was killed by a corporate rival wearing an Iron Man suit.

### She-Hulk

For Tony, one of the advantages of being Director of Shield, was coming into close contact with She-Hulk Jennifer Walters. The all-action heroine was every bit as keen on mixing pleasure with business as Tony. It wasn't long before the two found themselves in each other's arms—and later at each other's throats.

### Rae LaCoste

Although she and Tony were never serious about one another, Rae was one of the many women whose company Tony enjoyed on more than one occasion. Their frivolous affair evolved into a genuine friendship when Tony was paralyzed and Rae was able to overlook his disability.

### Kathleen Dare

She wouldn't take no for an answer. Their short-lived relationship ended due to Kathy's jealousy. The chemically-imbalanced Dare snuck then snuck into Tony's California home and shot her former lover. Later, when Tony seemingly died, Kathy took her own life out of grief.

### Veronica Benning

After cheating death, Tony worked his way back to health from a state of complete paralysis. Overcoming the odds with the help of his physical therapist Veronica Benning, Tony soon began to see her in a new light, and the two began a short-lived romance.

### Maya Hansen

A longtime friend of Tony's after meeting him at a technology conference, Maya Hansen went on to become a scientific pioneer. They met again when Tony was dramatically transformed by her Extremis serum (see pp. 156–7). Their relationship blossomed and they even moved in together for a while. Her commitment to her scientific career led her to end the affair by faking her own death.

### Countess Stephanie De La Spirosa

A pretty face from Iron Man's early years, the Countess was reunited with Tony when she hired his services during his days at Stark Solutions. The two managed to rekindle their romance in the brief pauses between Iron Man's battles.

### Pepper Potts

After years of flirting and dodging around the issue, Tony and his prized executive assistant Virginia "Pepper" Potts finally decided to curb their romantic feelings and just be friends. However, that decision was made just after they shared a passionate kiss. The fact remains that no matter how much they may deny it, Pepper and Tony share a connection that simply refuses to be held at bay forever.

### Dr Su Yin

Beautiful and gifted, Dr. Su Yin had little difficulty winning Tony's heart when he visited her native China to arrest a sudden rapid decline in his health. Unfortunately for Tony, not only could Yin not cure him, she was already married.

### Calista Hancock

When Tony briefly retired from his life as a multi-millionaire industrialist and took on the identity of humble computer technician Hogan Potts, he engaged in a brief affair with his boss Calista Hancock. Their fling ended when he resumed his former life as Tony Stark.

## And always...

## KEY DATA

**FULL NAME** Bethany Cabe

**ALIAS** War Machine 2.0

**OCCUPATION** War Machine project director, former CEO of Stark Enterprises, security chief, bodyguard

**AFFILIATIONS** Formerly Iron Legion, formerly partner in Cabe & McPherson, Security Specialists

**POWERS/ABILITIES** Expert hand to hand combatant, expert marksman

With a past as unusual as her career choice, perhaps no woman has challenged Tony Stark as much as...

# Bethany Cabe

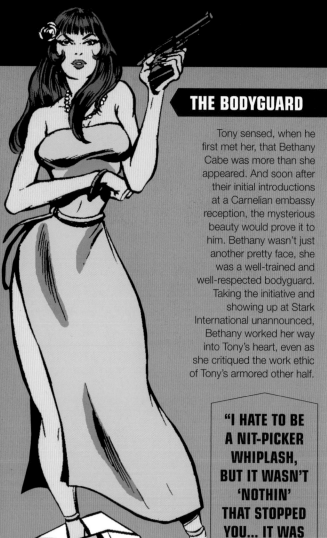

### THE BODYGUARD

Tony sensed, when he first met her, that Bethany Cabe was more than she appeared. And soon after their initial introductions at a Carnelian embassy reception, the mysterious beauty would prove it to him. Bethany wasn't just another pretty face, she was a well-trained and well-respected bodyguard. Taking the initiative and showing up at Stark International unannounced, Bethany worked her way into Tony's heart, even as she critiqued the work ethic of Tony's armored other half.

> "I HATE TO BE A NIT-PICKER WHIPLASH, BUT IT WASN'T 'NOTHIN' THAT STOPPED YOU... IT WAS A SMITH AND WESSON!"

# ALIVE!

Bethany was a woman of many secrets, and one of them was her marriage. At a young age, Cabe had married Alex van Tilberg, a German diplomat who, years ago, had seemingly died in a car crash caused by his addiction to pills.

Discovering that her husband was still alive, but a prisoner, Bethany traveled to East Germany and was also taken captive. Tony helped them both escape and also revealed his dual identity to his love.

**Safely back in America, Bethany was torn between her past and her present, ultimately choosing her husband over Tony.**

# SECURITY CHIEF

Bethany had lived a hard life and, in time, she bounced back from the heartbreak she had experienced with Tony. When fate brought them together once more, Bethany was able to keep a professional demeanor, at first anyway. While Tony was recovering from a drastic surgical procedure, Jim Rhodes, alias War Machine, formed an "Iron Legion" in order to mount an assault on the extra-terrestrial Ultimo. Alongside men with previous experience piloting Iron Men suits, Rhodes enlisted Bethany Cabe. Outfitted with old Iron Man suits, Rhodes led the team into battle. As Ultimo threatened to gain the upper hand, Tony Stark arrived in his new modular armor to help save the day. Afterwards, he offered Bethany the job of head of Stark Security, a position she eagerly accepted. Their romance was soon rekindled, only to be cut short again when Tony seemingly died under the control of the villain, Immortus. He posthumously promoted Bethany to co-CEO in his stead, but this role was taken away from her when the foreign company Fujikawa International mounted a successful hostile takeover.

## "TELL ME TONY... WHO'S GOING TO PROTECT YOU TONIGHT? MRS. ARBOGAST?"

## MIND SWAP

Shortly before Tony Stark first developed his silver centurion armor, Bethany was taken captive by his chief rival, Obadiah Stane. There she underwent an experimental procedure created by Dr. Theron Atlanta in which her personality was switched into the body of a clone of the villain Madame Masque. This new "Bethany" attempted to assassinate Tony, and the real Bethany was forced to come to his rescue in the form of Madame Masque. Fortunately, Tony managed to see through the deception and helped restore Bethany to her own body.

## WAR MACHINE RESEARCH DEPARTMENT

### Iron Man was her past. War Machine would be her future.

Years after Tony's return from the grave, Bethany once again found employment at Stark Industries. When Jim Rhodes was critically wounded during an explosion at a military complex, Bethany was placed in charge of his rehabilitation and unfortunate transformation into a cyborg. Working as Rhodey's researcher from her Colorado base, Bethany became instrumental in War Machine's missions. She even went so far as to don a set of armor to destroy a Roxxon facility as War Machine 2.0.

**Bethany helped coordinate War Machine's attack on mercenaries belonging to private defense contractor Eaglestar International.**

# IRON MAN #232

"How long have I been hunting it? All night? Forever? Doesn't matter. Nothing matters. I've got to keep on. Do whatever I have to. Got to find it. So I can kill it..."

IRON MAN

**MAIN CHARACTERS:** Iron Man (Tony Stark); Iron Man (Jim Rhodes)
**SUPPORTING CHARACTERS:** Various corpses
**LOCATIONS:** A dream world inside Tony Stark's mind; Tony Stark's coastal mansion, California

**PUBLICATION DATE**
July 1988

**EDITOR-IN-CHIEF**
Tom DeFalco

**COVER ARTIST**
Barry Windsor-Smith

**WRITER/PLOTTER**
David Michelinie

**PENCILER/PLOTTER**
Barry Windsor-Smith

**INKER/COLORIST**
Barry Windsor-Smith

**LETTERER**
Bill Oakley

## BACKGROUND

Barry Windsor-Smith was about to make history. Already well known for his groundbreaking artwork and storytelling skills on Marvel's *Conan the Barbarian* series in the 1970s, he had returned to Marvel in the 1980s, ready to breathe new life into a few of their Super Hero properties. He would soon reach comics superstardom by writing and drawing the landmark origin story of the X-Men's Wolverine in a series entitled *Weapon X*.

But before Windsor-Smith turned the life of Wolverine upside down, he dabbled in Iron Man's world. First coming into contact with the Golden Avenger in the second Machine Man limited series, he went on to plot, pencil, and color a surreal Iron Man adventure with the help of the current Iron Man team, writer David Michelinie and inker Bob Layton. An epilogue to the memorable *Armor Wars* storyline, readers were given a rare glimpse into the nightmares that haunt Tony Stark's psyche, while simultaneously shown the imagery of a breathtaking artist in his prime.

# The Story...

**Trapped in a vicious nightmare, Iron Man must come to terms with his inner demons and the many mistakes of his past.**

It was a labyrinth of wires, computer consoles, and shadows. Stalking through the mysterious landscape, was Iron Man, clad in his now outdated silver centurion armor **(1)**. He didn't know how long he had been on the hunt, he just knew that he had to continue. There was something out there in the darkness, and Iron Man was going to find it and kill it.

Suddenly an strange hum sounded in the distance. Iron Man lashed out towards it, firing his repulsors into the blackness **(2)**. But nothing happened, and the hum slowly turned into laughter.

Just then, Iron Man began to realize where he was. He was in his prey's lair. He felt overcome with fear, but it was too late. The creature was standing right in front of him. Iron Man again began to fire his blasters at full power, but the creature just absorbed it all, growing stronger and larger. The beast was an enigma. It was a gigantic robot husk, an elaborate tapestry of tubes and dials **(3)**. But its face, Tony Stark recognized all too easily. Because the creature was wearing the faceplate of an Iron Man.

As their battle raged, Iron Man fiercely attacked the robotic horror with his bare hands, managing to tear its head right off its shoulders. And just like that, it was over.

Tony could lie down for just a minute and catch his breath. But the ground below him had changed. He now found himself lying upon miles and miles of rotting corpses **(4)**.

Through the horrific landscape, a solitary figure trudged. It was Jim Rhodes, wearing his old Iron Man armor once more **(5)**. When Tony asked his friend where they were, Rhodey simply said that they were in a place Stark himself had made. The carnage was all Tony's fault and Rhodey was merely the custodian. With that, the landscape began to shift once more. Suddenly, Tony was standing in a bar, with Rhodey manning the counter. As Tony reluctantly ordered a vodka tonic, resigned to escaping his troubles at Rhodey's suggestion, thick cords began to appear around Tony's body. Restrained and helpless, Tony looked up once more at the creature he had been hunting. And this time, the horror was wearing his own face **(6)**.

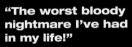

But Tony wouldn't give up without a fight. Channeling all his energy into one burst of his rocket boots, Stark freed himself, falling to the ground below him. But the beast was barely phased, and it was coming for him. Tony tried to run **(7)**, but the hands of his victims shot up from the metal cords below his feet. They grabbed at Tony, impeding his escape. Tony needed to think of another way to get free.

Realizing that his attacks on the creature only made it stronger, Tony set his repulsors to absorb energy, rather than release it. And with all the strength he could still muster, Tony charged the beast, sucking its raw energy into his armor. But Tony couldn't take much more and his frame exploded **(8)**, unable to contain all of the beast's powerful essence. And that's when Tony Stark woke up **(9)**.

**"The worst bloody nightmare I've had in my life!"**

Tony was safe and secure in his plush coastal mansion. It had all been a vivid nightmare, a way for his subconscious to tell him what he already knew deep down. Yes, the Armor Wars were over. Tony had succeeded in eliminating all the known cases of stolen and pirated Stark technology. But the guilt still remained, and Tony felt haunted by all the innocents killed or injured due to his misused innovations **(10)**. He could no longer keep fighting the guilt, or denying it. His mind was telling him to accept it as part of who he was now. And as Tony Stark looked out his bedroom window at the beautiful ocean beyond, he knew he would have to do just that. And continue the rest of his life as best he could.

# MAIN ENEMIES

As Iron Man, Tony Stark has faced down more criminals than he cares to remember. From violent fanatics clad in high-tech battlesuits, to moneyed masterminds who rarely leave the comfort of their plush offices, Iron Man has battled them all, and overcome every obstacle they have put in his way. But a select few of Iron Man's adversaries have proved relentless thorns in his armored side, and worthy opponents for the heroic Golden Avenger.

## The Mandarin

Believed to be the descendant of Genghis Khan, the warlord known only as the Mandarin considers himself destined to rule the world. A brilliant martial artist and strategist, the Mandarin continually plots to take over his native China and utilizes ten alien rings of almost limitless power to enforce his will. One of the Mandarin's least successful schemes involved the capture of Tony Stark by the warlord Wong-Chu. In the process, the Mandarin unwittingly helped create his nemesis: Iron Man.

## Obadiah Stane

Obadiah Stane was not one to let bygones be bygones. When Tony Stark interfered with Stane's illegal business affairs, Obadiah dedicated his life to destroying Tony. Over time, Stane manipulated Stark into becoming a drunk, acquired Stark International, destroyed Tony's new company Circuits Maximus, and purloined Iron Man technology to forge his own Iron Monger armor. Only after losing a physical battle to Iron Man, did Stane finally admit defeat. Rather than live with this failure, he committed suicide.

## Justin Hammer

The unscrupulous entrepreneur behind Hammer Industries, Justin Hammer has been an enemy of Iron Man's for years, constantly striking at Tony Stark from behind the scenes. Hammer's notoriety in the underworld first blossomed when he created his own network of Super Villains. Providing his amoral clients with enhanced technology in exchange for a cut of their profits, Hammer remained beyond the law's reach in his floating island hideout in international waters. Eventually, following a battle with Iron Man, Hammer was set adrift in space, frozen in a block of ice.

## Titanium Man

A Russian citizen and fanatical political activist, Boris Bullski's giant stature is only equaled by his unswerving adherence to outdated Marxist communist beliefs. Years ago, during the Cold War, Boris believed he had found a way to stand out from all other Soviet military personnel. He arranged to fight Iron Man, who in Boris' eyes symbolized the corrupt capitalist system, on live television. Boris lost the bout, despite bending the rules to suit his purposes, and developed an unquenchable hatred for his American counterpart.

## Blizzard

A disgruntled Stark Industries scientist, Gregor Shapanka attempted to rob the company's vaults but was foiled by Iron Man. Fired and humiliated, Gregor swore revenge on his former employer. Developing advanced freezing technology, Shapanka adopted the name Jack Frost, and set out as a career criminal, one destined to meet defeat at the hands of Iron Man. Later changing his name to Blizzard, Gregor was killed during a battle with an Iron Man from a possible future. He was later replaced by a new Blizzard, Donald Gill, who had been granted advanced freezing weaponry by another Iron Man archfoe, Justin Hammer.

## Fin Fang Foom

One of an alien race of dragon-like creatures from the peaceful planet Kakaranathara, Fin Fang Foom traveled the stars only to crash land with the rest of his crew on Earth. The true owner of one of the ten energy rings exploited by the villain Mandarin, Foom was awoken from a deep sleep by that selfsame warlord. These days, Fin Fang Foom has emerged into the world as if to perform the role of rampaging dragon to Iron Man's modern-day knight in shining armor.

## Spymaster

Three men have gone by the moniker Spymaster. The first, whose identity was never discovered, was a master of industrial espionage, targeting Stark Industries on many of his missions. Often working for Justin Hammer, he was murdered by the Ghost during an encounter with Iron Man. The second Spymaster was Nathan Lemon, a pupil of the criminal Taskmaster. He was killed on the orders of the newest Spymaster, supposed humanitarian Sinclair Abbott.

## Whiplash

A weapons designer with an eye for a quick buck, Mark Scarlotti became the mercenary Whiplash. Armed with cybernetically controlled whips of his own design, Whiplash (sometimes called Blacklash) sought assignments from various employers, including Justin Hammer. Despite upgrading his weaponry several times, even adding a flying platform to his arsenal, Whiplash was defeated by Iron Man on most occasions. When Iron Man's armor briefly gained sentience, Whiplash was killed by the artificially intelligent being. Recently, a new Whiplash has been spotted alongside a female partner named Blacklash.

## Crimson Dynamo

The product of scientific experiments dating back to the 1960s, the Crimson Dynamo is Russia's answer to Iron Man. Frequently reinvented over the years, the Crimson Dynamo armor has been worn by at least eight different individuals. The armor was originally invented by Anton Vanko, who was forced to attack Stark Industries by the Soviet government. After Vanko defected to the US, he died while opposing his successor as the Crimson Dynamo, Boris Turgenov. Today, the armor is usually piloted by Dimitri Bukharin, whose rivalry with Stark has developed into true friendship.

# OTHER FOES

## Kang the Conqueror

Nathaniel Richards, the time-traveling despot Kang, has wrought havoc in the life of Tony Stark. In fact, Kang's alternate future self, Immortus, was the one villain to truly defeat Iron Man, turning him into a murderer. Ironically, the teenaged Kang rebelled against his future destiny and decided to become the heroic Young Avenger Iron Lad.

## Unicorn

Using a power horn developed by Anton Vanko (the original Crimson Dynamo), Milos Masaryk became the saboteur Unicorn. He crossed Iron Man's path when on a mission to attack a Stark Industries plant that was manufacturing weapons for the US government. The unstable Unicorn is much more dangerous than his moniker might suggest.

## Firepower

The end result of a combination of stolen Stark technology and the devious mind of businessman Edwin Cord, Firepower was a destructive juggernaut without equal. Operated by mercenary Jack Taggert, Firepower seemed unbeatable until Iron Man redesigned his own armor specifically to take down the two-ton walking tank.

## The Melter

When industrialist Bruno Horgan was discovered to be using inferior materials in his construction of weaponry for the US government, his contracts were awarded to Tony Stark. Swearing revenge, Bruno became the Melter, utilizing a ray capable of reducing Iron Man's armor to dripping slag.

## Firebrand

Picking up his criminal career where the previous Firebrand, political zealot Gary Gilbert, left off, Rick Dennison, was even more hotheaded than his fiery predecessor. In his mutated form, Firebrand attacked an island business retreat, but was eventually defeated by the quick thinking of Iron Man.

## Count Nefaria

The birth father of Whitney Frost and the reason for her descent into a life of crime as Madame Masque, crime boss Luchino Nefaria has battled the Avengers and Iron Man more times than either care to remember. Believed dead for many years, Nefaria returned to wage a calculated assault on Iron Man's life.

## The Controller

Crippled in a lab accident, scientist Basil Sandhurst created an exoskeleton for himself and turned to a life of crime as the mind-manipulating Controller. Using his "slave discs" to control his unwitting pawns, the Controller has set up many illegitimate businesses to drain them of their energies.

## M.O.D.O.K.

The crowning achievement of the terrorist organization AIM, MODOK is the mutated form of George Tarleton. An acronym for Mobile Organism Designed Only for Killing, MODOK is bent on mass destruction, but so far his plans have been foiled by Iron Man, Captain America, and the Avengers.

### Wong-Chu

The heartless commander of the prison camp that unwittingly birthed Iron Man, Wong-Chu survived his first encounter with Stark only to plague him as a ruthless drug lord years later. Disfigured from his first encounter with Tony, Wong-Chu has seemingly perished, perhaps for good.

### Living Laser

Scientist Arthur Parks used his miniaturized laser weapons to embark on a life of crime. An accident involving Iron Man turned him into a much deadlier being composed of pure photons.

### A.I.M.

Iron Man has been thwarting the terrorist organization Advanced Idea Mechanics (AIM) for years. He recently put an end to a splinter faction called Advanced Genocide Mechanics.

### Ezekiel Stane

The son of one of Stark's greatest rivals, Obadiah Stane, Ezekiel followed in his father's footsteps and used pirated Stark technology to wage war against Tony.

### Sunturion

Iron Man and Arthur Dearborn, the energy-absorbing Sunturion, were enemies, until Sunturion realized his Roxxon employers were corrupt. He nearly gave his life for Iron Man's cause.

### Temujin

Son of the Mandarin, Temujin inherited his father's enemies when Mandarin was thought dead. Temujin clashed with Iron Man, relying on martial arts as much as on his father's rings.

### Morcedai Midas

The gold-obsessed crime boss has hired the likes of Madame Masque and Morgan Stark to do his bidding. Midas has set his greedy sights on Stark Industries many times.

### Iron Patriot

Former Green Goblin Norman Osborn commandeered one of Tony's Iron Man suits, repainting it and publicly declaring himself a hero, despite his evil intentions.

### Scarecrow

A contortionist by trade, Ebenezer Laughton left the stage behind when a chance encounter with Iron Man inspired him to become the flexible thief known as the Scarecrow.

### Doctor Doom

Iron Man's equal and opposite number, Victor Von Doom has used his brilliant scientific mind and advanced battlesuit not for the good of mankind, but to further his own selfish agenda.

### Madame Masque

Her scarred features reflect her disturbed mind. Whitney Frost has been Iron Man's lover, ally, and enemy. Her obsession with Tony Stark has grown to a near-fatal attraction.

### Ghost

Tony Stark first encountered the enigmatic saboteur the Ghost when Stark Enterprises was purchasing the electronics company Accutech. A frequent opponent of Iron Man's, the Ghost joined Norman Osborn's Thunderbolts team, after using his intangibility to help Osborn steal an Iron Man suit.

### Ultimo

A giant robot from outer space, Ultimo was unearthed by the Mandarin. Able to adapt to avoid defeat, Ultimo later merged with Tony's cousin Morgan Stark while battling War Machine.

### Raiders

A trio of high-tech thieves using stolen Stark technology and financed by Edwin Cord, the Raiders have recently upgraded and now work as enforcers for the Chinese government.

### L.M.D.

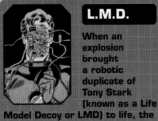

When an explosion brought a robotic duplicate of Tony Stark (known as a Life Model Decoy or LMD) to life, the android set out to replace the man he was created to serve. The LMD donned Iron Man's armor and battled his creator until he was destroyed in a vat of molten metal.

### Vibro

Seismologist Alton Vibereaux gained power over earthquakes and became the unstable criminal Vibro. He fought and lost to both Tony Stark and Jim Rhodes during their Iron Man terms.

# IRON MAN
# VOL. 3 #1

MARVEL COMICS **HEROES RETURN**

COLLECTOR'S ITEM 1st ISSUE! **IRON MAN**

FEB 1998

WWW.MARVEL.COM

BUSIEK CHEN CANNON

DIRECT EDITION

0 01111

7 59606 04457 3

$2.99 US $4.20 CAN

**PUBLICATION DATE**
February 1998

**EDITOR-IN-CHIEF**
Bob Harris

**COVER ARTIST**
Sean Chen & Eric Cannon

**WRITER**
Kurt Busiek

**PENCILER**
Sean Chen

**INKER**
Eric Cannon

**COLORIST**
Liquid!

*"You want to come after Mr. Stark—you want to hurt him, kill him, stop him from doing what he's setting out to do—you do it over Iron Man's dead body. That's all I've got to say."*

IRON MAN

**MAIN CHARACTERS: Iron Man (Tony Stark),**
**MAIN SUPPORTING CHARACTERS: Death Squad;**
**Georgie Avalon; Ms. Denton; Vittorio Silvani;**
**Rosalind Sharpe; Foggy Nelson; Norman Osborn;**
**Sunset Bain; Pepper Potts; Jim Rhodes**
**MAIN LOCATIONS: Avalon Trading Co.; Stark Tower;**
**Maria Stark Community Center; Baintronics (all New**
**York); AIM hideout**

## BACKGROUND

The heroes were returning, and Marvel fans couldn't be more relieved. After all, Iron Man had been through a lot lately. He had turned evil, died, been replaced by a younger version of himself, died again, and been reborn in a pocket universe as an adult version of himself. Fans were tired of the ever-shifting status quo, and when the *Heroes Return* mini series event catapulted Marvel's famous heroes back to their old familiar selves and realities, they welcomed them back with open arms.

Enter Kurt Busiek. Already a fan-favorite writer for his groundbreaking *Marvels* mini series and his innovative take on super-heroics in the pages of *Thunderbolts*, Busiek set out to not only restore Iron Man to his past glory, but to also control the fate of the Avengers comic. Busiek didn't disappoint. He told consistently classic tales that paid tribute to the past, while always moving forward in new, unexpected directions. The result was a true rebirth for the Golden Avenger, worthy of a new first issue heralding his fresh start.

# The Story...

**As Iron Man returns to his proper dimension and to his life as a millionaire playboy, he faces new threats hired by old foes, and is forced to adapt and change with the times.**

"Wide-beam, shallow-effect repulsor blasts turn the glass fragments to powder. Don't want anyone getting hurt..."

New York City was abuzz. Not only was Tony Stark back from the seeming dead, but so was his fabled bodyguard, the armored hero known as Iron Man **(1)**. And as all of Manhattan wondered if Tony was going to attempt to take back his old company, now merged with the Japanese conglomerate Fujikawa Industries, Iron Man had other priorities on his mind. There was a hostage situation at the Avalon Trading Company that needed the hero's attention **(2)**.

After dealing with the violent mercenary Vittorio Silvani and his hired help, Iron Man headed back to Stark Tower, situated in the heart of Manhattan's flatiron district. After all, the evening was drawing close, and Tony Stark had quite a homecoming gala to attend **(3)**.

With a guest list including such luminaries as the Fantastic Four's Reed Richards and Sue Storm, Daily Bugle founder J. Jonah Jameson, and famous crusading attorney Foggy Nelson, Tony Stark spent the majority of the black tie affair shaking hands and making small talk. After turning down the advancements of the beautiful, and quite available Leah Sheffield, Tony stood outside on Stark Tower's rooftop balcony, reminiscing about a tour of a Southeast Asia plant he went on years ago that went horribly wrong **(4)**. He thought about the guerrilla leader Wong-Chu, and the death of his friend Ho Yinsen. But most of all, Tony thought about donning his Iron Man armor for the first time in order to escape Wong-Chu's custody **(5)**, and about the start of his own long-lasting war on crime that began soon after.

Deciding to get a bit of fresh air from a vantage point other than his ivory tower, Tony walked over to the construction site of a housing development he was spearheading through his charitable Maria Stark Foundation. As he toured the grounds, finding comfort in the bare steel and rivets surrounding him **(6)**, Stark's musings were interrupted by gunfire. Behind him were five heavily armed assailants, calling themselves the Death Squad.

Led by the militant Firefight, and containing members Rocket-Launcher, Airborne, Smokescreen, and Boobytrap, the Death Squad wasted no time in attacking Stark on behalf of their mysterious employer. With his trademark briefcase in hand, Tony sprinted away from the villains until he found a nice deserted hole in the ground, perfect for a quick costume change. And seconds later, the Death Squad was no longer facing a helpless millionaire playboy. Now they were up against the updated and extremely advanced technology of Iron Man **(7)**.

As the fight raged on and Iron Man gained the upper hand, the mercenaries made their getaway with the help of Smokescreen's blackout blast **(8)**. And it wasn't until the villains were safely out of sight that Iron Man realized the damage the battle had cost him. True, Tony Stark was still alive, but the housing project he had worked so hard to construct was now nothing more than expensive smoking rubble. Something had to change. He'd lost too many things that truly mattered to him.

After a sleepless night spent lost in thought **(9)**, Tony Stark called a press conference the following morning. There, to the surprise of friends and enemies, Tony announced the creation of Stark Solutions, a new company offering aid, advice or, appropriately enough, solutions, to any client willing to pay his extremely high fees. Profits would largely be turned over to the Maria Stark Foundation for reconstruction projects to help make the world a better place. And as Tony Stark turned the press conference over to questions from the audience **(10)**, he felt he could rest easier that night. He knew there would be problems yet to face, and foes yet to fight, but at least now he knew where he was going. And for Tony Stark, that was all that mattered.

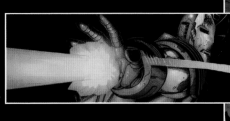

"As dawn starts to break, I make a few decisions."

# AVENGERS ASSEMBLE!

"And there came a day, a day unlike any other, when Earth's mightiest heroes and heroines found themselves united against a common threat. On that day, the Avengers were born—to fight the foes no single Super Hero could withstand! Through the years, their roster has prospered, changing many times, but their glory has never been denied! Heed the call, then—for now, the Avengers Assemble!"

THOR

HULK

ANT-MAN

## THE BEGINNING

Thor's brother Loki was up to his old tricks again. Despite being imprisoned on a barren island in the mystical dimension of Asgard by his brother Thor, the Norse god of thunder, Loki still had access to his magical abilities. After manipulating the Hulk into attempting to wreck a passenger train, Loki diverted a radio call requesting help to Thor's civilian identity of Dr. Donald Blake. However, Loki's ploy worked a little too well. He successfully lured Thor into a battle with the Hulk, but he also accidentally summoned Iron Man, as well as Ant-Man and the Wasp. Discovering Loki's ruse, the newly formed team of heroes defeated the god of mischief. As they celebrated their triumph, they realized that working together certainly had its advantages. And so the Avengers, Earth's mightiest hero team, was born.

WASP

IRON MAN

It wasn't long before the Avengers set up shop in Tony Stark's childhood mansion and began to hold regular meetings. Bankrolled by Stark's seemingly limitless funds, the fledgling team soon faced a scheming alien dubbed the Space Phantom. Unfortunately, the battle bred more suspicion against the team's loose cannon, the incredible Hulk. Tired of the evident mistrust of heroes that were supposed to be his teammates, the Hulk quit the Avengers' ranks. In the Avengers very next adventure, the Hulk joined forces with Namor the Sub-Mariner and ruler of the undersea kingdom of Atlantis to battle the team. Fighting these two powerhouses to a standstill, the Avengers were unable to prevent Namor's escape. While searching for the disgruntled sea king, they chanced upon a body frozen in ice—and realized they had found the comatose form of the long-lost World War II icon, Captain America.

Reviving the fallen war hero, the Avengers soon accepted Cap to their ranks. The inspiration of an entire generation, Captain America naturally gravitated towards a leadership position, and cemented the team's reputation as the Earth's Mightiest Heroes.

Right from the start, the Avengers' roster was destined to be constantly in flux. Heroes would join and depart, depending on their politics or the circumstances of their own often-complex personal lives. Iron Man soon decided that he could no longer carry on his duties as a permanent member. However, he still contributed to the team's funding and housing. He also continued to supply them with innovative modes of transport, such as their famed, high-speed Quinjet airplanes, and recommended Clint Barton, the archer who had once opposed the Golden Avenger as the masked vigilante Hawkeye, for Avengers membership.

Over the years, Iron Man has returned to the Avengers' fold many times. He's been a constant influence on the team's direction, helping to found several different incarnations of the team, including the West Coast Avengers, the New Avengers and the Mighty Avengers. And even though Tony sometimes finds himself at odds with the group (on one occasion he was so frustrated with his teammates that he created his own super-powered splinter group called Force Works), Iron Man is always drawn back to the team he has invested so much of his money, energy, and heart into.

After the earth-shattering Super Hero Civil War, Tony Stark became head of the government peacekeeping agency SHIELD, and was thus in a position to shape the Avengers team to his liking.

# TEAM UPS

These team-ups have played a big part in Iron Man's career, giving him a wide array of fellow heroes to call on when the need arises.

## Ms. Marvel

Carol Danvers has had many names over the course of her long career. She has been known as Warbird, Binary, and Ms. Marvel. Carol lost her powers for a while when the mutant Rogue (then a member of the Brotherhood of Mutants) absorbed them; however, she gained new ones while fighting alongside the X-Men in space. She was Iron Man's first choice as field leader when he formed the Mighty Avengers, but has more in common with Tony than merely their crime-fighting past. Like Tony, the stress of her double life took its toll and she turned to alcohol to cope with her problems. Recognizing the signs from his own troubled past, Tony offered Carol his help, even revealing his dual identity to her. While it took Ms. Marvel time to acknowledge her addiction, she was able to conquer it, just as she had overcome many other hurdles in her life.

## Reed Richards and the Fantastic Four

Tony Stark has found few men that equal or surpass his intellect, but Reed Richards is one of them. The founding force behind the super family of heroes known as the Fantastic Four, Reed (the Fantastic Four's super-malleable Mr. Fantastic) has formed a firm friendship with Tony, each respecting the other's scientific achievements. With many common interests, including a regular chess game, it's no surprise that the two friends have come to each other's aid on the battlefield as well. Alongside his wife, Sue Richards (the Invisible Woman), his brother-in-law Johnny Storm (the hotheaded Human Torch), and his old friend Ben Grimm (the irrepressible Thing), Mr. Fantastic has used his elastic powers to help Iron Man many times. On one occasion, Iron Man and the Fantastic Four squared off against a barrage of monsters on the streets of Tokyo, Japan, as well as a giant creature from another dimension. Tony and Reed were also both members of the top secret group known as the Illuminati and pivotal players on the government's side during the Civil War (see pp. 162–163) that ravaged the Super Hero community.

## Spider-Man

Possessing a curious scientific mind like Stark's, Peter Parker has always looked up to Tony as a role model and a mentor. Even when fighting side-by-side as Spider-Man and Iron Man, or during their time on the same Super Hero team, the New Avengers, Spider-Man looks to Iron Man for guidance and advice.

Sharing many of the same mutual foes, such as the armored Beetle, the criminal mastermind Justin Hammer, and the poisonous Radioactive Man, Iron Man and Spider-Man have teamed up many times over the years. Side by side with the other New Avengers, they've faced down threats such as Hydra doppelgangers and armies of deadly Hand ninja. And as partners, they've tackled the likes of Radioactive Man, the Terrible Thinker, and Big Wheel. Peter Parker even served as Tony's right-hand man before the complex issues of the Super Hero Civil War tore their friendship apart.

## Ka-Zar of the Savage Land

Over the years, Iron Man has paired with some unlikely partners. Perhaps none was more improbable than Lord Kevin Plunder, the jungle dwelling Ka-Zar. Iron Man met up with Ka-Zar when the hero left his home in the lost world named the Savage Land, situated somewhere in Antarctica, and journeyed to the Avenger's West Coast compound in California. Touring the grounds, contemplating life as a fully fledged Super Hero, Ka-Zar was taken by surprise when the Avengers' old enemy Fixer, in an attempt to steal Iron Man's armor, attacked the compound. Pitting his basic survival techniques against the high-tech arsenal of the Fixer, Ka-Zar captured the villain with a little help from Iron Man's ingenuity.

In more recent times, Ka-Zar and his wife, Shanna helped Iron Man fight the Skrull invasion when the Skrulls attempted to set up a base in the Savage Land.

## The Champions

A short-lived team of unlikely allies, the Los Angeles-based Champions teamed with many heroes during their brief existence. Consisting of super spy Black Widow, spirit of vengeance Ghost Rider, former founding X-Men members Iceman and Angel, and the demigod Hercules, the Champions were a force to be reckoned with in their heyday.

On one particular adventure, the team crossed paths with Iron Man while the Golden Avenger was busy battling his enemy MODOK on the west coast of America. After contacting his two former Avenger colleagues, Black Widow and Hercules, Iron Man and the Champions set out to track down MODOK.

Iron Man finally discovered MODOK's hiding place and, with the Champions by his side, expelled excess energy directly at the robot villain, seemingly finishing him once and for all.

## The Thunderbolts

Formerly the criminal Masters of Evil, the Thunderbolts appeared on the scene after the Avengers disappeared following their battle with the mysterious creature called Onslaught. Winning the public's support before revealing their former Super Villain identities, (members included Blizzard, Songbird, Jolt, Joystick, Charcoal, Moonstone, Beetle, Atlas, Speed Demon, and Radioactive Man) the Thunderbolts remained controversial figures in the minds of the Avengers upon that team's return from exile in a pocket dimension.

On one occasion, Iron Man masqueraded as the villain known as the Cobalt Man in order to infiltrate the Thunderbolts' ranks. Iron Man's deception was discovered by the Thunderbolt Moonstone, when she lost control of the vast energy she possessed. With the Avengers' help, Iron Man and the Thunderbolts took down the crazed villainess. During the Civil War, Iron Man utilized the Thunderbolts to help track down unregistered heroes.

## Namor the Sub-Mariner

Ruling the underwater kingdom of Atlantis has done nothing for Namor the Sub-Mariner's modesty. With a hair-trigger temper and the brute strength to back it up, Namor has flip-flopped from hero to villain in the eyes of the public and their Super Hero protectors. Nevertheless, Namor possesses his own unique and unswerving moral code, which has led him to partnering with Iron Man from time to time and both have been members of the Avengers but were only briefly teammates.

On one occasion, Namor put himself at odds with the Golden Avenger after the sea king's reckless actions accidentally knocked a passenger plane out of the sky. Realizing that Namor's tantrum was caused by the activities of the corrupt Roxxon Oil company, Iron Man joined forces with the Atlantian and helped him destroy the company's criminal naval operation.

# OTHER IRON MEN

There have been times when Tony Stark has reluctantly stepped down and allowed other men and women to take up the Iron Man mantle.

**HAPPY HOGAN**
When the public began to suspect Tony's connection to Iron Man, his chauffeur Happy Hogan decided to save his boss's reputation by taking a turn in the Iron Man armor. By appearing in public, Happy put to rest any lingering suspicions that Tony Stark and Iron Man were one and the same.

**EDDIE MARCH**
Drawing inspiration from Iron Man's heroic exploits, prize-fighter Eddie March seemed the ideal choice to take over as Iron Man when Tony Stark decided to retire due to health complications. Unfortunately, March had a secret blood clot, and so Tony was soon forced to renew his role as the Golden Avenger.

**BETHANY CABE**
A trusted ally, though she never wore an Iron Man suit herself, Bethany Cabe first stepped into the role of Iron Man when Jim Rhodes recruited a team to pilot Tony's spare suits and battle the alien robot Ultimo. Bethany took to the equipment like a natural and played a crucial role in the ensuing battle.

**MICHAEL O'BRIEN**
Originally meeting Iron Man on the battlefield as the second Guardsman, Michael O'Brien later became a trusted friend of Tony Stark, and even wore the Iron Man armor to aid Tony in battle. Mistaken for the real Iron Man, O'Brien was captured by the Mandarin, forcing Iron Man to rescue him.

**CARL WALKER**
Formerly known as Clay Wilson, Carl Walker embarked on a criminal career as Force, until he became plagued by nightmares involving his misdeeds. With the help of his old enemy Iron Man, Walker left his criminal past behind him and even stood in as Iron Man when Tony needed his help against the notorious Fixer.

**JIM RHODES**
The only other person to take up the Iron Man role on a long-term basis, Jim Rhodes led the attack of Iron Men against Ultimo.

# "Spare Parts Man"

When he discovered Iron Man's recovery armor on the ocean floor, the villainous Dr. Demonicus took the opportunity to take his revenge upon his hated foe. After meticulously scrutinizing the mechanics of the suit, Demonicus donned the armor and headed in search of the West Coast Avengers' hideout.

As luck would have it, his path soon crossed that of Tony Stark who, without an Iron Man suit for the time being, was clad in a makeshift uniform that he had assembled from spare costumes found around the West Coast Avengers' compound. Dubbed

"Spare Parts Man" by his old teammate Hawkeye, Tony was soon forced to put his rough and ready costume to work battling Demonicus aboard an Avengers' Quinjet. Managing to save his own life and subdue his twisted enemy, Tony was then in a position to retire "Spare Parts Man" for good.

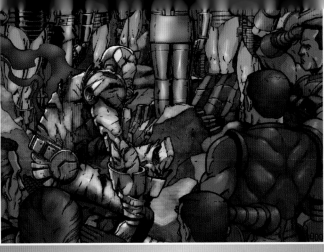

While briefly serving as the US government's Secretary of Defense, Tony was able to regulate the use of the technology that the government had appropriated from him over the years. However, owing to the political scheming of Under-Secretary Sonny Burch, dozens of malfunctioning Iron Men suits were developed without Tony's knowledge and they were about to be put into use. Luckily, Tony discovered the plot and when the Iron Men were being transported across the skies of Washington, Tony rescued the plane carrying them, just before it was about to crash.

# WOLVERINE

When hunting down the super criminal known as Nitro, the villain responsible for the destruction of the town of Stamford, Connecticut, Wolverine called upon his New Avenger teammate Iron Man for help. Borrowing a suit of Tony's hydro armor, Wolverine was able to travel to the ocean floor to the ancient city of Atlantis, in order to see to it that Nitro was brought to justice.

# TIMELINE

- The only child of wealthy arms manufacturer Howard Stark and his wife Maria, Tony is raised in a mansion neighboring New York City's Central Park. His father's strict discipline and alcohol abuse turns Tony into a quiet, withdrawn child.

- To escape his family's troubles, Tony becomes fascinated with his erector set and builds a toy Iron Man.

- At age seven, Tony is sent away to boarding school—an attempt by his father to "toughen" him up.

- Finding it difficult to relate to other children, Tony escapes into the realms of science fiction and Thomas Mallory's tales of King Arthur and his Knights of the Round Table.

- A child prodigy, Tony enrolls at MIT at age 15, double majoring in physics and engineering and studying under many esteemed professors, including Ted Slaught.

- Tony begins dating Meredith McCall, his first serious relationship.

- Tony begins work for his father at Stark Industries. He doesn't take the job very seriously, preferring the life of a millionaire playboy.

- While driving to Long Island from a function in the city, Howard and Maria Stark lose control of their luxury sedan owing to a brake failure secretly engineered by a group of corrupt industry competitors who would go on to form Roxxon Oil. Howard and Maria are both killed in the wreck, leaving the apparently irresponsible Tony in charge of their entire estate.

- As his first act as head of Stark Industries, Tony buys the manufacturer of his parents' car and fixes the design flaw that caused their supposed accident.

- Tony promotes secretary Pepper Potts to be his executive assistant after the alert young woman corrects an oversight when typing up papers for a government contract, saving the company over a half million dollars.

- As Tony flounders as head of Stark Industries, Pepper takes on more and more of his responsibilities.

- Tony and his girlfriend, Joanna Nivena, become engaged.

- On a trip to Afghanistan as a consultant to the US military, Tony is caught in the explosion of one of his own company's land mines when terrorist forces attack his convoy. With shrapnel lodged in his chest next to his heart, Tony is taken captive by the rebels and told to build a weapon that they can use against the Americans. With the help of fellow inventor and prisoner Ho Yinsen, Tony instead builds a primitive Iron Man suit that keeps him alive and allows him to escape the insurgents' camp.

- Still clad as Iron Man, Tony meets pilot Jim Rhodes and the two help each other escape enemy territory, finally returning to a US base.

- Back in the US, Tony wears his life-saving Iron Man chest plate to survive, but makes it thinner and more compact. He also develops a way to store the suit of armor in his briefcase. He decides to continue as Iron Man to combat crime, but keeps his dual identity a secret, announcing that Iron Man is his bodyguard and a Stark Industries' employee.

TIMELINE

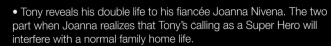

• Tony reveals his double life to his fiancée Joanna Nivena. The two part when Joanna realizes that Tony's calling as a Super Hero will interfere with a normal family home life.

• After wrestling escaped lions at a circus as Iron Man, Tony paints his armor gold, realizing that his gray armor frightens the public.

• When testing his "Stark Special" racecar, Tony crashes and is pulled from the wreckage by former boxer Happy Hogan. Tony hires Happy as his chauffeur, and the two become fast friends.

• The villain Jack Frost attacks Stark Industries, rebelling against his own employer.

• Iron Man joins Ant-Man, the Wasp, Thor, and the Hulk to form the Avengers to thwart the trickery of Thor's evil brother, Loki. The team's headquarters is the Manhattan mansion that was Tony's childhood home.

• Iron Man battles Professor Vanko, the Crimson Dynamo, convincing the villain to defect to the US and work for Stark Industries.

• Bruno Horgan attacks Stark Industries as the Melter after the military contracts weapons from Stark Industries instead of his own company.

• Tony constructs a new red and gold Iron Man suit out of lighter material to help him defeat the villainous Mr. Doll.

• Iron Man heads to China at the behest of the US government and first battles the Mandarin.

• After a failed robbery, the contortionist known as the Scarecrow flees to Cuba to escape Iron Man.

• The Avengers unearth Captain America and add him to their ranks.

• Tony has a fling with the Soviet spy known as the Black Widow before learning of her treachery and foiling her schemes.

• Iron Man streamlines his "horned" helmet into a rounded shape.

• Iron Man fights the Unicorn when the villain decides to pit his strength against the hero.

• Black Widow returns to plague Iron Man, this time with marksman Hawkeye in tow as her love-struck partner.

• After besting the villain known as the Saboteur who was out to ruin Stark Industries' government contracts, Tony finally devotes himself fully to his company, to the relief of the overworked Pepper Potts.

• Iron Man quits the Avengers, yet remains their main financial supporter. He also backs reformed villain Hawkeye for team membership.

• Iron Man bests the communist Titanium Man in a televised fight for national pride. During the epic battle, Happy Hogan reveals that he has deduced Iron Man's double identity.

• Tony Stark helps found the government super spy agency SHIELD and is instrumental in recruiting Nick Fury as its director.

• The Mandarin discovers the alien android Ultimo and unleashes the 25-foot-tall behemoth on Iron Man.

• Pepper Potts and Happy Hogan get married.

• Whiplash slugs it out with Iron Man for the first time, and fights the hero to a standstill.

• Tony begins a romance with Janice Cord.

• Iron Man faces a batch of new threats, including Madame Masque, Mordecai Midas, and the Controller.

• When Iron Man suffers a heart attack in battle, Dr. Jose Santini transplants a synthetic heart into Tony's chest, freeing the hero from dependency on his Iron Man chest plate.

• Boxer Eddie March steps in as Iron Man when Tony retires. When Eddie suffers a severe injury at the hands of a new Crimson Dynamo, Tony returns as Iron Man, fighting the Crimson Dynamo in a battle that costs Janice Cord her life.

• The political activist Firebrand first comes into conflict with Iron Man.

• The original Spymaster and his Espionage Elite attack Stark Industries, taking Tony Stark hostage.

• Tony creates the Guardsman armor for engineer Kevin O'Brien, but the armor causes O'Brien to go insane, and attack Tony's new girlfriend Marianne Rodgers. Iron Man accidentally kills O'Brien in a later skirmish.

• Iron Man fights alongside the Avengers in the Kree/Skrull War. He later forms the Illuminati alongside Mr. Fantastic, Namor, Professor X, Dr. Strange, and Black Bolt in order to prevent such conflicts recurring in future.

• Tony changes the name of his company to Stark International to better reflect his role in the global marketplace. He abandons his work in munitions in favor of the more beneficial innovations of electronics development.

• Jack Frost returns as the criminal Blizzard.

• Michael O'Brien, the brother of the original Guardsman, investigates his brother Kevin's death and eventually takes up his mantle after briefly posing as Iron Man.

• Jim Rhodes, Bethany Cabe, and Bambi Arbogast all come to work at Stark International.

• Justin Hammer wages war on Stark's business.

• With Iron Man framed for murder, Tony undergoes training by Captain America in martial arts and other fighting techniques.

• Although Tony manages to escape Hammer's clutches, the stress of the ongoing skirmish and the threat of a hostile company takeover drive Tony to drink.

• With the help of his budding romance with Bethany Cabe, Tony manages to kick his drinking habit and reclaim his life.

• Iron Man tries out his first armor variation, his space armor, while investigating an orbiting Roxxon satellite.

• Industrialist Edwin Cord orders the Raiders to attack Iron Man, and is jailed.

• Dr. Doom and Iron Man travel back to the time of King Arthur and the Knights of the Round Table.

• Iron Man uses his new stealth armor to invade a top-secret East German research complex resulting in an ongoing feud with the villainous Living Laser.

• Obadiah Stane begins a hostile takeover of Stark International, setting his sights on destroying Iron Man while simultaneously scheming to return Tony Stark to the bottle.

Tony lapses into alcoholism once more, becoming incapable of operating the Iron Man suit.

• Pilot Jim Rhodes takes over Tony Stark's duties as Iron Man while Tony roams the New York City streets, reduced to little more than a penniless vagrant.

• Obadiah Stane takes over Stark International, renaming it Stane International.

• Iron Man Jim Rhodes is transported to Battleworld with many other heroes to fight at the whim of the mysterious Beyonder. There his armor is augmented by fellow hero Mr. Fantastic.

After befriending a homeless pregnant woman and saving her son's life, Tony becomes sober again.

• Tony and a few friends move to California and create a new company called Circuits Maximus.

Iron Man battles the seismic-powered Vibro.

• As Iron Man, Jim Rhodes joins the West Coast Avengers.

When his new company is destroyed by Stane, Tony Stark dons new silver armor and reclaims his title as Iron Man. Iron Man attacks Stane, who has designed his own Iron Monger battlesuit, and defeats him. Stane takes his own life.

• Tony sets up a new company called Stark Enterprises.

• Iron Man dons his underwater armor for the first time when searching for chemical weapons at the bottom of the ocean.

• The Ghost attacks a new subsidiary of Stark Enterprises, bringing him into conflict with Iron Man for the first time.

• Tony hires reformed villain Force and discovers his new employee's armor contains stolen Stark components. This prompts Iron Man to embark on a renegade mission, dubbed the Armor Wars, to destroy all of his technology that has been appropriated by other hands over the years.

• Tony's extreme actions in the Armor Wars lead to Iron Man being kicked out of the Avengers and Tony creating a new Iron Man suit.

• The emotionally disturbed Kathy Dare becomes obsessed with Tony Stark and shoots and paralyzes him. Tony employs an experimental microchip to regain the ability to walk.

• Iron Man faces manipulation and control from outside forces, along with the revenge of a more powerful Living Laser in the second Armor Wars.

• Tony travels to China in an attempt to find a cure for his worsening spinal condition and instead encounters the Mandarin and Fin Fang Foom in the Dragon Seed Saga.

• Iron Man joins with the Avengers to fight in Operation: Galactic Storm during an interstellar war between the Kree and the Shi'ar.

• Undergoing experimental treatment to cure his ailing condition, Tony fakes his own death, promoting Jim Rhodes to CEO of Stark Enterprises and once again into the position of Iron Man.

• Tony is successfully revived, prompting Rhodes, sick of being kept in the dark, to angrily quit his employ. Rhodes adopts the War Machine identity and embarks on his own crime fighting career.

TIMELINE

• War Machine joins the West Coast Avengers.

• In a battle with Ultimo, Iron Men past and present join forces after Tony's remote controlled NTU Iron Man fails to stop the giant alien android. The group defeats the villain only after Tony arrives clad in a new advanced Iron Man armor.

• Iron Man employs his Hulk-Buster armor during a fight with an intelligent Hulk regarding the destruction of a factory that produces gamma ray bombs.

• The West Coast Avengers disband, allowing Tony to form his own team of heroes, Force Works.

• Tony Stark and Jim Rhodes put aside their personal differences during a battle with the Mandarin.

• Tony is corrupted by the forces of Immortus in the guise of Kang the Conqueror and goes on a killing spree in service of his new master. This prompts the other Avengers to travel back in time and seek the aid of a young Tony Stark.

• In a final moment of heroism, the older Tony Stark sacrifices his life to help defeat Kang and his allies. The young Tony decides to carry on his duties as Iron Man in the present.

• The young Tony Stark, along with many other heroes, seemingly dies in order to save the world from the rampaging powerhouse Onslaught. In reality, the heroes are transported to an alternate pocket dimension.

• Iron Man returns to his rightful dimension as an adult, wearing a new suit of Iron Man armor.

• With the merger of Stark Enterprises and Fujikawa Industries occurring in Tony's absence, Tony decides to start a new proactive subsidiary called Stark Solutions.

• Iron Man joins a new incarnation of the Avengers with a familiar classic roster after an epic battle with Morgan le Fay.

• Tony meets Rumiko Fujikawa when fighting a new version of Firebrand on a tropical island, and the two begin dating.

• When his reputation is destroyed by Tiberius Stone, Tony Stark gives his fortune to the Avengers and the Maria Stark Foundation and begins life anew as computer tech Hogan Potts.

• Iron Man dons a new liquid metal Iron Man suit with the help of Askew Labs.

• Tony reclaims his fortune and, with Rumiko's help, reclaims his original company as well. He also adopts a new suit of armor.

• Iron Man decides to go public with his dual identity to save the life of a dog about to be hit by a car.

• Tony dons magic Thor-Buster armor for the first time during a conflict with the thunder god on foreign soil.

• When he discovers that several of his designs are being employed by the US government without his permission, Tony decides to regulate their use by becoming the US Secretary of Defense.

• After a scandal caused by the machinations of his fellow Avenger, the mentally imbalanced Scarlet Witch, Tony resigns from his government position in disgrace.

• Rumiko Fujikawa is killed by Tony's former business rival Clarence Ward, who is wearing a stolen suit of Iron Man armor at the time of the assassination.

• The Avengers officially disband after their ranks are decimated by the magic abilities of the Scarlet Witch.

With the help of his old friend Maya Hansen, Tony applies experimental Extremis technology to his Iron Man armor, allowing him to link directly into the Iron Man suit and other machinery with his mind, and making him more powerful than ever.

After a breakout at the maximum holding facility known as the Raft, Iron Man joins with several other heroes to form the New Avengers.

• The Scarlet Witch alters reality completely so that mutants are the dominant species, forcing Iron Man and other heroes to topple her new regime and restore the world to normal.

• Iron Man becomes a mentor figure to Spider-Man and even builds the hero his own suit of armor dubbed the Iron Spider.

Civil War breaks out between two factions of heroes when congress passes the Superhuman Registration Act. Iron Man spearheads a team of government-sponsored, legally registered heroes while Captain America leads a clan of vigilantes who refuse to give up their right to privacy. Iron Man and his allies ultimately win the war, resulting in Captain America's death.

• Happy Hogan is killed fighting the Spymaster, leaving Pepper Potts a widow.

• Iron Man is promoted to Director of SHIELD and instigates the Fifty State Initiative, a program that installs a Super Hero team in every state. Iron Man oversees a team of new Mighty Avengers, while assigning Pepper Potts to oversee the California-based premier team of new blood called the Order.

Exiled in outer space by the Illuminati, the Hulk returns and declares war on Super Heroes. Iron Man battles him and helps the heroes triumph by employing satellite technology.

• Ezekiel Stane, son of Tony's former arch-foe Obadiah Stane, steals and upgrades Stark technology and wages war on Iron Man and his companies, severely injuring Pepper Potts.

Jim Rhodes is nearly killed while on a military base in Dubai, but is rebuilt by Tony into a half-human cyborg as a newly advanced version of War Machine.

Earth falls victim to a Secret Invasion led by the alien shape-shifters called the Skrulls. During the devastating war, all Stark technology is rendered inert by the aliens, including Tony's Extremis technology.

Former Green Goblin, Norman Osborn, kills the Skrulls' queen, causing an upswing in public opinion for the one-time villain. He soon replaces Stark at the head of the reformed SHIELD organization (now called HAMMER) and frames Tony for war crimes. Osborn even steals an old Iron Man suit of Stark's and claims it for himself, leading a new group of Dark Avengers as the Iron Patriot.

• A fugitive from the law, Tony closes the doors to the financially crippled Stark Industries and erases all the files of the Superhuman Registration Act, even from his own mind, causing him to slowly lose his intelligence and subsequently downgrade his armor.

Pepper Potts adopts the identity of Rescue and her own set of defensive armor powered by the repulsor technology Tony used to save her life after her injury at the hands of Zeke Stane.

• After a fierce battle with the Iron Patriot, Tony is placed in a coma, virtually brain dead. Meanwhile, his old allies rally around a mysterious disc that could possibly be the key to his recovery.

TIMELINE

# IRON MAN
# Vol. 5 #10

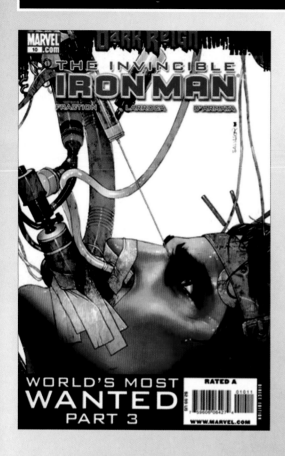

WORLD'S MOST WANTED PART 3

RATED A

**"And while you're there doing your thing... and Pepper is at Stark doing her thing... I'm doing my thing and running like hell."**

TONY STARK

**MAIN CHARACTERS: Iron Man; Maria Hill; Pepper Potts; Iron Patriot (Norman Osborn)**
**SUPPORTING CHARACTERS: Kat Farrell; Victoria Hand; HAMMER employees**
**LOCATIONS: Stark Industries; Funtime, Inc.; Restoration Park, NYC; Chicago; Los Angeles; Rome; Berlin; Hong Kong; Seattle**

**PUBLICATION DATE**
April 2009

**EDITOR-IN-CHIEF**
Joe Quesada

**COVER ARTIST**
Salvador Larroca

**WRITER**
Matt Fraction

**ARTIST**
Salvador Larroca

**COLORIST**
Frank D'Armata

**LETTERER**
Joe Caramagna

## BACKGROUND

Following his support of the Superhuman Registration Act that helped spark the Civil War between heroes, Iron Man was almost being regarded as a villain by the majority of the heroes in the Marvel Universe. As such, it was growing harder and harder for writers to create sympathy for the character, or to paint him in a heroic light. Tony Stark was in need of an adventure or two that would restore his previous status as a modern-day knight in shining armor. So when writer Matt Fraction helped relaunch Iron Man's fifth series, he looked to Tony's long and storied history, charm, and good nature to restore the hero to his former glory. By turning Iron Man from a government employee to a noble fugitive from that same institution, Fraction superbly achieved his aim. Fraction also fleshed out Tony's supporting cast, giving new prominence to longtime love interest Pepper Potts, and also the most recent villain to challenge Tony's legacy, Norman Osborn.

# The Story...

With her boss, Tony Stark, on the run from Norman Osborn and his newly-formed HAMMER organization, Pepper Potts stumbles upon an Iron Man suit tailor-made just for her.

Blamed for not anticipating the recent invasion of the alien Skrulls, Tony Stark had been proclaimed a criminal by Norman Osborn, the Director of a new government security organization named HAMMER. He was now on the run, and his former, computer-based Iron Man powers had been shut down. Furthermore, Tony possessed the only copy of the Superhuman Registration data files, a directory of every hero's secret identity, downloaded into his brain, and was forced to slowly delete his intelligence in order to make sure that Osborn never got his villainous hands on them. And yet, despite all this mayhem, Tony Stark had a plan, and he was determined to see it out.

While Norman Osborn engaged in the latest of a number of press conferences regarding Iron Man's fugitive status **(1)**, Pepper Potts was doing her best to figure out why Tony Stark had just recently placed her in charge of Stark Industries **(2)**. The former multi-billion-dollar national conglomerate had been reduced to a virtually bankrupt shell staffed by a skeleton crew. Tony's company was dying, and it seemed that Pepper's job was simply to pull the plug.

Meanwhile, at one of Tony Stark's subsidiaries, Funtime, Inc., Tony and his former right-hand woman at SHIELD, Maria Hill, were discussing their plans now that Osborn had made both of them into wanted criminals. Tony needed Maria to break into his Futurepharm plant in Austin, Texas and, using a jump drive **(3)** locate a hard drive containing crucial information. She should then take the hard drive to Captain America. Maria agreed and, knowing that she might be embarking on her very last mission, kissed Tony. Overcome by passion, Tony and Maria forgot grim reality for a few brief moments.

Back at Stark Industries, Pepper was growing ever more frustrated with the responsibilities of her new position **(4)**. In a fit of rage, she threw her chair across the room, knocking a framed picture askew. And that's when she discovered just why Tony had placed her in charge of his company. She had accidentally tripped a trigger that opened a panel to a secret room. Inside this futuristic chamber was a female version of the Iron Man armor, made to fit Pepper's body **(5)**.

But Pepper wouldn't be the only person trying out an Iron Man suit that day. Across town, in the newly christened Restoration Park, Norman Osborn was hosting yet another press conference, this time clad in a suit of armor appropriated from Stark Tower: a red, white, and blue version of Iron Man's own suit **(6)**. With the public now referring to him as the Iron Patriot, Osborn announced that since Tony had failed to meet him at this public forum, he had ordered the seizure of all of Tony's companies all over the world. He was going to bring Tony Stark to justice **(7)**.

Of course, Osborn wouldn't get everything. Back at Funtime, Inc., Maria Stark was busy blowing up the main building, ensuring that dozens of Iron Man suits wouldn't fall into the wrong hands **(8)**. And as Tony Stark flew through the sky in one of his older suits of armor to continue his mission, yet another Iron Man suit was escaping Osborn's clutches. Because back on Long Island, on the rooftop of Stark Industries, Pepper Potts stood in her new suit of armor, about to take to the skies for the first time, realizing that there would truly be no turning back now **(9)**.

### "Oh, I think going bonkers is completely imperative."

**Tony Stark**

# The Character of Wolverine

## ...FIVE THINGS YOU SHOULD KNOW ABOUT WOLVERINE...

**1** Wolverine's real name is James Howlett, *NOT* Logan, which was an alias he adopted after fleeing his family home. Thomas Logan was the groundskeeper on the Howlett estate in Alberta, Canada.

**2** Wolverine is over 100 years old, but his remarkable regenerative powers keep him looking as he did in his early forties.

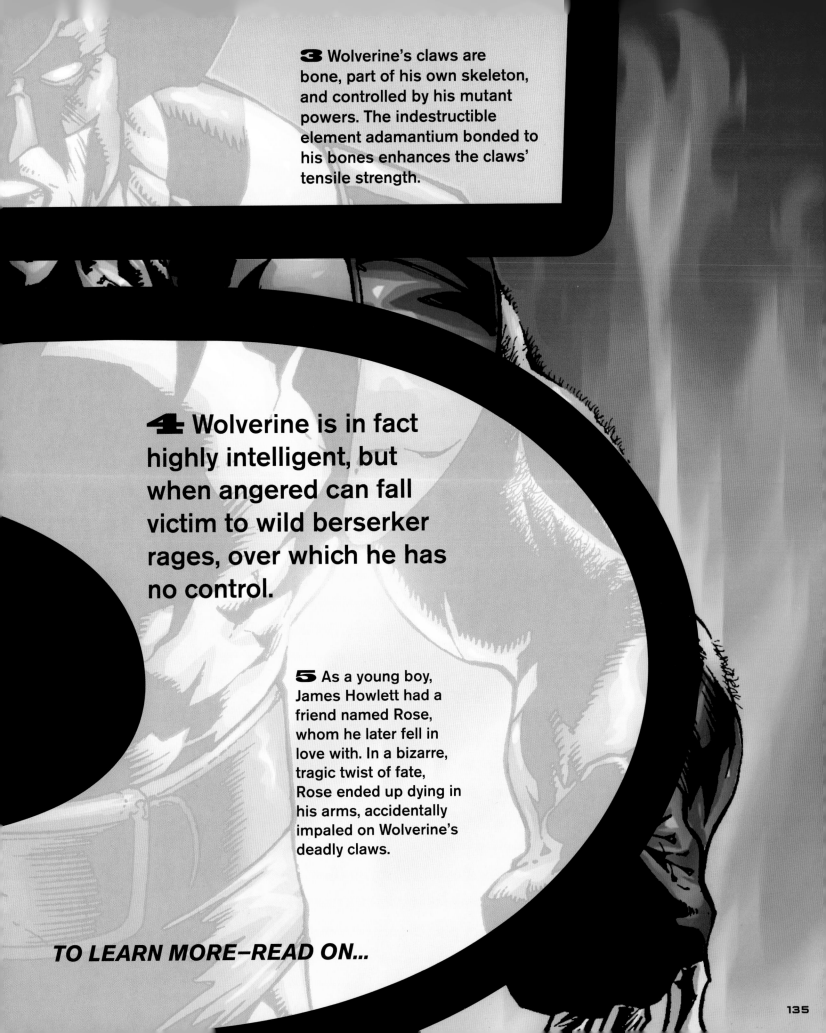

**3** Wolverine's claws are bone, part of his own skeleton, and controlled by his mutant powers. The indestructible element adamantium bonded to his bones enhances the claws' tensile strength.

**4** Wolverine is in fact highly intelligent, but when angered can fall victim to wild berserker rages, over which he has no control.

**5** As a young boy, James Howlett had a friend named Rose, whom he later fell in love with. In a bizarre, tragic twist of fate, Rose ended up dying in his arms, accidentally impaled on Wolverine's deadly claws.

*TO LEARN MORE—READ ON...*

# THE STORY OF WOLVERINE

*"IF YOU REALLY WANT TO TANGLE WITH SOMEONE...*

*...TRY YOUR LUCK AGAINST...*

# ...the Wolverine!"

Wolverine can take a bullet. With his high tolerance to pain and mutant healing ability, he has proven that he can shrug off more than his fair share of spent ammunition. However, when the character was first being developed by writer Len Wein and artist John Romita Sr., it seemed that *dodging* bullets might be his greatest strength.

The first bullet was his name. Editor-in-Chief Roy Thomas decided that the Marvel Universe needed a character whose roots were planted firmly in the Canadian wilderness. Thomas toyed with the name Badger, before opting for Wolverine, an idea he passed to Wein to develop.

As Wein collaborated with art director, John Romita Sr., the character of Wolverine would dodge his second bullet. Knowing next to nothing about the animal in question, Romita was under the impression that a wolverine was a female wolf. Fortunately, this misconception was quickly discovered when Romita began to research the furry creature.

The final bullet Wolverine successfully dodged during his creation was his intended origin. Originally, Wein conceived Wolverine as simply a highly evolved version of his animal namesake. However, the notion of a talking woodland creature was soon nixed and the character given a more realistic background.

Wolverine's claws were always intended to be retractable; however Len Wein never intended for them to be a part of his actual body. Instead, Wein saw the claws as part of Wolverine's gloves, but was overruled by writer Chris Claremont, when Wolverine made his way onto the X-Men. Claremont thought that natural claws made the character irreplaceable.

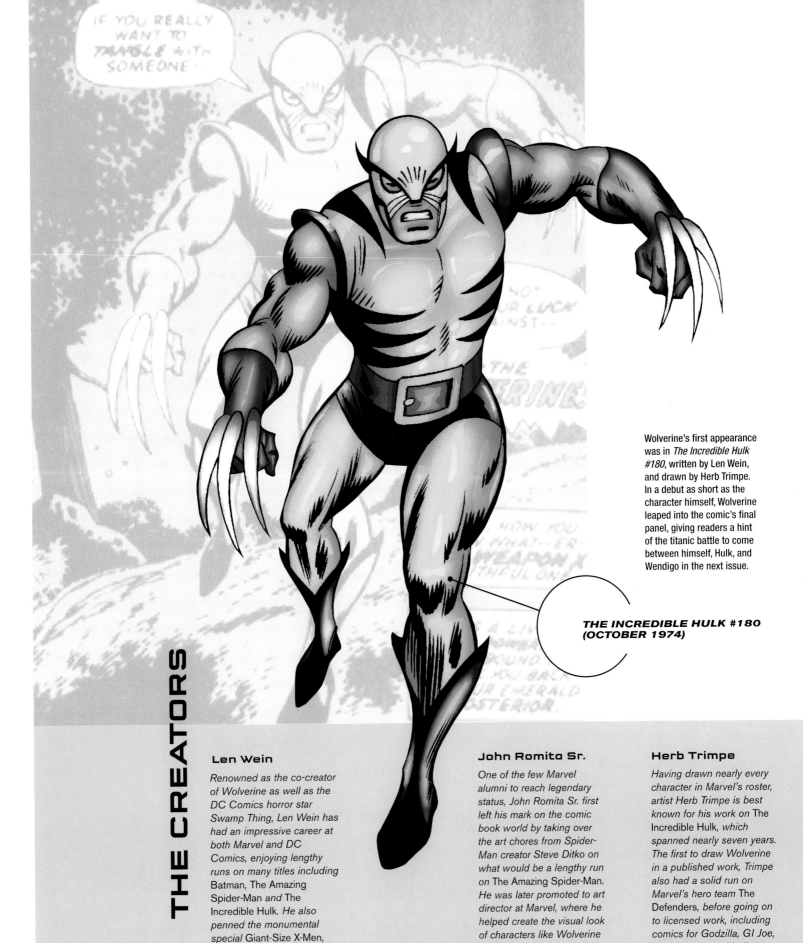

Wolverine's first appearance was in *The Incredible Hulk #180*, written by Len Wein, and drawn by Herb Trimpe. In a debut as short as the character himself, Wolverine leaped into the comic's final panel, giving readers a hint of the titanic battle to come between himself, Hulk, and Wendigo in the next issue.

**THE INCREDIBLE HULK #180 (OCTOBER 1974)**

# THE CREATORS

### Len Wein

*Renowned as the co-creator of Wolverine as well as the DC Comics horror star Swamp Thing, Len Wein has had an impressive career at both Marvel and DC Comics, enjoying lengthy runs on many titles including* Batman, The Amazing Spider-Man *and* The Incredible Hulk. *He also penned the monumental special* Giant-Size X-Men, *before serving for a time as Marvel's Editor-in-Chief.*

### John Romita Sr.

*One of the few Marvel alumni to reach legendary status, John Romita Sr. first left his mark on the comic book world by taking over the art chores from Spider-Man creator Steve Ditko on what would be a lengthy run on* The Amazing Spider-Man. *He was later promoted to art director at Marvel, where he helped create the visual look of characters like Wolverine and the gun-toting vigilante, the Punisher.*

### Herb Trimpe

*Having drawn nearly every character in Marvel's roster, artist Herb Trimpe is best known for his work on* The Incredible Hulk, *which spanned nearly seven years. The first to draw Wolverine in a published work, Trimpe also had a solid run on Marvel's hero team* The Defenders, *before going on to licensed work, including comics for Godzilla, GI Joe, Transformers and Indiana Jones.*

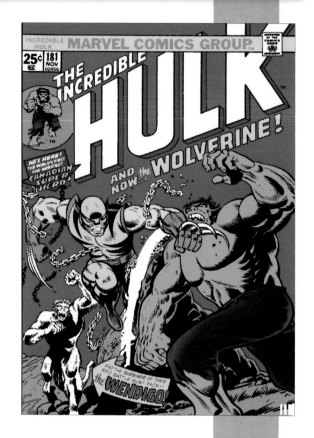

## The Incredible
# HULK
## #181

> "**Little man tried to trick Hulk... but Hulk was smarter... Hulk was stronger... ... and that is why Hulk won!**"

**HULK TO A DEFEATED WOLVERINE**

**MAIN CHARACTERS:** Hulk, Wolverine, Wendigo
**SUPPORTING CHARACTERS:** George Baptiste, Holeridge, Marie Cartier, Matthews
**LOCATIONS:** Quebec, Canada (including Department H)

**Publication date**
*November 1974*

**Editor-in-chief**
*Roy Thomas*

**Cover artist**
*Herb Trimpe*

**Writer**
*Len Wein*

**Penciller**
*Herb Trimpe*

**Inker**
*Jack Abel*

**Colorist**
*Glynis Wein*

**Letterer**
*Artie Simek*

## Background

Roy Thomas had recently discovered Canada. In 1974, as editor-in-chief of Marvel Comics, Thomas had become aware that his company had been selling more and more comics to his country's northern neighbors, and therefore thought the creation of a Canadian Super Hero was in order. Inspired by the real-life woodland animal that finds its home on both sides of the American/Canadian border, Thomas handed over the character concept of Wolverine to *Incredible Hulk* scribe Len Wein with instructions to use this new creation in Hulk's own title. Wein shaped the hero into a "small, nasty guy," and passed the idea along to the art director, legendary Marvel artist John Romita Sr. Even though Wein had pictured Wolverine as a fiery teenage brawler, Romita gave the hero an older look. He researched the real-life wolverine animal and gave the character a height of just 5 ft 3 in to reflect the relatively small size of this fierce creature. And soon, with a one-panel introduction on the last page of issue *#180* of *The Incredible Hulk*, Wolverine was born, leaping into battle with a furious energy that would prove typical of the future hero's hair-trigger temper.

# The Story

Wolverine makes his action-packed debut as he throws himself in between two seeming forces of nature, the incredible Hulk and the brutal woods-beast Wendigo...

Nothing in the life of Dr. Robert Bruce Banner ever went smoothly. First there were the gamma rays, the ones that transformed him from a simple mild mannered scientist into a raving behemoth known as the Hulk. Then there was the government. They'd pursued him in both of his identities, demanding Bruce Banner pay for the damage caused by his monstrous alter ego. Even when Banner tried to do good, things seemed to blow up in his extremely frightening face. Take his latest attempt at heroics. The Hulk traveled to Quebec, Canada at the insistence of the beautiful Marie Cartier in order to find a cure for the mythic albino monster, known only as the Wendigo, that haunted the nearby wilderness. But instead of helping the brutal beast the Hulk found himself battling him, the two nearly evenly matched in both strength and stamina. And if that wasn't bad enough, soon a third equally savage player entered the arena. A mean little man calling himself Wolverine.

Clad in a bright yellow uniform complete with drawn on whiskers and claws, Wolverine immediately leapt into the fray. A secret agent for Department H, a faction of the Canadian government, Wolverine, also known as Weapon X, was embarking on one of his first missions: to take down the Hulk using whatever means necessary. It was a formidable task, but one Wolverine didn't balk at, despite the noticeable size differential.

Using his speed to his advantage, Wolverine vaulted from the Hulk to the Wendigo, and back again, barely even coming into contact with the ground below. As ferocious as his namesake, Wolverine soon fell into favor with the Hulk, and teamed up with the Green Goliath in order to knock the Wendigo unconscious (1). As the two took in a moment of silence to gaze at their fallen opponent, Wolverine quickly turned on the Hulk, taking the opportunity to catch his true target off guard.

While in a not-too-distant secret complex, military personnel argued over his capabilities (2), Wolverine continued to battle the Hulk as night slowly gave way to the rising sun. Meanwhile, Marie Cartier along with her friend, Georges Baptiste, emerged from the nearby bushes and dragged Wendigo's limp body away from the conflict. As it turned out, Marie's brother was actually the Wendigo, the victim of an ancient curse that she intended to transfer to the Hulk through the use of the black arts. Though Georges seemed weary of Marie's plan, he nevertheless followed her as she cast the spell of subjugation (3), creating an almost invisible gas that rendered both Wolverine and the Hulk unconscious (4), and made the Hulk revert back to his form as Bruce Banner. Seeing Banner in his true form, Georges refused to be a part of Marie's twisted plan any longer, and left her to bind Wolverine by herself (5) in order to remove the mutant from the action. While she was otherwise occupied, Banner awoke from his slumber and changed back into the Hulk, now furious at Marie as well as Wolverine. As Marie ducked into a nearby cave, the Hulk shattered Wolverine's chains (6) so as to resume their fight unencumbered.

But their battle would be interrupted once more as Marie ran into the Wendigo itself in her attempt to flee, the young woman letting out a shrill scream that distracted Wolverine. The Hulk capitalized on his foe's momentary lapse, knocking the hero unconscious (7), and then watched the Wendigo flee the nearby cave, followed by a distraught Marie Cartier. It seems that Marie's plot had worked indeed, but just not in the way she had devised. Yes, her brother was free of the Wendigo's curse, but at a high cost, as the creature's monstrous burden had been unwittingly transferred to her good friend, Georges Baptiste.

**2**

**3**

**4**

**5**

**5**

**"Hulk will break little man's chains... and little man with them!"**

**6**

# TO KILL

Although he's comfortable fighting a barroom brawl in a leather jacket and jeans, Wolverine nevertheless feels the need to dress for the occasion, finding a proper uniform helps him to get in the right mindset to do what he does best.

## 1 X-MEN

The costume Logan wears most frequently is a variation on his original Wolverine uniform. While serving with the X-Men or off on his own adventures, Wolvie's classic blue and yellow duds let his opponents know exactly what kind of trouble is headed their way.

## 2 X-FORCE

As the field leader in Cyclops's new mutant strike team, X-Force, Wolverine has to dress to fit the part. And with his covert attacks mostly occurring in the dead of night, black and grey seems a natural choice.

## 3 ORIGINS

After getting his memory back in the House of M epic, Logan regained his knowledge of all who wronged him in his long and storied history. So, to Wolverine's way of thinking, it makes sense for him to don his brown and tan costume from yesteryear in order to hunt those responsible for past injustices.

# WOLVERINE style

Over the years, Wolverine has undergone many a costume change, his look often representing a new era or incarnation of his team, the X-Men. But when not dressed in full battle gear, Logan's unique style proclaims his outsider stance.

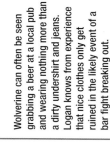

As co-owner of the Princess Bar, a small saloon in the island nation of Madripoor, Wolverine sometimes feels the need to dress up. Perhaps in an attempt to give his establishment the same air as a classic film from cinema's golden age.

Wolverine can often be seen grabbing a beer at a local pub and wearing nothing more than a dirty undershirt and jeans. Logan knows from experience that nice clothes only get ruined in the likely event of a bar fight breaking out.

Even though Logan spent months nude in the freezing wilds of Canada in his past, these days he'd much rather throw on a coat and boots when heading to colder climates.

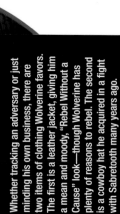

Whether tracking an adversary or just minding his own business, there are two items of clothing Wolverine favors. The first is a leather jacket, giving him a mean and moody, "Rebel Without a Cause" look—though Wolverine has plenty of reasons to rebel. The second is a cowboy hat he acquired in a fight with Sabretooth many years ago.

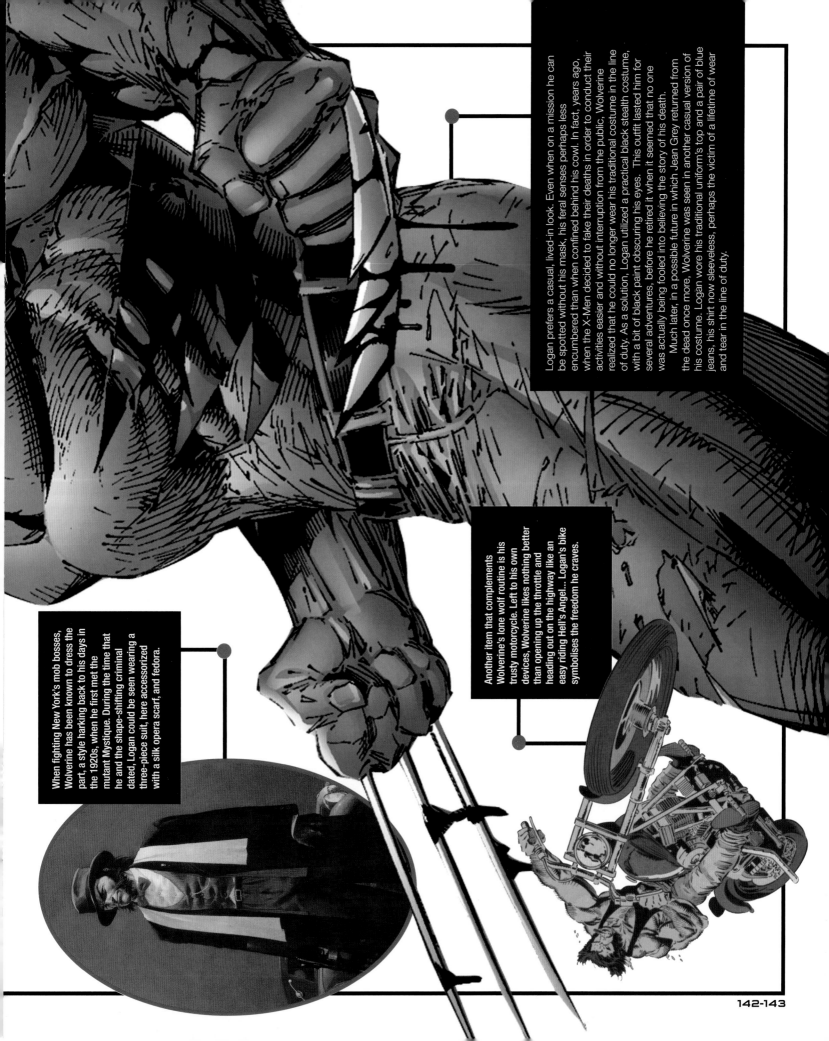

Logan prefers a casual, lived-in look. Even when on a mission he can be spotted without his mask, his feral senses perhaps less encumbered than when confined behind his cowl. In fact, years ago, when the X-Men decided to fake their deaths in order to conduct their activities easier and without interruption from the public, Wolverine realized that he could no longer wear his traditional costume in the line of duty. As a solution, Logan utilized a practical black stealth costume, with a bit of black paint obscuring his eyes. This outfit lasted him for several adventures, before he retired it when it seemed that no one was actually being fooled into believing the story of his death.

Much later, in a possible future in which Jean Grey returned from the dead once more, Wolverine was seen in another casual version of his costume. Logan wore his traditional uniform's top and a pair of blue jeans, his shirt now sleeveless, perhaps the victim of a lifetime of wear and tear in the line of duty.

Another item that complements Wolverine's lone wolf routine is his trusty motorcycle. Left to his own devices, Wolverine likes nothing better than opening up the throttle and heading out on the highway like an easy riding Hell's Angel... Logan's bike symbolises the freedom he craves.

When fighting New York's mob bosses, Wolverine has been known to dress the part, a style harking back to his days in the 1920s, when he first met the mutant Mystique. During the time that he and the shape-shifting criminal dated, Logan could be seen wearing a three-piece suit, here accessorized with a silk opera scarf, and fedora.

# Fightin' MAD!

## With his unique combination of brute strength and training, Wolverine is the perfect fighting machine.

He punches with the power of a freight train. His body is always at the peak of human perfection. And he has a near limitless internal catalog of learned martial arts techniques to pick and choose from. Even without his enhanced senses and razor-sharp claws, Wolverine can best most any opponent foolish enough to face him. But when combined with his feral nature, instinctive predatory abilities, healing factor, and adamantium-laced bones, Wolverine is an almost unstoppable threat.

In an attempt to keep his berserker animalistic nature in check, Wolverine has traveled all over the globe mastering civilized fighting styles. Besides the training he underwent in order to become a member of the CIA and Canadian military, Wolverine has studied under a variety of masters in a variety of countries. In Japan, he studied under Ogun, a master who had no peer in his day. Wolverine also journeyed to Jasmine Falls in order to study under Bando Suboro, and later had his anger forged into a tangible weapon by the fabled immortal known as Muramasa.

Through the years, with the help of other instructors, Wolverine built upon the techniques he acquired from these masters. He perfected his fighting styles training with the mercenary Cyber and in various military institutions. With this vast bank of martial arts knowledge to draw from, combined with his considerable experience in battle and his training beside Professor Charles Xavier and his mutant teammates in the X-Men, Wolverine is a master of virtually every fighting style known to man or mutant.

### SUPERHUMAN STRENGTH

Besides being a natural born brawler, Wolverine was also blessed with a degree of superhuman strength alongside his other mutant abilities. When his skeleton was bonded with unbreakable adamantium by the clandestine Weapon X project, his inherent power was increased as well, with reinforced bones that added about 100 lbs to his already hefty small frame. Wolverine's powerful blows are capable of giving even Marvel's mightiest heavyweights, such as the Incredible Hulk and Colossus, a moment's pause.

A GIGANTIC SENTINEL ROBOT PROVES NO MATCH FOR WOLVERINE

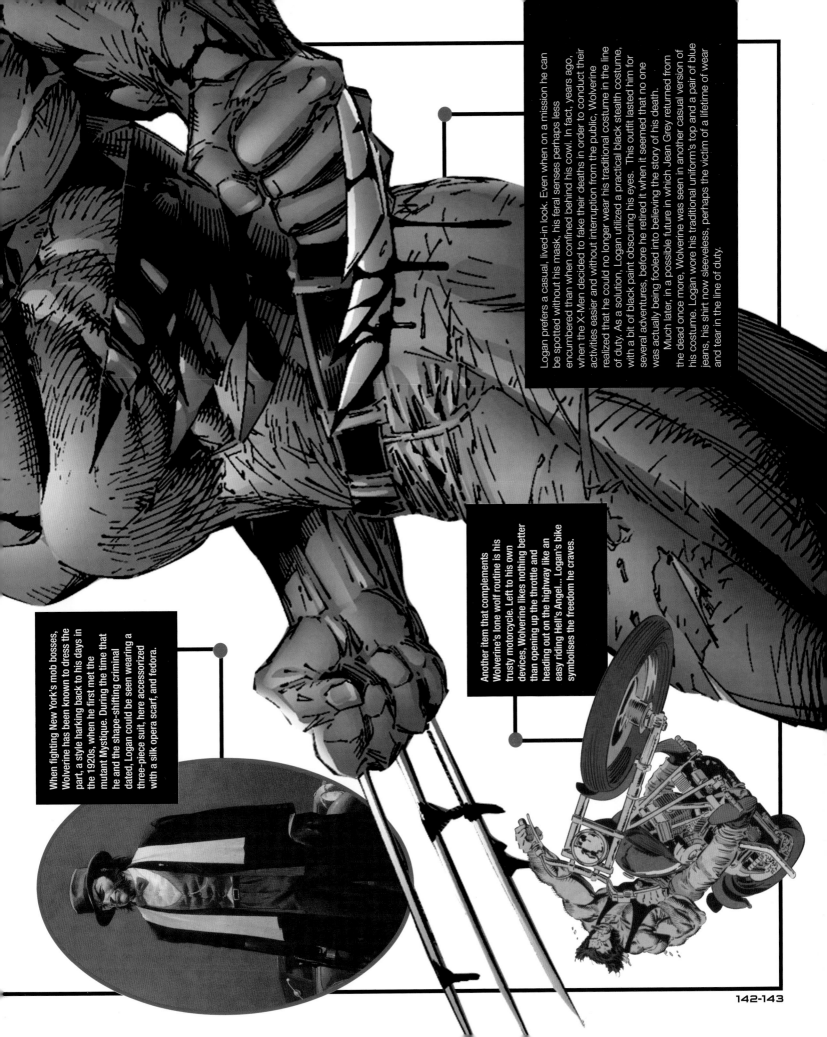

Logan prefers a casual, lived-in look. Even when on a mission he can be spotted without his mask, his feral senses perhaps less encumbered than when confined behind his cowl. In fact, years ago, when the X-Men decided to fake their deaths in order to conduct their activities easier and without interruption from the public, Wolverine realized that he could no longer wear his traditional costume in the line of duty. As a solution, Logan utilized a practical black stealth costume, with a bit of black paint obscuring his eyes. This outfit lasted him for several adventures, before he retired it when it seemed that no one was actually being fooled into believing the story of his death.

Much later, in a possible future in which Jean Grey returned from the dead once more, Wolverine was seen in another casual version of his costume. Logan wore his traditional uniform's top and a pair of blue jeans, his shirt now sleeveless, perhaps the victim of a lifetime of wear and tear in the line of duty.

Another item that complements Wolverine's lone wolf routine is his trusty motorcycle. Left to his own devices, Wolverine likes nothing better than opening up the throttle and heading out on the highway like an easy riding Hell's Angel... Logan's bike symbolises the freedom he craves.

When fighting New York's mob bosses, Wolverine has been known to dress the part, a style harking back to his days in the 1920s, when he first met the mutant Mystique. During the time that he and the shape-shifting criminal dated, Logan could be seen wearing a three-piece suit, here accessorized with a silk opera scarf, and fedora.

# POWERS

ALTHOUGH WOLVERINE IS NOT DEFINED
SOLELY BY HIS SUPERHUMAN ABILITIES,
THEY DO COME IN HANDY IN A FIGHT

When his mutant powers were activated, James Howlett went from being a weak and sickly adolescent to a life as a clawed, super-strong fighting machine. His dormant abilities were triggered by the stress of seeing his father murdered before his eyes. That traumatic moment forever shattered James's seemingly normal life.

## HEALING FACTOR

Probably the biggest advantage garnered by Wolverine's mutant genetic makeup is his uncanny ability to heal rapidly from virtually any wound inflicted upon him. This healing process is many times quicker than the average man's, but varies in speed depending on the severity of the wound. During his adventures, Wolverine has bounced back from having his body shot, burned, and stabbed. His mutant abilities also enable him to heal rapidly from poisons and disease, and resist the ravages of old age. Despite being more than a hundred years old, Logan only appears to be in his early forties because of his amazing mutant healing factor.

## FERAL SENSES

Due to his mutant gene, Wolverine possesses incredibly fine-tuned senses. He can see in near pitch darkness, and view an enemy perfectly from far distances. His sense of smell rivals that of the finest hunting dog, and allows him to track a target for miles. His hearing is so acute, he can identify an unseen threat from blocks away, just by detecting the slightest rustling of clothing.

## ADAMANTIUM

When captured by the clandestine Weapon X program, Wolverine's bones were bonded with adamantium, a virtually unbreakable metal. The weight of metal in his body increases Logan's strength and density, and helps protect his vital inner organs.

## PHYSICAL STRENGTH

Wolverine's already extraordinary strength is increased by his adamantium-enhanced skeleton. Possessing punches that feel like a collision with solid steel, Wolverine can lift between 600 and 800 lbs (272 and 363 kg). He also possesses superhuman endurance, speed, and stamina, and when in one of his mindless berserker rages he is capable of releasing a barrage of attacks in a few frenzied moments.

## THE CLAWS

Wolverine's claws first sprang from his fists after a traumatic encounter triggered his latent mutant abilities when he was a young boy. First consisting only of rock-hard bone, his claws were later laced with adamantium, making them unbreakable and able to cut through nearly any known surface. Wolverine maintains absolute control over his claws, and can "pop" one at a time if it suits his purposes. The skin on his hands breaks each time the claws emerge.

# Fightin' MAD!

## With his unique combination of brute strength and training, Wolverine is the perfect fighting machine.

He punches with the power of a freight train. His body is always at the peak of human perfection. And he has a near limitless internal catalog of learned martial arts techniques to pick and choose from. Even without his enhanced senses and razor-sharp claws, Wolverine can best most any opponent foolish enough to face him. But when combined with his feral nature, instinctive predatory abilities, healing factor, and adamantium-laced bones, Wolverine is an almost unstoppable threat.

In an attempt to keep his berserker animalistic nature in check, Wolverine has traveled all over the globe mastering civilized fighting styles. Besides the training he underwent in order to become a member of the CIA and Canadian military, Wolverine has studied under a variety of masters in a variety of countries. In Japan, he studied under Ogun, a master who had no peer in his day. Wolverine also journeyed to Jasmine Falls in order to study under Bando Suboro, and later had his anger forged into a tangible weapon by the fabled immortal known as Muramasa.

Through the years, with the help of other instructors, Wolverine built upon the techniques he acquired from these masters. He perfected his fighting styles training with the mercenary Cyber and in various military institutions. With this vast bank of martial arts knowledge to draw from, combined with his considerable experience in battle and his training beside Professor Charles Xavier and his mutant teammates in the X-Men, Wolverine is a master of virtually every fighting style known to man or mutant.

### SUPERHUMAN STRENGTH

**Besides being a natural born brawler, Wolverine was also blessed with a degree of superhuman strength alongside his other mutant abilities. When his skeleton was bonded with unbreakable adamantium by the clandestine Weapon X project, his inherent power was increased as well, with reinforced bones that added about 100 lbs to his already hefty small frame. Wolverine's powerful blows are capable of giving even Marvel's mightiest heavyweights, such as the Incredible Hulk and Colossus, a moment's pause.**

A GIGANTIC SENTINEL ROBOT PROVES NO MATCH FOR WOLVERINE

# Always on top!

## 5 OF WOLVERINE'S UNBELIEVABLE BATTLES

**1** Despite being unable to breath underwater, Wolverine once faced down the aquatic villain Tiger Shark, and narrowly avoided drowning when his claws became embedded in a coral reef. He later bested the villain in a fierce battle in a helicopter, knocking Tiger Shark into the water below and into the jaws of the villain's hungry namesake.

**2** While in China, Wolverine found himself locked in combat with the mysterious White Shadow and Black Shadow, seemingly indestructible energy creatures. Tracking the mystical enigmas back to their lair, Wolverine was finally able to defeat these untouchable manifestations by destroying their host body.

**3** On a mission to destroy the high priest of the secret criminal organization called the Hand, Logan fought his way through hundreds upon hundreds of expert ninjas in search of the villain known as Gorgon. He also had help help from his old friend and brilliant martial artist in her own right, Elektra.

**4** While being pursued by a near-unbeatable combination of mind-controlled versions of his former X-Men allies, Phoenix, Rogue and Psylocke, as well as martial artists Jessica Drew, Yukio, and Tyger Tiger, Wolverine defeated his brainwashed friends and his own feral rage with the help of former sidekicks Jubilee and Shadowcat.

**5** In Belgium during World War I, as he fought for the Canadian cause, Wolverine encountered Lazaer, also known as Azrael, the angel of death himself. Undaunted by his supernatural opponent, Logan seemingly killed his foe by impaling him through the chest with his own sword.

# The HEALING FACTOR

It's probably his most powerful weapon. Wolverine was born a mutant, possessing an enhanced X gene in his genetic makeup. Like most of his kind, his abilities were triggered during his adolescence. From that time forward, Logan has found his body has the amazing ability to recover from most any wound. When combined with his unbreakable adamantium skeleton, he becomes almost indestructible, and has proven over the years that he's able to bounce back from any injury, given time for his body to knit itself back together.

Wolverine's body is able to grow back damaged tissue, fight off disease and infection at a rapid rate, retard the normal human aging process, and quickly battle most poisons and drugs. It has also been theorized that some of Wolverine's most traumatic memories have been eradicated by this same mutant ability, in an attempt by his body to protect his mental health.

During the Civil War, Wolverine was turned into a fireball by Nitro, but he emerged with only slightly singed hair.

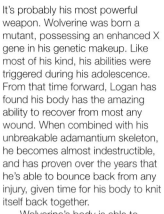

Both Wolverine and Sabretooth possess the uncanny mutant power to heal both muscle and skin tissue, an ability that only serves to prolongs their violent clashes.

# 10 things Wolverine has survived

1 Logan proved just how bulletproof he was when he received a gunshot in the forehead while facing off against a Japanese crime family.

2 Fighting alongside the Silver Samurai, Wolverine once had the majority of his skin burnt in an explosion and his adamantium skull partially exposed.

3 Wolverine's body was sent into shock when Magneto ripped out the adamantium metal coating his skeleton. Logan just barely pullied through the trauma.

4 When fighting the anti-hero the Punisher, Wolverine was run over by a steamroller but still managed to survive.

5 While partnering with Daredevil and Spider-Man, Logan was shot by a bazooka, but lived to fight again.

6 After escaping a Japanese prison camp near the end of World War II, Wolverine recovered despite being trapped in the nuclear blast at Hiroshima.

7 Logan was left for dead after being blown up by a bomb by an agent of the terrorist organization known as Scimitar.

8 Wolverine once deliberately set off an explosion in a car he was in so, as a supposed corpse, he would be carried behind enemy lines unnoticed.

9 Trapped on an asteroid headed for the sun, Logan opened a hatch and exposed himself to the star. Badly burned, he was saved by Phoenix.

10 Caught in an artificial nuclear explosion caused by the villain Nitro, Wolverine's adamantium-enhanced skeleton was forced to heal itself from scratch.

## The New Deal

But there are some injuries even a mutant healing factor can't mend. When Wolverine pushes himself past the limits of his regenerative abilities, he finds himself in a limbo of sorts, facing off against Lazaer, the angel of death. Only by winning these duels can Logan continue to return to the land of the living. Recently Wolverine struck up a bargain with Lazaer in order to regain a piece of his soul. In exchange, not only is Logan's healing factor less powerful, but now he can no longer return from the dead.

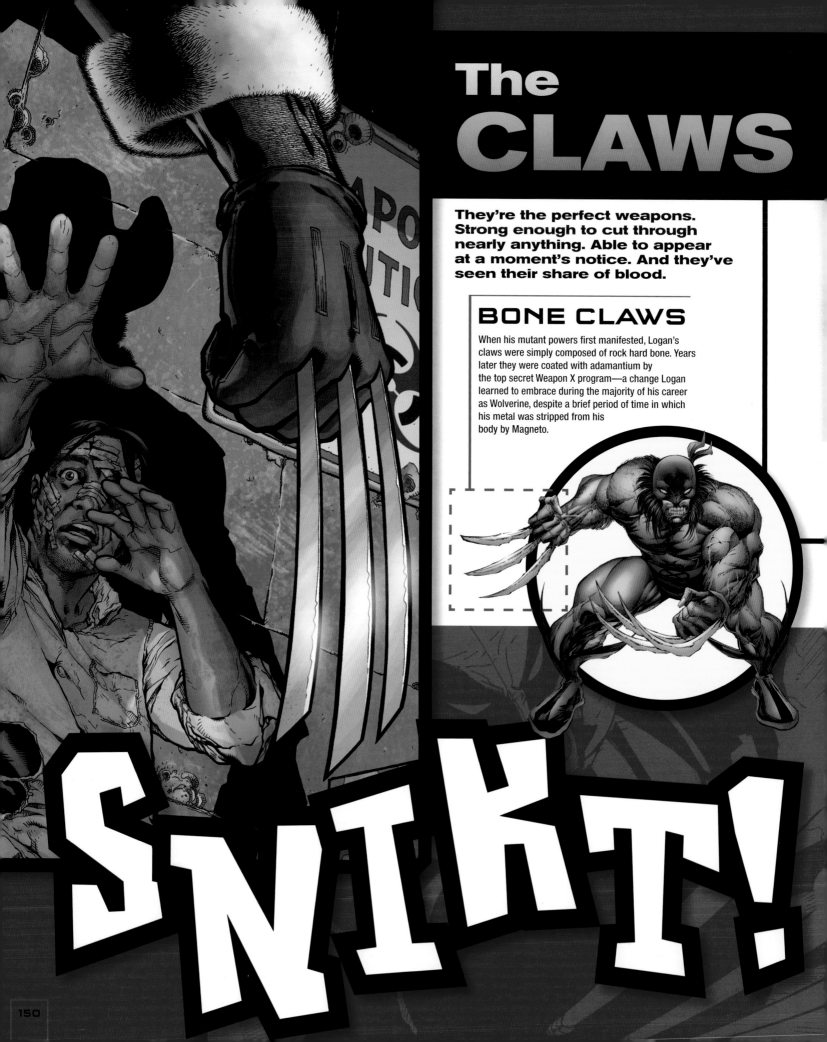

# The CLAWS

They're the perfect weapons. Strong enough to cut through nearly anything. Able to appear at a moment's notice. And they've seen their share of blood.

## BONE CLAWS

When his mutant powers first manifested, Logan's claws were simply composed of rock hard bone. Years later they were coated with adamantium by the top secret Weapon X program—a change Logan learned to embrace during the majority of his career as Wolverine, despite a brief period of time in which his metal was stripped from his body by Magneto.

# SNIKT!

Laced with the near-unbreakable steel alloy, adamantium, Wolverine's claws can cut through virtually anything. This, combined with Wolverine's enhanced mutant strength and heavy adamantium skeleton, means that he has rarely met a target he couldn't slice—even the solid metal of a gun barrel is no contest for the mutant's claws.

The only exception to this rule is adamantium itself. Adamantium is impervious even to other adamantium, and Wolverine's previous attempts at disproving this fact have only served to send his claws back into his arms, causing him immense pain in the process.

# CUTTING POWER

WHIFF

SLAAAAAA...AAASSHH

Logan's claws can't slice Silver Samurai's mystic blade, but they can easily penetrate his flesh.

# LEARNING CURVE

Though handy in a fight, Wolverine's claws took some getting used to. When not extended, the claws rest in Logan's forearm, and are almost undetectable. In fact, there have been several times in Logan's life when, after being brainwashed, he has been unaware of even possessing his claws in the first place. Back in 1963, during Logan's time with the CIA's Team X division, he was waiting in a holding facility in Dallas, Texas by order of his boss, the shadowy puppet master known as Romulus. On that occasion, Logan avoided the brainwashing procedure he was supposed to undergo, and in a violent fit of rage, popped his claws, for what seemed to him the first time. Soon after he quit Team X, now once again aware of his status as a mutant.

In order to project his claws, Logan uses a mental command that forces the blades through his skin, actually puncturing his flesh each time they are drawn. Popping his claws causes him a small degree of pain, but it is a short-lived sensation, due to Wolverine's healing factor which causes his skin to quickly mend around the small puncture wounds.

# SKILLS

## MARTIAL ARTS

In an effort to curb his primitive instincts and develop a more civilized fighting method, Logan spent many of his past years abroad, studying various martial arts and fighting techniques. When traveling through China as a merchant marine, Logan attracted the interest of Ogun, a master of martial arts who invited Logan to join his dojo in Kanazawa, Japan, an offer Logan accepted years later. Not content with the teachings of just one master, Logan also studied under master Bando Suboro as well as many other mentors over the years.

Throughout his training, Wolverine always possessed an affinity for bladed weapons.

Logan is a master of precise technique, though he rarely displays this quality in a fight.

### SPECIAL SKILLS

- Expert at most unarmed traditional fighting styles, including ju-jitsu, judo, karate, escrima, muay thai, and kali
- Master of the samurai sword
- Master of the *bokken*, a wooden practice sword
- Expert with the machete and other wide knives
- CIA advanced training in espionage and surveillance
- Expert with a crossbow
- A crack shot with most types of firearms

Though not his style these days, Logan has amassed much experience with firearms.

## WEAPONS

Wolverine has felt a kinship with sharp objects ever since his claws first emerged from the back of his hands during his youth. Since his mind has often been tampered with, making his memories of past events inaccessible to him, it was only natural for Logan to adopt the use of similar blades during the periods of his life when he was not aware that he in fact possessed his claws. Also during these times, Logan has become adept at handling a variety of guns. However he has never showed the same level of inborn appreciation for firearms as he has felt toward a sword or dagger.

## SENSES

A natural-born hunter, Wolverine is endowed with enhanced senses. He utilizes his senses together in order to locate his prey, giving him the tracking ability of a bloodhound.

### SIGHT
Wolverine's sight is much more acute than a normal human's, allowing him to see targets at great distances. He also possesses enhanced night vision.

### SMELL
Logan often relies on his magnified sense of smell to detect the presence of people nearby, recognizing the particular scents of those he has met in the past.

### HEARING
Aware of a predator's location from the slightest rustling in the surrounding brush, Wolverine's intensified hearing also enables him to eavesdrop on others' conversations.

### TASTE
Presumably, Logan also enjoys a heightened sense of taste. However he rarely remarks on this ability, not seeming to mind even if his meat is served to him raw.

SNIFF

"THE EQUIVALENT OF AN OLYMPIC GYMNAST DOING A GOLD MEDAL ROUTINE WHILE SIMULTANEOUSLY BEATING FOUR CHESS COMPUTERS IN HIS HEAD!"

FORGE DURING DANGER ROOM TRAINING SESSION

## LANGUAGES

Wolverine's extensive travels during his long lifetime have led him to become fluent in many different languages apart from English, including Japanese, Russian, Chinese, Cheyenne, Lakota, and Spanish. He also has a passing knowledge of French, Thai, and Vietnamese.

Regardless of the tough guy image he likes to maintain, Wolverine is an avid reader. *Walden, or Life in the Woods* by Henry Thoreau is one of his favorite books.

# WOLVIE'S WIT AND WISDOM

**Wolverine's dry sense of humor reveals a lifetime of hard knocks and training in the ways of the eastern world. His one-liners range from the flippant to the philosophical.**

"The day I quit fightin' is the day I die."

## "I'm the best there is at what I do. But what I do best isn't very nice"

"This wilderness has bite. It has claws. So what—so do I."

**"They should have stamped 'Loser' on your forehead when you were born."**

**"I hear ya don't like mutants. Well we don't much like you!"**

**"A man comes at me with his fists, I'll meet him with fists. But if he pulls a gun —or threatens people I'm protectin'— then I got no sympathy for him."**

"I said huntin' honeybunch—I said nothin' about killin'. It takes no skill t'kill."

**"I never used my claws on someone who hadn't tried to kill me first."**

## "Just think how I might've turned out. I might've wound up a pastry chef."

**"We're heroes... We're supposed to stand for something. We're supposed to play by the rules. Because if we don't, why should anybody?"**

"I'm the best there is at a couple of things in this world... but what we just did ain't one of them."
Wolverine to Atsuko

Little Girl: "Are You Spider Man?"
Logan: "No darlin'… Spider Man is a sissy."

**"I SHOULD HATE MYSELF WHEN I GET LIKE THIS. EVERYTHING GOES RED."**

"Let's just say I'm a fast healer."

**"I've done a lotta bad things in my life. More than most folks. But then, I've lived a lot longer than most folks."**

154

**"Who won? Musta been me, 'cause I'm still breathing..."**

"I leave him with his honor. I've got no use for it."

**"Human being's an animal, bub—though most animals probably wouldn't take that… as much of a compliment."**

**"Ninety percent of accidents happen at home, bub."**

"I know what you're thinkin', punk. Question is: 'Can I get Wolverine before he turns me into shish-kabob with those claws?'"

"He's in perfect condition. I'm not. I figure that makes us even."

**"Funny thing about this mutant healing factor o' mine... it sure doesn't cancel out any of the pain."**

"I lost control. I feel sick. I feel great."

"...And if you're looking for death... you've come to the right place."

"Place still smells the same... just cleaner. Less bloody. But that's probably 'cause I haven't been here in so long."

**"HE'S BIG AN' MEAN—A ROGUE GRIZZLY BEAR. NO MORE FEARSOME— OR DEADLY—CREATURE EXISTS ON EARTH. 'CEPT ME."**

Wolverine to Professor X:
"Thought this was the Danger Room. Oughtta rename it, or you could be sued for fake advertisin'."

**"I'M THE BEST THERE IS AT WHAT I DO. BUT WHAT I DO BEST ISN'T SHOPPING."**

"Maybe I don't *like* hospitals. Last time, I was on an operatin' table, it didn't turn out so well.

**"Mine'll grow back. Yours, on the other hand..."**

# Does Wolverine have WEAKNESSES?

At first glace he seems to be the ultimate fighter, a natural born scrapper devoid of any Achilles' heel. But despite appearances, Wolverine is not immortal, and it is said that a dire injury could kill him, especially now that his healing factor has been weakened after his encounter with the Angel of Death. However, while there are several elements in the world that could easily bring about his end, it is also believed that even Logan could not recover from decapitation.

## THE MURAMASA BLADE

*During one the blackest days of Logan's past he gave in to his anger and paid a visit to Muramasa, an ancient Japanese master of the dark arts. With the feral mutant's consent, Muramasa molded the brutal hatred inside of Logan into an actual object, a blade able to cause permanent injury to even Logan's hide. Possessing mystic properties, the Muramasa Blade can negate Logan's healing factor, and cause him lasting injury, or even death.*

## CARBONADIUM

*Created by the Soviets in an attempt to duplicate adamantium, carbonadium is a tough, yet malleable metal which gives off a radioactive aura. During his time as an agent for the mastermind Romulus, Logan ingested carbonadium, and his body's healing factor was negated, making him no more powerful than any other mortal man. With villains such as Omega Red possessing carbonadium tentacles, Wolverine is constantly on the alert for this dangerous alloy.*

## MAGNETISM

*Probably his most obvious weakness, magnetism has taken its toll on Wolverine during more than one encounter. Since his skeleton was bonded with adamantium, Logan has proven fairly ineffectual when battling magnetic-powered villains, particularly the mutant Magneto. Instead, Wolverine often finds himself tossed around like a rag doll at the whim of his opponent, Magneto even using his abilities on one occasion to rip the adamantium from Logan's bones.*

# MEMORIES and RAGE!

There is more than one way to skin a Wolverine. As many of his villains can attest, Logan is also susceptible to a subtler form of attack. With a past rich in mind manipulations and brainwashings, Logan's head has been a virtual stomping ground for many of his adversaries. With his memories ripe for the picking and altering, Logan can often be stopped dead in his tracks with a psychic attack, especially one that dredges up painful memories or perverts the few cherished recollections that he still possesses.

Perhaps the greatest weakness Wolverine possesses is his limited control over his emotions. When his patience is at and end, or when he has received an injury that wounds him too deeply, Logan's mind snaps into a state of frenzy. This uncontrollable berserker rage grips him on a primal level, and reduces his actions to pure instinct. Without control of himself, Wolverine becomes like a wild animal and therefore greatly susceptible to enemies who rely mainly on their wits.

Logan has always lived a lonely, tortured life.

Having lived for over a century, Wolverine has had several lifetimes' worth of romances. But nearly every one, long or short, has ended in heartbreak.

After discovering that his intended, Mariko, was married to someone else, Wolverine had a brief fling with Yukio. But the impetuous daredevil proved too much—even for him.

# WOLVERINE IN *Love*

## Ladies' Man

Despite being the runt of the litter, Wolverine still manages to attract more than his fair share of women. Perhaps they are attracted to his confidence and brute strength, or even by the natural pheromones he emits. Whatever the reason, the many women who have touched Logan's heart were all able to look past his apparently crude nature and gruff attitude and find the gentle soul that resides beneath.

Perhaps Wolverine's greatest love was the largely unrequited romance he shared with former X-Man Jean Grey. Jean was usually involved with teammate Cyclops while Wolverine knew her, but Logan stole a kiss from her more than once.

When demonic presences took over Manhattan, Logan's wicked side got the better of both him and Miss Grey.

A Madripoor crime boss and a business associate of Logan's, Tyger Tiger was partial to Wolvie's rough-hewn charm. The two enjoyed a romantic evening together every so often.

At one time, Wolverine had an on-off affair with tricksy, shape-shifting Mystique.

When ATF agent Cassie Lathrop became obsessed with Wolverine, the two had a brief affair. It ended when Logan's past came back to haunt him.

In return for saving his life, he married his longtime foe Viper, a union that helped stabilize the nation of Madripoor.

Wolverine and Storm once shared a kiss on the battlefield, convinced they were at death's door; however their relationship never developed beyond strong friendship.

Wolverine and Amir first met during the Super Hero Civil War. The two enjoyed a whirlwind romance before her untimely death at the hands of an agent of Scimitar.

When Wolverine visited the Savage Land years ago, he met the native Gahck, and the two had a brief affair that may have resulted in the birth of a child.

Back before World War II, Wolverine and Seraph, the unscrupulous former owner of Madripoor's Princess Bar, became lovers. Years later, she died at Sabretooth's hands.

Wolverine has no problem finding love, but keeping it is another matter. His trail of lost loves ensures that he remains a lonely and tortured soul.

# Love Kills

Wolverine's curse is that nearly every woman he falls in love with dies a violent death. From his childhood love Rose, to Silver Fox, the Native American with whom he spent arguably his happiest moments; from Janet, a fellow operative he loved in the days before World War I, to the Native, a fellow survivor of the Weapon X program, each woman died tragically and without cause. A sinister mind was behind it all, a shadowy figure going by the name Romulus, who was manipulating Wolverine's life for his own twisted agenda.

# Mariko

Wolverine and Mariko Yashida, a wealthy Japanese businesswoman with ties to organized crime, carried on a long-distance relationship for years during Wolverine's early time with the X-Men. They were even once engaged, but fate continually kept them apart, separating them either by location, honor, or the interference of a third party. Though Wolverine held the Yashida Blade as her clan's prized warrior, Mariko was determined not to marry him until she had cleaned up her family's criminal enterprises, a feat she only accomplished on her deathbed.

After Wolverine killed her evil father, Lord Shingen, he and Mariko were free to get married. However, their union was delayed by the criminal Mastermind, and then later by a debt of honor Mariko felt she owed to her future husband.

# FRIENDS & ALLIES

Wolverine's not really a social sort of animal. If his childhood taught him anything, it was to build a wall around his emotions, and never trust anyone. But Wolverine has lived a long life, and from time to time he has let his guard slip. Over the years he has created everything from dedicated lasting friendships, to the bond found only between loyal brothers-in-arms. And today, just as there are many dangerous men and women who consider Wolverine their enemy, there are nearly as many who are proud to call him their friend.

## NIGHTCRAWLER

Just as Logan was able to see beyond Kurt Wagner's frightening exterior to the hero that lay beneath, so too was Nightcrawler able to look past Wolverine's gruff manner. Wolverine and Nightcrawler quickly became friends during their original tenure with the X-Men, and Kurt even volunteered to join Logan on an excursion back to Canada. Even after Nightcrawler became a priest, the two remained close—Logan always knowing he has a sounding board if he needs to get something off his chest.

## YUKIO

Although not much is known about the past of Wolverine's one-time lover, Yukio, the feral mutant trusts her implicitly and even asked her to serve as a guardian to his ward, Amiko. Although she has turned away from her former life as an assassin and mercenary, Yukio still manages to find her way into more than enough trouble.

## AMIKO

Having witnessed the tragic death of Amiko's mother in Japan, Wolverine agreed to watch over the young girl, accepting her as his ward. But with his dangerous life as an X-Man proving an inappropriate environment for a foster father, Logan soon arranged for his lover Mariko to take care of Amiko, followed by Yukio, after Mariko's death.

## PUCK

Although Wolverine and Puck know each other from their days with the Canadian Super Hero team Alpha Flight, the relationship between these two fishing buddies stems back much further, to before the Spanish Civil War. Puck was not always so short in stature, but, despite his height, he has always been good in a fight—a plus when drinking at a pub with Logan.

## TYGER TIGER

After an encounter with cyborg villains the Reavers changed her life forever, Jessan Hoan decided to become Madripoor's newest crime boss Tyger Tiger—a position Wolverine let her keep as long as she avoided dealing in drugs. Today, Wolverine and Tyger Tiger maintain their bond as trusted allies, with the benefit of the occasional romantic fling.

## VINDICATOR

If Logan had had his way, he and Heather Hudson—the Super Hero known as the Vindicator— would have been much more than friends. After all, it was Heather who discovered him roaming the Canadian wild, and Heather who held him until he regained his humanity. Unfortunately, Heather did not feel the same way, and Logan had to settle for her friendship.

## NICK FURY

Nick Fury first met Logan during Operation: Blueboy in World War II. They continued to work together many times after the war, both keeping active as intelligence agents for their respective nations. So when Fury became the head of the world peacekeeping organization SHIELD, it was no surprise when he asked Wolverine for help on the occasional mission.

## HAVOK

Alex Summers and Logan have not fought alongside each other as X-Men for anywhere near as long as Wolverine and Havok's brother Scott, and they have also never found themselves competing over the affections of a girl. Instead, the two would settle for a beer, a good bar fight, and the occasional road trip to Mexico.

## AGENT ZERO

Formerly called Maverick when he and Logan were members of the CIA-sponsored Team X, Christoph Nord changed his name to Agent Zero when he was genetically modified by the Weapon X program. Later losing his powers on M-day, Nord is nonetheless still viewed with such respect by Logan that Logan even placed the deadly carbonadium synthesizer in his care for a time.

## JESSICA DREW

Although she has had a lengthy career as Spider-Woman, Jessica Drew didn't become friends with Wolverine until she moved to the Asian island of Madripoor. Working there as a private investigator, she would often partner with Logan and later both heroes served as members of the New Avengers.

## ELSIE-DEE AND ALBERT

Artificial beings crafted in the labs of inventor Donald Pierce, Elsie-Dee and Albert were created as the perfect weapons against Wolverine. Appearing as a Wolverine duplicate, Albert was meant to lure Logan into a fight, while the innocent-looking Elsie-Dee self-destructed. However, both androids developed a moral center, and became staunch allies of their intended target.

## CAROL DANVERS

Wolverine and Carol Danvers, the woman known today in the Super Hero set as Ms. Marvel, have had a long relationship that dates back to Logan's espionage days. Logan first met Carol when she and Nick Fury rescued him from an attacking pack of Hydra agents during a visit to Washington. The two later flew a mission together to gather intelligence on the Russians.

## THE HUNTER IN DARKNESS

The legendary wild beast called the Hunter in Darkness first met Logan in the Canadian wild soon after the feral mutant escaped the Weapon X facility. After freeing the albino beast from a bear trap, Logan stumbled away in the snow, unaware that he had made a new ally who would help him save a young woman from an attacker years later.

SHEATHE THOSE CLAWS, WOLVERINE, OR SO HELP ME --

-- MY NEXT OPTIC BLAST GOES DOWN YOUR THROAT!

I'VE JUST ABOUT HAD IT WITH YOUR "MAD KILLER" ACT PAL.

IT'S NO ACT LEADER-MAN--

-AN' IF YOU DON'T BELIEVE ME, KEEP PUSHIN'!

# TEAM PLAYER

He likes to think of himself as a lone wolf. But as Logan is well aware from his own childhood in the Canadian wild, wolves tend to work best in a pack. Despite himself, Logan has been a team player since his debut, even though he constantly finds himself at odds with many of his colleagues. In his long life, Wolverine has served with the Canadian military, various government agencies, and many Super Hero teams. Even on solo mission, Wolverine has a tendency to attract partners, from sidekicks Jubilee and Kitty Pryde, to team-ups with other people of the Super Hero ilk like Spider-Man and Captain America. Wolverine has even been brainwashed into teaming with the terrorist organization Hydra, as well as into joining in with the evil mutant Apocalypse as one of his Horsemen. It seems being a team player is in Logan's blood, whether he likes to think so or not.

## X-Men

Above all else, Wolverine is first and foremost an X-Men member. Truly believing in Professor Charles Xavier's vision of a peaceful coexistence between mutants and mankind, Wolverine will make any sacrifice for his fellow mutant teammates.

## New Avengers

When fate forced Wolverine to team up with Captain America, Iron Man, Spider-Man and others on an adventure in the Savage Land, he soon found himself accepting membership into the world's premier Super Hero team.

## X-Force

## Team X

In this CIA-sponsored strike force, Logan's mind was manipulated by the Weapon X program, so much so that he willingly teamed with his arch foe Sabretooth, as well as his former love Silver Fox, among other shady characters.

## Alpha Flight

Wolverine was the first recruit to this Canadian Super Hero team, brought into the fold by James MacDonald Hudson. Wolverine's tenure with the Flight was short however, as he soon quit in order to join the X-Men.

## Other Teams

Logan has been a part of many other groups over the years, including serving as one of the rotating members in Dr. Strange's Secret Defenders, as well as spending a short stint in a new incarnation of the Fantastic Four.

X-Force

# X-Force

Wolverine recently joined this covert mutant strike team as their field leader, under the overall supervision of the team's founder, Cyclops. Serving on X-Force is second nature to Logan, as their deadly tactics allow him to really cut loose.

# PARTNERS

He lives in a world packed with mutants and superhumans, so it's only natural that Wolverine would cross paths with other heroes now and again. Although often reluctant to allow anyone else to join in on one of his violent escapades, Logan also recognizes that there are some jobs that require an extra set of helping hands.

## SPIDER-MAN

Logan and Peter Parker have almost nothing in common. With his way of finding humor in almost every situation, Spider-Man's personality is the opposite of Wolverine's tough, no-nonsense persona. So how the two have managed to team-up on dozens of occasions is anyone's guess.

As Super Heroes are wont to do, Logan and Spidey have often started their missions together with a fight. During the period in the X-Men's career where the world at large believed them to be dead, Spidey attacked Wolverine on a rooftop, thinking the man in costume was an imposter. However, Parker discovered his mistake fairly quickly, and soon he and Logan were pairing up in order to rescue a little girl from a group of evil mutants.

Despite their fundamental differences, over the years Wolverine and Spider-Man have developed a mutual respect for one another. On one occasion Peter even invited his mutant ally over for dinner after a particularly harrowing SHIELD mission.

## THE PUNISHER

After Frank Castle's family was killed by members of New York's mafia, he started a brutal war against the city's underworld. Calling himself the Punisher, he killed any criminal dumb enough to cross his path. With such a single-minded vendetta, Castle has caught Logan in his crosshairs several times, and the two troubled Super Heroes only combine forces when given no other choice. This was the case when they encountered each other in the South American jungle outside a town known as Erewhon. On a normal day, the two seem much more comfortable at each other's throats, and over the course of their many fights, the Punisher has run Logan over with a steamroller, shot him with a bazooka, and even sicced the Hulk on his feral adversary.

## KITTY PRYDE

When Kitty Pryde first came to the Xavier School for Gifted Youngsters she was a wide-eyed innocent young girl, still struggling to master her newly discovered power to pass through solid matter. But Charles Xavier, the school's headmaster and founder of the secret Super Hero team the X-Men, had plans for his shy new student. Pairing Kitty with the battle-hardened veteran Wolverine, Xavier unwittingly awarded Logan a faithful and unswerving sidekick.

Although at first he found Kitty a hindrance and her presence annoying, Wolverine soon grew fond of the young girl's optimistic attitude, and began to view her as a sort of surrogate daughter. As Kitty continued to develop her crime fighting skills, she accompanied Logan on many different missions, including a recruitment drive to locate a new mutant, one of Wolverine's birthday brawls versus Sabretooth, and even a trip to the bizarre Wundagore Mountain.

## ELEKTRA

Wolverine has teamed up with the female assassin Elektra many times over the years. They formed an unbreakable bond when she helped coach him back to his normal self after a battle with the demented mutant Genesis left him in a primitive state. Logan even became a sounding board for her when she attempted to restart her life as a dancer. But the two lost touch when Elektra fell back into her old ways and resumed her career as an assassin.

## GHOST RIDER

When an attack at a Madripoor bar led Wolverine to Manhattan, he found himself partnering Danny Ketch—the cursed supernatural avenger known as Ghost Rider—in order to take down a villain named Deathwatch. Soon after, the two joined forces with Spider-Man and the Hulk to form a brief incarnation of the Fantastic Four.

## BEN GRIMM

Before Ben Grimm was bathed in cosmic rays and became the Fantastic Four member known as Thing, he and Logan partnered on a few occasions, while Logan worked for Canadian intelligence. On their first meeting, Grimm flew his mutant companion to Washington. On their second, the two piloted a spy plane into Russian airspace.

## GAMBIT

Logan and Gambit have much experience fighting side by side while serving together on the X-Men, but the two have also enjoyed a few missions without their other mutant cohorts. They once journeyed to England to combat the female mutant Mastermind, and her partner, Arcade.

## JUBILEE

Orphan Jubilation Lee, aka Jubilee, was a California mallrat with pyrotechnic abilities who helped rescue Logan from an attack by the cyborg gang known as the Reavers. Using her street survival instincts as well as her mutant pyrotechnic displays to get the injured Wolverine out of harm's way, she soon became a fixture in Logan's life and accompanied him on dozens of adventures as his sidekick.

## HULK

The Hulk and Wolverine have fought each other as many times as they have fought alongside each other and have developed a mutual animosity, resulting in anything from fairly harmless pranks to extreme violence. Once, when the Hulk visited Madripoor, Wolverine began to torment his old rival by immediately arranging for the behemoth's expensive clothing collection to be replaced with dozens of pairs of embarrassing purple pants instead.

# Wolverine's enemies

## SABRETOOTH

Perhaps Wolverine's oldest and most hated enemy, Victor Creed became a lifetime foe when he murdered Logan's Native American lover Silver Fox. After that, the two spent years at each other's throats, in a conflict drawn out by their evenly matched mutant physiques and healing factors, until Logan finally managed to slay his rival.

## LADY DEATHSTRIKE

Daughter of a shamed kamikaze pilot and scientist, Yuriko Oyama became obsessed with the adamantium bonding process, a formula she felt was created from notes stolen from her deceased father. Because Logan's body was laced with that very metal, he became the focus of her hatred.

## WILD CHILD

Like Wolverine, Kyle Gibney, led a life as an unwilling guinea pig and later overcame his feral instincts to serve as a member of Alpha Flight. However, under the influence of Romulus, Wild Child recently succumbed to his darker side.

## LORD SHINGEN

The father of Wolverine's beloved, Mariko Yashida, and the head of the ancient Yashida Clan, Lord Shingen battled with Logan to the death over the corrupt man's crimes. Although Logan triumphed at the time, Shingen was mysteriously resurrected, renewing his old campaign against the man who took his life.

## SHIVA

A series of robots designed by the Weapon X program, the Shiva units were meant as a defense system against surviving test subjects. With an adaptive program that never falls prey to the same method of defeat twice, the Shiva androids proved to be dangerous adversaries for Wolverine when he accidentally activated them.

## SILVER SAMURAI

The mutant son of Lord Shingen, Kenuichio Harada possesses the ability to focus his body's energy through his sword, making his blade able to cut through most any substance. He hated Wolverine for his involvement in the Yashida Clan. This hatred deepened when Wolverine severed his hand.

## OMEGA RED

Serial killer turned super-soldier by the Russian Government, Arkady Gregorivich was trained by the KGB to be the ultimate warrior. Arkady was outfitted with carbonadium tentacles in each of his forearms. The tentacles served as conduits for his formidable natural powers, which included an energy-draining "mutant death factor." As Omega Red, Arkady has clashed with Wolverine many times.

## EPSILON RED

Another super-soldier developed by the Russian government, Epsilon Red's body was altered to withstand exposure to the extremes of outer space. Though Logan originally met Red on an assignment organized by the CIA to assassinate him, the next time he crossed paths with the misunderstood multi-tentacled mutant, he greeted him as an ally.

With a fuse to match his stature, Wolverine's temper has gotten him into many scraps in his lifetime. And after amassing over a century's worth of fights to his credit, Logan has racked up a small army's share of enemies, many of whom, like an incurable virus, keep coming back time and time again to plague the diminutive mutant hero.

# BLOODSCREAM

Also known as Bloodsport, the vampiric Bloodscream possesses the ability to suck the life force out of his prey, merely by touch. Having encountered Wolverine several times during his century-spanning lifetime, Bloodscream is a frequent partner of the super-strong Roughouse, the pair often working as hired muscle.

# DAKEN

The son of Logan and his wife Itsu, Daken was presumed dead by his father when a pregnant Itsu was slain by the Winter Soldier. Only years later, when Daken had been conditioned by Romulus to hate his birth father, did Wolverine and son finally meet.

# CYBER

Originally Logan's drill sergeant back when he trained with a shadowy outfit of killers during his brainwashed days working for Romulus, Silas Burr continued to haunt Wolverine as the adamantium-armored Cyber, a twisted, super-strong sadist with a healing factor and poison-tipped finger claws.

# ROUGHOUSE

Hailing from the fabled home of the Norse gods, Asgard, the man-mountain named Roughouse first came into contact with Wolverine in Madripoor as hired muscle. Although they have teamed up on occasion, Roughouse and Wolverine are more commonly found trading thunderous punches.

# GORGON

A member of the criminal organizations Hydra and the Hand, Tomi Shishido possessed the mutant ability to turn people into stone with just a glance. Extremely intelligent, and possessing superhuman stamina, speed, and strength, the Gorgon proved more than a match for Wolverine and even succeeded in killing, resurrecting, and subsequently brainwashing his feral opponent.

# WENDIGO

A mystical albino brute normally found wandering the Canadian wilderness, the super-strong Wendigo is the result of a magical curse. Several people have been turned into the cannibalistic monster, and many of them have faced Wolverine, his relationship with the creature dating back to one of his first missions for Canada's Department H.

# ROMULUS

With a past as shrouded in mystery as any enemy Wolverine has faced, little is known about Romulus, save his name and that he stems from the lupine order of mutants. Whatever his motivations, Romulus has spent the last century of his ancient life manipulating and controlling Logan's life.

# OGUN

An old friend and sensei of Logan's, Ogun trained the future Wolverine years ago in the ways of the martial arts. Later, when Ogun strayed from the path of honor, the two met again when Kitty Pryde succumbed to Ogun's brainwashing, a slight Wolverine was not prepared to ignore.

# OMEGA RED

Like his archenemy Wolverine, Arkady Gregorivich's past is something of a mystery. A captured serial killer handed over to the KGB, Gregorivich was to be the ultimate weapon for the communist agenda. Codenamed Omega Red, Gregorivich's transformation into a super-soldier was interrupted when Wolverine and his teammates of the CIA-sponsored Team X, Sabretooth and Maverick, sabotaged the operation by stealing the Carbonadium Synthesizer, the tool instrumental in the soldier's creation, and freed double agent Janice Hollenbeck. However Sabretooth was given another mission on the orders of Romulus, the mysterious figure who was secretly manipulating Wolverine's life. Sabretooth's attempting to recruit Omega Red to Romulus's cause, ended in an impromptu battle. Logan secured the Synthesizer, and the trio managed to escape, at the cost of Hollenbeck's life (something Sabretooth had planned from the start, in a play to keep Wolverine in check).

**CAUGHT UP**
Omega Red possesses the ability to sap a person's life energy, his carbonadium tentacles serving as the conduits for this mutant power. And since carbonadium cancels out Wolverine's healing factor, this makes Omega Red twice as deadly to him.

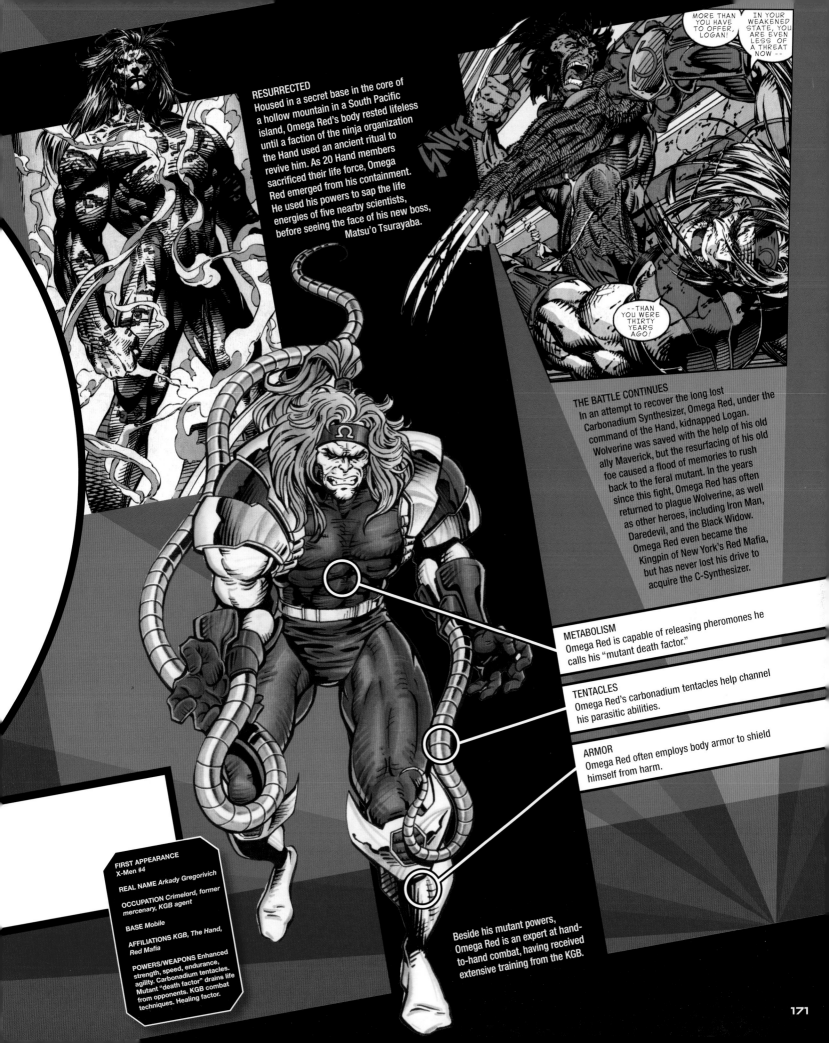

**RESURRECTED**
Housed in a secret base in the core of a hollow mountain in a South Pacific island, Omega Red's body rested lifeless until a faction of the ninja organization the Hand used an ancient ritual to revive him. As 20 Hand members sacrificed their life force, Omega Red emerged from his containment. He used his powers to sap the life energies of five nearby scientists, before seeing the face of his new boss, Matsu'o Tsurayaba.

MORE THAN YOU HAVE TO OFFER, LOGAN!

IN YOUR WEAKENED STATE, YOU ARE EVEN LESS OF A THREAT NOW --

--THAN YOU WERE THIRTY YEARS AGO!

**THE BATTLE CONTINUES**
In an attempt to recover the long lost Carbonadium Synthesizer, Omega Red, under the command of the Hand, kidnapped Logan. Wolverine was saved with the help of his old ally Maverick, but the resurfacing of his old foe caused a flood of memories to rush back to the feral mutant. In the years since this fight, Omega Red has often returned to plague Wolverine, as well as other heroes, including Iron Man, Daredevil, and the Black Widow. Omega Red even became the Kingpin of New York's Red Mafia, but has never lost his drive to acquire the C-Synthesizer.

**METABOLISM**
Omega Red is capable of releasing pheromones he calls his "mutant death factor."

**TENTACLES**
Omega Red's carbonadium tentacles help channel his parasitic abilities.

**ARMOR**
Omega Red often employs body armor to shield himself from harm.

**FIRST APPEARANCE**
X-Men #4

**REAL NAME** Arkady Gregorivich

**OCCUPATION** Crimelord, former mercenary, KGB agent

**BASE** Mobile

**AFFILIATIONS** KGB, The Hand, Red Mafia

**POWERS/WEAPONS** Enhanced strength, speed, endurance, agility. Carbonadium tentacles. Mutant "death factor" drains life from opponents. KGB combat techniques. Healing factor.

Beside his mutant powers, Omega Red is an expert at hand-to-hand combat, having received extensive training from the KGB.

# Timeline

James Howlett is born to John and Elizabeth Howlett in Alberta, Canada in the late 1800s.

A sickly child, James befriends Rose, a young servant girl, and Dog, the son of the groundskeeper Thomas Logan.

James discovers his mutant powers when Thomas Logan murders his father. At this time, James's mother also takes her own life.

Rose and James flee the Alberta estate, and head to the Yukon Territory where James adopts the name Logan in order to keep his anonymity. He begins a job working in a quarry. Logan's mutant healing factor helps erase his memories of his parents' traumatic deaths.

Now a young adult, Logan accidentally kills Rose when Dog attacks him. Logan flees into the woods, renouncing his humanity to live like an animal.

Resurfacing into civilization, Logan begins work for the Hudson Bay Company.

Logan meets the Blackfoot tribe and battles a mystical monster called Uncegila. He is referred to as Skunk-Bear by them, a name which translates as Wolverine.

While in Tokyo, Logan is abducted by a man he later realizes was the master manipulator Romulus. At Romulus's request, Logan encounters Sabretooth for the first time when Creed is attacking a prostitute. Logan stops Creed's attack, and Sabretooth swears payback for Logan's interruption.

In the Canadian Rocky Mountains, Logan settles down in a cabin with a Native American woman named Silver Fox. The two live a quiet, happy life until Sabretooth seemingly murders Silver Fox on Logan's birthday.

Logan loses the ensuing fight with Sabretooth and is left in a pit. There he is manipulated by Romulus and Sabretooth into giving in to his anger.

Venturing to Madripoor for the first time, Logan has a romantic liaison with the owner of the Princess Bar, Seraph.

In 1912, Logan is trained in a Canadian covert military camp run by a mysterious man named Hudson.

Logan takes a girlfriend, a fellow operative named Janet. His drill sergeant Silas Burr then kills her on orders from Romulus, sending Logan into an animalistic state. He is retrieved by Sabretooth and Burr, his healing factor and brainwashing making him forget the event.

Logan fights for Canada in World War I in Belgium in 1915. He defeats Lazaer, the angel of death, on the battlefield, and falls into a deep depression.

Mystique and Logan meet in Mexico in 1921 and escape a firing squad to move to Kansas City together. They become lovers, but part ways following a botched bank robbery.

As a merchant marine, Logan travels to Shanghai, China and meets his future mentor, ninja and martial arts Master Ogun.

Logan begins work for the interdimensional firm of Landau, Luckman, and Lake after encountering a mysterious man named Chang.

Logan journeys to Madripoor in 1932 and reunites with Seraph, where he works in her employ as an assassin.

Along with writer Ernest Hemingway and future Alpha Flight member Puck, Logan fights in Spain in 1937 during the Spanish Civil War.

On a mission in the Soviet Union, Logan meets Natalia Romanova, the future Black Widow, for the first time, and begins to train her. He later murders her father.

Back in Japan, Logan trains with Master Ogun, becoming an expert in the martial arts and learning the Japanese language.

Heading back to Madripoor in 1941, Logan meets Captain America for the first time, and the two help rescue Natasha Romanova from Baron Von Strucker.

In 1942, Logan fights once again alongside Captain America, this time in the Italian Alps. There he meets Wild Child for presumably the first time. During World War II, Logan participates in Operation: Blueboy on orders from Seraph and Romulus, and teams up with Captain America, meeting Bucky and Nick Fury for the first time. Cap and Logan part ways as enemies, despite Logan disobeying Romulus's orders in an effort to save Captain America's life.

Later, in Poland, Wolverine is taken prisoner at the Sobibor Nazi death camp, where he successfully torments the installation's various leaders.

In Normandy in 1944, Logan jumps with the 1st Canadian Parachute Division during the D-Day invasion.

In the closing days of World War II, Logan is taken prisoner in a Japanese POW camp. He manages to escape and meets a woman named Atsuko. The two share a passionate night together before Atsuko is murdered and Logan is caught in the explosion of a nuclear bomb dropped on Hiroshima by the Americans in 1945.

Logan travels to Jasmine Falls in Japan at the suggestion of his former sensei, Ogun. There he meets Itsu, and the two fall in love. Logan trains under sensei Bando Suboro.

Itsu and Logan are finally married. After she becomes pregnant with Logan's child, she is murdered by the Winter Soldier. Logan heads to the nearby camp of the ancient Muramasa, and Muramasa creates a sword out of Logan's anger.

Logan is abducted by the Winter Soldier, who is under orders from Romulus to take Logan back to Madripoor.

Having survived the death of his mother, Logan's son Daken is given to a man named Akihira and his wife in Sendai, Japan, in 1946.

In 1953, brainwashed and working again for Romulus, Logan aids in the death of Charles Simpson in Dayton, Ohio, helping to destroy the life of his son Frank, the future villain Nuke.

Logan starts to work for Team X, a CIA-sponsored strike force run by the Weapon X department. His travels take him all over the world on various missions. During this time, Logan is subjected to various fake memory implants, and his past memories are altered.

After his first encounter with the evil Soviet super-soldier Omega Red, Logan quits Team X when Sabretooth murders a female double agent in cold blood in order to teach Logan a lesson.

In 1968, under orders by Romulus, Logan tortures Frank Simpson, finalizing his transformation into the twisted super-soldier called Nuke.

Logan begins solo intelligence work for Canada, and becomes an alcoholic, despite his healing factor, accidentally shooting a fellow agent at the firing range.

Logan is abducted by the secret Weapon X project, and has his skeleton bonded with adamantium, with the intention of making him the perfect killing machine for the government. In a Canadian complex, he is subjected to hundreds of tests and experiments, and has his mind and memories once again tampered with.

Escaping Weapon X in a veritable bloodbath with the help of the Winter Soldier, Logan retreats into the Canadian wild, where he lives like an animal in the forest.

Logan meets the mythical Canadian beast known as the Hunter in Darkness, and frees the creature from a hunter's trap.

In a modest cabin in the Pacific Northwest, Logan begins a life with a female Weapon X escapee known as the Native.

In Canada's Wood Buffalo National Park, Logan is discovered by James and Heather Hudson, the young couple taking Wolverine in and helping him calm down and regain his senses.

Logan enrolls in James Hudson's project, the Canadian government's Department H program. There he is given the codename Weapon X, as well as Wolverine, and adopts a Super Hero uniform to match his new persona.

Despite being a part of Department H, Logan continues his intelligence work for the Canadian government, teaming with other future heroes such as Ben Grimm (later the Thing) and Carol Danvers (later Ms. Marvel).

On a mission for Department H, Wolverine attempts to take down the Hulk, but is interrupted when the two encounter the Wendigo.

Wolverine helps lead Alpha Flight, a band of Canadian Super Heroes, before quitting on unfriendly terms when recruited by Professor X into his X-Men.

On a mission to Krakoa, Wolverine cements his membership with the X-Men and decides to stay with the team on a permanent basis.

Logan falls in love with X-Man Jean Grey after she seemingly dies on a mission and is resurrected as the Phoenix.

Venturing to Japan alongside the X-Men, Logan meets his future love Mariko Yashida for the first time.

The X-Men battle Jean Grey's supposed alter ego the Dark Phoenix, and Wolverine watches as Jean seemingly perishes for a second time.

Logan dons a new brown and tan version of his costume, and then makes peace with his old allies of Alpha Flight.

Mariko journeys to New York, and she and Logan begin a formal courtship that continues for years.

Unable to reach Mariko by phone, Logan travels to Japan and discovers she has been forced to marry another by her cruel, criminal father, Lord Shingen. Mariko's husband and father are killed in the subsequent skirmish, and Logan and Mariko become engaged.

As the X-Men travel to Japan for Logan's wedding ceremony, Mariko calls off the festivities while under the mind control of villain Mastermind. She later regains her true emotions, but still refuses to marry Logan until she has severed all ties to the Yashida's criminal empire.

Logan meets Amiko, and promises her dying mother to watch over the young girl. He soon leaves Amiko in Mariko's care as he returns to the United States.

Again finding himself in Japan, Wolverine kills Ogun when his former sensei tries to brainwash fellow X-Man Kitty Pryde.

Wolverine meets Lady Deathstrike while being paid a visit by Heather Hudson, now a Super Hero in her own right called the Vindicator.

The X-Men face the threat of the Marauders in what would later be known as the Mutant Massacre, providing the setting for one of Wolverine's most brutal battles with Sabretooth.

As the X-Men relocate their base to Australia, faking their deaths, Logan begins to spend much of his time again in Madripoor.

Logan travels to the Savage Land and has a relationship with a native woman named Gahck, their bond seemingly resulting in the birth of a child.

Wolverine is ambushed in Australia by the Reavers and is saved from a torturous death by the young Jubilee.

While in Madripoor, Logan once again tangles with his former drill sergeant Silas Burr, the villain now calling himself Cyber.

Wolverine returns to the Weapon X complex with Jubilee and once again adopts his blue and yellow costume, struggling with his many fake memories.

During another trip to Japan, Logan watches helplessly as his love Mariko is poisoned by the Hand criminal organization. Wolverine kills his love in an act of mercy to ease her suffering.

Logan reunites with some of his former Team X allies and realizes that Silver Fox is still alive, only to watch her die once more at the hands of the vicious Sabretooth.

While storming the Avalon space satellite, the adamantium in Wolverine's body is ripped from his bones by the villain Magneto. Logan barely survives the attack, and from that day forward, is forced to rely on his natural bone claws.

The unbalanced mutant Genesis kidnaps Logan in an attempt to recreate him as a Horseman for the mutant overlord Apocalypse. Attempting to bond adamantium once more to Logan's frame, Genesis reduces Wolverine to a feral state when Logan manages to reject the transfusion.

With the help of the ninja Elektra, Wolverine regains control of his faculties, and regains his human demeanor.

Forced to return to Madripoor, Logan fulfills an old debt to his enemy Viper, marrying her in order to help unite the country's citizens under her rule.

During a trip through time to battle the planet-eating villain Galactus, Wolverine and the X-Men are frozen in stasis. The shape-shifting aliens known as the Skrulls use this opportunity to abduct Logan and replace him with one of their own.

The Skrulls give Wolverine to Apocalypse, where he becomes the evil mutant's brainwashed servant Death, receiving his adamantium back in the process.

With the help of the X-Men, Logan regains control of his mind, and rejects Apocalypse's programming.

In Madripoor, Viper divorces Wolverine in exchange for medical treatment following a clash with the spirit of Logan's old master, Ogun.

Logan returns to Xavier's school in Westchester as a part of the New X-Men. He begins a teaching position there, serving as a rather unusual mentor.

Along with Cyclops and the mysterious Fantomex, Logan invades a Weapons Plus base, learning more about his past traumas.

Wolverine and Jean Grey are trapped in space during a visit to Asteroid M. As they hurtle toward the sun, Logan is forced to kill Jean in order to hasten her death and end her pain. Set free, Jean accesses the Phoenix force, and brings them both back to Earth, only to truly die at the hands of the villain Xorn.

Logan reunites with the Native in their old cabin, only to watch her die at Sabretooth's hands.

Wolverine is killed by the mutant Gorgon during a return visit to Japan, and resurrected under the ninja clan Hand's control. He finally regains his true personality through the help of SHIELD, and slays his former killer.

During an adventure in the Savage Land, Wolverine teams up with several other heroes, unwittingly becoming one of the New Avengers.

The former Avenger Scarlet Witch reforms the world so that mutants are in the majority. Wolverine regains all his lost memories, and retains them even as the world is returned to normal.

Logan sets out to avenge past wrongs, once again garbed in his brown and tan costume. On a quest that brings him into conflict with many of his old enemies, Logan traces his origins, and discovers that his son Daken is still alive.

After an explosion at Stamford, Connecticut, and the subsequent start of the Super Hero Civil War, Logan tracks down Nitro, the villain responsible for the tragedy.

Wolverine joins with the so-called Secret Avengers, helping the group of heroes hide from the Super Hero Registration Act.

Logan kills Sabretooth after discovering their lupine mutant history, and realizing the scope of their connections to the evil manipulator Romulus.

In a battle involving Lazaer and Mariko's resurrected father, Lord Shingen, Logan reclaims a piece of his soul that was missing since Gorgon killed him. His healing powers are severely lessened as a result.

After the events of the Messiah Complex event, Wolverine joins the new X-Men strike force team X-Force as field leader.

Wolverine takes part in fending off the Earth from an invading hoard of Skrulls during the Secret Invasion event.

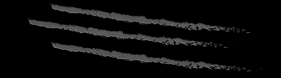

As a boy, James Howlett grew up in a giant mansion in Alberta, Canada, raised as an only child to solemn parents who were affected deeply by the death of his older brother.

## CHILDHOOD FRIENDS

James lived a lonely life. His only friends were Dog, the son of the cruel groundskeeper Logan, and Rose, a young orphan sent to the house by her aunt as a servant. The three became fast companions despite their differences in social status and manners. While Dog was the rough and tumble result of an abusive home, James was a sickly child, often bedridden due to various allergies.

# THE ORIGIN

*JAMES HOWLETT WAS BORN INTO A TRAGIC FAMILY WITH DARK, LINGERING SECRETS, INCLUDING A DEAD OLDER BROTHER.*

## JOHN HOWLETT

James's older brother John had died at the tender age of 12 by causes known only to the Howlett family. The young boy's death, however it occurred, proved too much for his mother, and Elizabeth was soon put into a madhouse in order to cope with her grief. When she returned to the estate, she was a shadow of her former self. The only souvenir she possessed of this strange, tragic episode was a set of mysterious claw marks that scarred her back. She locked herself away in her room, not even bothering to visit with her still living son James.

## REVENGE

As Thomas Logan fired his shotgun, killing the senior John Howlett in front of the eyes of his son, young James was overcome with a berserker rage. Razor-sharp claws of bone emerged from the backs of his hands for the first time in his life. James charged Logan, accidentally stabbing the killer in the stomach.

## BREAKING POINT

Thomas Logan had had enough. The longtime groundskeeper for the Howlett family, he was rumored to have had a torrid affair with the lady of the house, Elizabeth. Logan was finally fired from his position after the violent acts of his son, Dog. Deciding to seize what he considered his own property, Logan and Dog stormed the mansion in an attempt to kidnap Elizabeth, and take a good chunk of the Howlett family fortune as well. Only the timely intervention by Elizabeth's husband and son prevented Logan from seeing his plan through.

*"YOU KILLED MY PAPA! I'LL KILL YOU BACK! I'LL KILL YOU!"*

Whether caused by the onset of adolescence or a surge of adrenaline, James Howlett's mutant abilities were triggered that night.

After scarring Dog's face with his claws, James fled into the nearby woods with Rose, his senses heightened and his mind in a state of shock. Feeling pity for the helpless boy, who seemed to remember nothing of what had happened, and realizing she would be implicated in the bloodbath, Rose took James and quit their home forever.

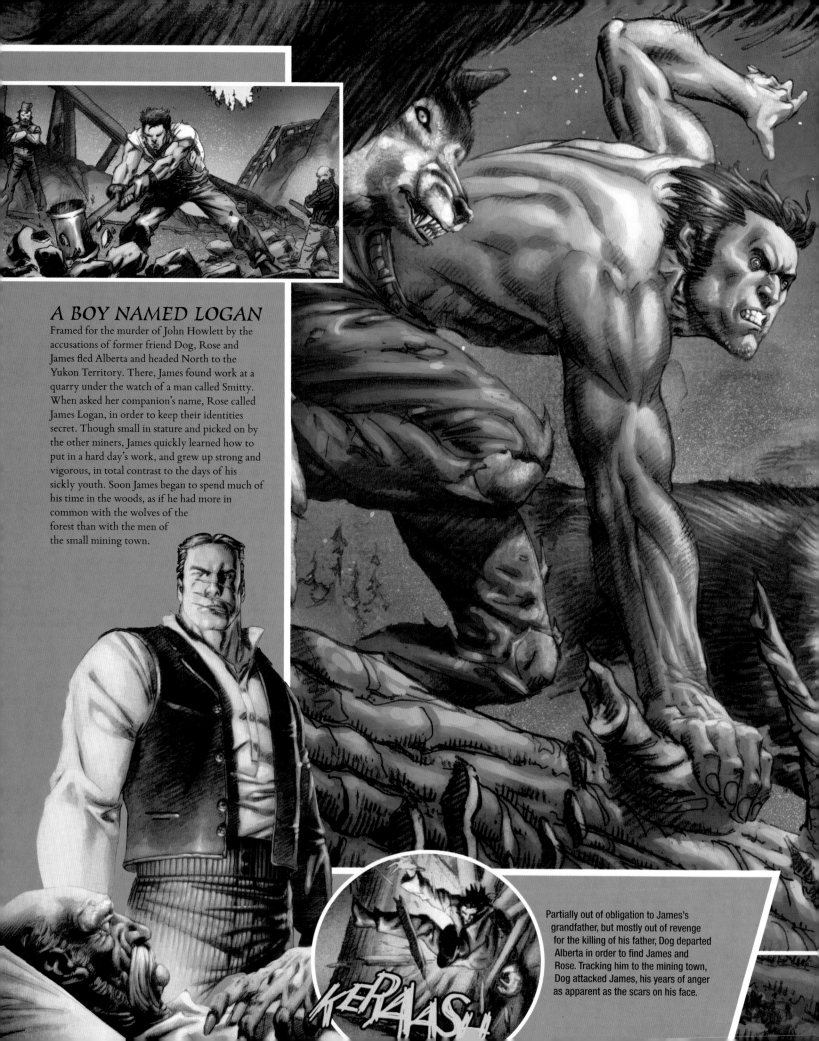

## A BOY NAMED LOGAN

Framed for the murder of John Howlett by the accusations of former friend Dog, Rose and James fled Alberta and headed North to the Yukon Territory. There, James found work at a quarry under the watch of a man called Smitty. When asked her companion's name, Rose called James Logan, in order to keep their identities secret. Though small in stature and picked on by the other miners, James quickly learned how to put in a hard day's work, and grew up strong and vigorous, in total contrast to the days of his sickly youth. Soon James began to spend much of his time in the woods, as if he had more in common with the wolves of the forest than with the men of the small mining town.

KERAASH

Partially out of obligation to James's grandfather, but mostly out of revenge for the killing of his father, Dog departed Alberta in order to find James and Rose. Tracking him to the mining town, Dog attacked James, his years of anger as apparent as the scars on his face.

## JAMES AND ROSE

Carving out a simple life for themselves, James and Rose lived in a small cabin in the woods. As James worked at the mine and developed into a fine hunter in his spare time, Rose kept a written account of their life in her journal, wishing her childhood friend would open up to her and discuss what had happened on that fateful night back in Alberta. As "Logan" started to become as wild and uncouth as his namesake, fighting with other miners and hunting with the wolves by night, he started to lust after Rose. However Rose began to develop a close relationship with Smitty, who had taken a shine to the pretty young woman. Soon Smitty and Rose decided to be married and move to a new town, putting this hard life behind them. Logan took the news poorly, and took out his frustration in a local barroom cage match. But when pitted against Smitty himself for the grand prize, Logan's feelings for Rose got the better of him and he nobly and deliberately lost the fight in order to ensure that Rose and Smitty would have enough money to begin a new life together.

## ROSE'S DEATH

Hearing of Logan's injuries in the cage fight, Rose ran to the bar to make sure he was okay. But Logan was anything but okay. Attacked by Dog after exhausting himself in the cage matches, Logan was pinned by his foe, until memories of his father's murder flooded his mind. Possessed by berserker rage, Logan was about to kill Dog, until Rose stepped between them, trying to protect her childhood friends. Logan's claws pierced her chest and she fell dead. In despair, Logan retreated into the wilderness, abandoning his life and his humanity.

# X-MEN MEMBERS

## PROFESSOR X

Charles Xavier, also known as Professor X, is the founder and guiding voice behind the X-Men Super Hero team. A mutant himself, he initially used his School for Gifted Youngsters in Westchester, New York as a cover for secretly training young mutants. Xavier later went public, revealing to the world his vast psychic abilities and quickly becoming a respected authority on mutants.

## SHADOWCAT

Katherine "Kitty" Pryde has been known by many names over the years—Ariel, Sprite, Shadowcat, and Kitten, to name a few. Just like her name, Kitty's personality has changed too. Once a wide-eyed pupil at Professor X's School for Gifted Youngsters, she is now an invaluable team player and dedicated teacher. Thanks to her mutant abilities she is able to shift through solid matter.

## NIGHTCRAWLER

Although his close friend Wolverine often refers to him affectionately as "Elf," Kurt Wagner is more than capable of holding his own in any X-Men fight. Able to teleport himself, or even a few others from one location to the next with merely a thought, Nightcrawler is as evasive as he is surprising in the field of battle.

## COLOSSUS

Already quite imposing at a hulking 6ft 6in, Piotr Rasputin becomes downright intimidating when he uses his mutant abilities to increase his size and mass. He is able to transform his body tissue into a nearly unbreakable steel-like organic material, and gains super-strength as a result of this metamorphosis.

## WOLVERINE

Joining the X-Men during their crucial mission to the mutant island Krakoa, Wolverine found a family as well as a team while fighting beside his fellow mutants. Although he will always find the need to indulge in a solo mission now and again, Logan has long ago acknowledged that he will keep returning to the X-Men for the rest of his life.

## JUBILEE

Serving as Logan's surrogate daughter and sidekick for a time, Jubilation Lee used her firework-like mutant pyrotechnics, her street smarts, and her upbeat attitude to fight alongside the X-Men as well as Generation X. She eventually lost her mutant abilities during the House of M event, and joined up with the underground hero team the New Warriors, using advanced technology to become the hero known as Wondra.

## ARCHANGEL

Warren Worthington III, another of the X-Men's founding members, changed from a rich teen heartthrob into the hated and feared high-flying mutant Angel. After undergoing a transformation by the evil mutant overlord Apocalypse, Warren adopted the identity of Archangel, the moniker somehow seeming a better fit for his now harder image.

## CYCLOPS

He was the X-Men's first leader, and he has rarely relinquished that title since. Having recently accepted even more responsibility after taking over Professor X's position, Scott Summers continues to use his shrewd mind and concussive eye blasts to guide the X-Men's future.

Although he usually prefers to work alone, Wolverine has come to realize that sometimes teamwork is the only option. When six claws and a bad attitude just aren't enough, Logan partners with his fellow mutants of the amazing X-Men.

## ROGUE

Although her past is largely a mystery, it is known that Anna Marie was raised by the mutants Mystique and Destiny, and that she embarked on a criminal life before changing sides and joining the X-Men. Possessing super-strength as well as the ability to absorb the powers and energy of others, Rogue has more than made up for her past sins during her time with the X-Men.

## ICEMAN

Robert "Bobby" Drake was one of the original X-Men, but often felt out of place because he was the team's youngest member. Today, Bobby displays expert control over his mutant ice projecting powers, and serves as an inspiration to the young mutants of the Xavier Institute for Higher Learning (as the School for Gifted Youngsters is now known.)

## STORM

Although she is the new bride of the hero known as the Black Panther, and therefore the queen of the African nation of Wakanda, Ororo Iquadi T'Challa (née Munroe) is an old hand to the ranks of the X-Men. She has lent her mutant weather-manipulation abilities in many a battle.

## BEAST

Henry "Hank" McCoy has been evolving his whole life. A former child prodigy and a scientist by inclination, as the X-Men's Beast, Hank has changed from being an agile man with large feet, to a furry humanoid blue creature, to his current secondary mutation as a lion-like renaissance man.

## PHOENIX

The heart and soul of the X-Men from the very beginning, Jean Grey took a piece of every one of her teammates with her when she died. A formidable telepath with telekinetic skills as well, Jean always struggled to contain the cosmic power of the Phoenix force, a battle she endured until the day she died.

## HAVOK

Always feeling second best to his brother Cyclops, Alex Summers nonetheless became an important part of the X-Men, even leading the team on occasion. Possessing the ability to fire concussive blasts of plasma out of his hands, Havok continues his on-again/off-again relationship with both the mutant team and his girlfriend Polaris.

## GAMBIT

Born in the bayou of Louisiana, Remy LeBeau possesses a unique outlook on life—one that has gotten him into quite a lot of trouble with the law as well as with women. Despite his lapses, Remy normally uses his energy-charging abilities for the greater good.

## WHITE QUEEN

Formerly the headmistress of the Massachusetts Academy and Professor X's chief rival in recruiting new mutant finds, Emma Frost has since reformed her ways, and lends her impressive telepathic abilities to the X-Men, as well as to her lover, Scott Summers.

## MAGNETO

Eric Magnus Lehnsherr grew up in a Nazi death camp. He survived the ordeal and was left with a lifelong appreciation for his fellow mutants. His violent campaign to see mutants freed from human oppression has brought him into conflict with the X-Men many times, but his mastery of magnetism has always kept them at bay.

## MR. SINISTER

Nathaniel Essex was given the name Sinister by the mutant overlord Apocalypse when the two crossed paths in the 19th century. A brilliant geneticist and strategist, Mr. Sinister was a thorn in the X-Men's side until his murder at the hands of the shape-shifting Mystique.

## SEBASTIAN SHAW

The Black King of Manhattan's clandestine Hellfire Club, Sebastian Shaw led a campaign against the X-Men, kidnapping Jean Grey in the process. Although he has been defeated time and again by the heroes, Shaw nevertheless continues to utilize his kinetic energy redirection powers to challenge his foes.

## JUGGERNAUT

Cain Marko thought that when he was originally granted super-strength and invulnerability by the mystical Crimson Gem of the Cyttorak, that he could finally end his rivalry with his stepbrother Charles Xavier. Yet somehow, all the behemoth managed to achieve was defeat at the hands of the X-Men.

## CASSANDRA NOVA

One of the bodiless parasites known as Mummudrai, Cassandra Nova copied Charles Xavier's DNA while he was in the womb, bringing herself into the physical world as his twin sister. As an adult, she set out to destroy all mutants, and even caused the destruction of the nation of Genosha.

## MASTERMIND

Although now deceased, Jason Wyngarde was a formidable mutant in his time, using his abilities to manipulate others to see and hear what he wished them to. At his prime, he even influenced Jean Grey into joining the corrupt Hellfire Club as his lover.

## STRYFE

The clone of the mutant Cable, Stryfe embarked on a mission to destroy his would-be family, consisting of Cable's father, Cyclops, and his X-Men teammates. A powerful telekinetic mutant, Stryfe was rewarded for his cruel ways with an untimely death.

## THE SENTINELS

The brainchildren of mechanical genius Bolivar Trask, the giant robots called the Sentinels were originally created to put an end to mutant life everywhere. Having gone through several upgrades over the years, ironically now a handful of Sentinels are used by the government to protect mutant life.

While Wolverine has amassed an impressive rogues' gallery in his personal life, most villains can't hold a candle to the dire universal threats he's faced during his time with the X-Men.

## DARK PHOENIX

A duplicate of Jean Grey's body, and possessing a shred of the female mutant's conscience, the Dark Phoenix was a force of nature, destroying an entire solar system before it committed suicide after convincing itself and the X-Men that it was truly the heroine Jean Grey.

## BLACK TOM CASSIDY

The brother of former X-Man Banshee, Black Tom Cassidy was the black sheep of the family. Having transformed from a mutant able to generate concussive blasts into a plant-manipulating master and back again, Black Tom still continues his vendetta with the X-Men despite his brother's death.

## THE BLOB

Although he lost his powers on M-Day in the wake of the House of M event, Fred J. Dukes had been a longtime member of the Brotherhood of Evil Mutants, utilizing his enormous girth and immovable weight to constantly stand in the X-Men's way.

## ARCADE

Obsessed with video games of all varieties, paid assassin Arcade has used his genius level intellect and his penchant for technology and design to run the X-Men through his various gauntlets in his Murderworlds, deadly theme parks that seemingly bring video games to life.

## BASTION

The combination of the artificial intelligence of the future Sentinel Nimrod and the Sentinel Master Mold, Bastion took on a human form, and began to follow his original programming in a campaign against all mutants, even manipulating a faction of the US government to help him in his cause.

## MOJO

The undisputed ruler of Mojoworld, Mojo runs his media-obsessed dimension with a remote of iron, constantly using the X-Men and other earthlings as pawns in his demented movie productions and reality TV experiments, not caring if his "actors" live to see the season finale.

## GOBLYN QUEEN

An identical clone of Jean Grey, Madelyne Pryor was birthed in Mr. Sinister's labs, and was quickly accepted by a heartbroken Cyclops as a replacement for his seemingly dead lover, Jean. After giving birth to Cyclops's son Cable, Madelyne soon revealed her truly demented colors when Jean Grey resurfaced.

## DANGER

When the X-Men's complex training facility known as the Danger Room slowly gained a mind of her own, Danger was born, a cybernetic life form able to exploit the limitations and fighting nuances of the entire X-Men team she knows so well.

# WOLVERINE AND JEAN GREY

**He was attracted to her right away. Possessing a kind soul and a resemblance to Logan's first love, Rose, Jean Grey quickly became the object of his unrequited affection.**

When first they met, Jean didn't much care for Logan's attitude or for the nickname of "Jeannie" that he gave her, but she slowly warmed to him.

## Early years

From the beginning, she was somebody else's girl. By the time Wolverine joined the X-Men, the telepathic Jean Grey and Scott Summers, aka Cyclops, had been in a relationship for years. So when Logan developed a crush on the young woman who called herself Marvel Girl, he didn't stand much chance of winning her heart.

But when Jean seemingly died on a mission to space only to be reborn as the powerful Phoenix, Logan decided to make his affections known. However, he thought better of it when he realized how many other people cared for the young woman and instead decided to bury his feelings deep inside himself. But things weren't as they seemed. Jean grew more and more powerful until she almost appeared to be a different entity entirely.

The insidious Hellfire Club kidnapped Jean, subjecting her to mind control, and the Jean Grey the X-Men knew and loved was no more.

**"HEAR ME, X-MEN! NO LONGER AM I THE WOMAN YOU KNEW! I AM FIRE! AND LIFE INCARNATE! NOW AND FOREVER"**

## The Birth of Phoenix

It turned out that a cosmic entity had merged with Jean Grey. With her all-too human emotions corrupting the Phoenix Force within her, Jean Grey became the Dark Phoenix, and carved a path of destruction throughout the cosmos, even obliterating an entire solar system. With the help of the alien Shi'ar race, the X-Men fought the Phoenix for a time, allowing Jean Grey's tortured personality to emerge if only for a moment. Realizing the scope of what she had done, Jean took her own life, and thus saved the entire universe.

However, as the X-Men would come to learn, the Phoenix that had died that day was not Jean Grey. In fact, the real Jean had been in a cocoon of sorts at the bottom of Jamaica Bay—the place she had apparently been reborn as the Phoenix all those months ago. At that time, the cosmic entity of the Phoenix Force had tapped into her potential power, and made itself into her doppelganger, its performance so perfect, even the Force believed itself to be the real deal.

--I AM PHOENIX!

BOOM!

Fooled by the Phoenix Force's duplicate into thinking she was their friend Jean Grey, the X-Men were truly devastated by Jean's apparent betrayal and then her death.

## "FORGIVE ME, DARLIN'"

## "D-DO IT, WOLVERINE!"

### Love and Marriage

Resurrected and returned to her place beside the founding X-Men in the newly formed team X-Factor, Jean Grey's return shocked her longtime friends. As X-Factor soon rejoined with their fellow mutants of the X-Men, Jean resumed her relationship with Cyclops, although she could not deny her attraction to the feral Logan. The two even shared a few fleeting moments of passion during the life-threatening situation known as the Inferno event, where Manhattan became a literal hell on Earth, as well as during the X-Tinction Agenda, when Jean believed Logan to be dying while locked in a prison. But in the end, Jean always chose Cyclops, and finally, the two were married. Although he could not bring himself to attend the ceremony, Wolverine nevertheless watched the proceedings from afar, with a small part of himself even happy for his two old friends.

### The Death of Jean Grey

Lured by the demented mutant Xorn onto an Asteroid satellite that was then hurled towards the sun, Wolverine and Jean Grey realized they had no chance of escape. As their quarters began to slowly get hotter and hotter, Jean could no longer stand the pain, and asked for Logan to end her life with his claws. Obliging his love her last wish, Jean's death unlocked the power of the Phoenix once more. Thus empowered, Jean returned Logan and herself to Earth, as Logan slowly healed from being burned alive.

However, as the duo confronted Xorn alongside their fellow X-Men, Xorn injected Jean with a lethal electromagnetic pulse and she died in her husband's arms.

# WOLVERINE
## AND THE X-MEN

With only one solo adventure to his credit, Wolverine didn't find his true home until he was enlisted by Professor X into the elaborate world of the X-Men.

A handshake sealed the deal. Recruited by the X-Men's founder Professor Charles Xavier on a mission to rescue the original X-Men members, Wolverine became an integral part of the mutant team's second generation. As members of the old guard moved on to new adventures, leaving only Cyclops and Marvel Girl behind to train the band of newcomers, Wolverine found himself part of something much larger than he originally anticipated. At first, Wolverine masked his true emotions beneath his trademark cowboy hat, opting to play the role of the runt with a chip on his shoulder and something to prove. He slowly developed into a proud team player, even orchestrating coordinated attacks with his other teammates, like his famous "fastball special," where Colossus would pick him up and literally pitch him at their intended target. Little by little, Logan began to reveal more and more of his true personality to the X-Men, even as he started to fall in love with Cyclops's girlfriend, his teammate Jean Grey. Wolverine's feelings towards the mutant telepath also known as Marvel Girl only helped to strengthen the animosity Wolverine and Cyclops had felt since their first meeting. Indeed while Wolverine was quickly becoming a close friend of Nightcrawler and Colossus, he and Cyclops would never see eye to eye.

## "I've just about had it with your 'MAD KILLER' act, pal."

Logan always struggled to keep his bestial side in check, but sometimes it resurfaced and caused trouble between himself and his teammates.

Wolverine's feelings for Jean Grey blossomed when she supposedly died and was reborn as the Phoenix. However, he pushed his feelings to the back of his mind, the activities of numerous Super Villains keeping him occupied. During this era, Wolverine and the X-Men tangled with Professor X's hulking stepbrother Juggernaut, teammate Banshee's scheming brother Black Tom Cassidy, and of course, the master of magnetism, Magneto. The team also faced robotic duplicates of the original X-Men and the cosmic power of Firelord, and journeyed into space to meet the alien race known as the Shi'ar. The X-Men proved their loyalty to Wolverine when they chose to stick by his side even after Guardian, calling himself Weapon Alpha, of Canada's Department H, attempted to drag Wolverine back to his native country.

## "It's NO ACT, leader-man."

**X-Men #106 (Aug. 1977)**
After their teammate Thunderbird's death, Cyclops began to drive the team harder than usual, an action Wolverine refused to tolerate.

**X-Men #107 (Oct. 1977)**
Traveling into space to battle the Shi'ar aliens, Wolverine was forced to don a brown and tan costume belonging to savage alien Fang when his own uniform was shredded.

**X-Men #109 (Feb. 1978)**
Wolverine battled James Hudson with the help of the X-Men, when his old friend tried to force him return to Canada's Department program.

# WOLVERINE
## AND THE X-MEN

Wolverine was growing up. Comics were becoming more sophisticated, and Logan was following suit, his character gaining a whole new level of depth.

As the decade began, Logan slowly began to grab more moments in the spotlight. His past a well-guarded secret, he nevertheless grew closer to his teammates. His unrequited love for Jean Grey resurfaced, and he watched the object of his affection undergo brainwashing by the notorious Mastermind of the evil elite Hellfire Club. This deviant programming corrupted Jean's already fragile mind and the former heroine transformed into the evil entity known as Dark Phoenix. Wolverine was forced to help the X-Men battle her, as she had grown so powerful that her mere existence threatened the entire universe. But in a brief moment of clarity, Jean realized the errors of her ways and killed herself, forcing Logan to watch his love die yet again. As the years continued, Wolverine faced the demons of his past while clearing his name with the Canadian government and their super-team Alpha Flight, and also

## "OKAY, suckers— you've taken yer BEST SHOT!"

Wolverine clawed and scraped his way through the sewers in order to sneak into the headquarters of the Hellfire Club unnoticed, determined to save his love, Jean Grey.

## "Now it's MY turn!"

got a glimpse into his future as an older version of his teammate Kitty Pryde traveled back in time from the days of future past. He was instrumental in defeating the forces of a new incarnation of the Brotherhood of Evil Mutants led by his old flame Mystique, and he faced the horror of the Marauders when this band of evil mutants massacred hundreds of mutants living in the tunnels below Manhattan. Logan opposed the government itself as they imposed registration on his mutant brothers, and battled his own temptations as he fought the Goblyn Queen when New York City became a living inferno.

Uncanny X-Men #141 (Jan. 1981)
The Wolverine of a dystopian future, one of the last of the dying mutant race, struggled against the murderous Sentinels.

Uncanny X-Men #227 (Mar.1988)
As the government passed strict mutant registration laws, Wolverine found more than merely his civil rights in jeopardy.

Uncanny X-Men #251 (Nov. 1989)
Crucified by the evil cyborg Reavers in the Australian outback, Wolverine escaped an agonizing death with the help of Jubilee.

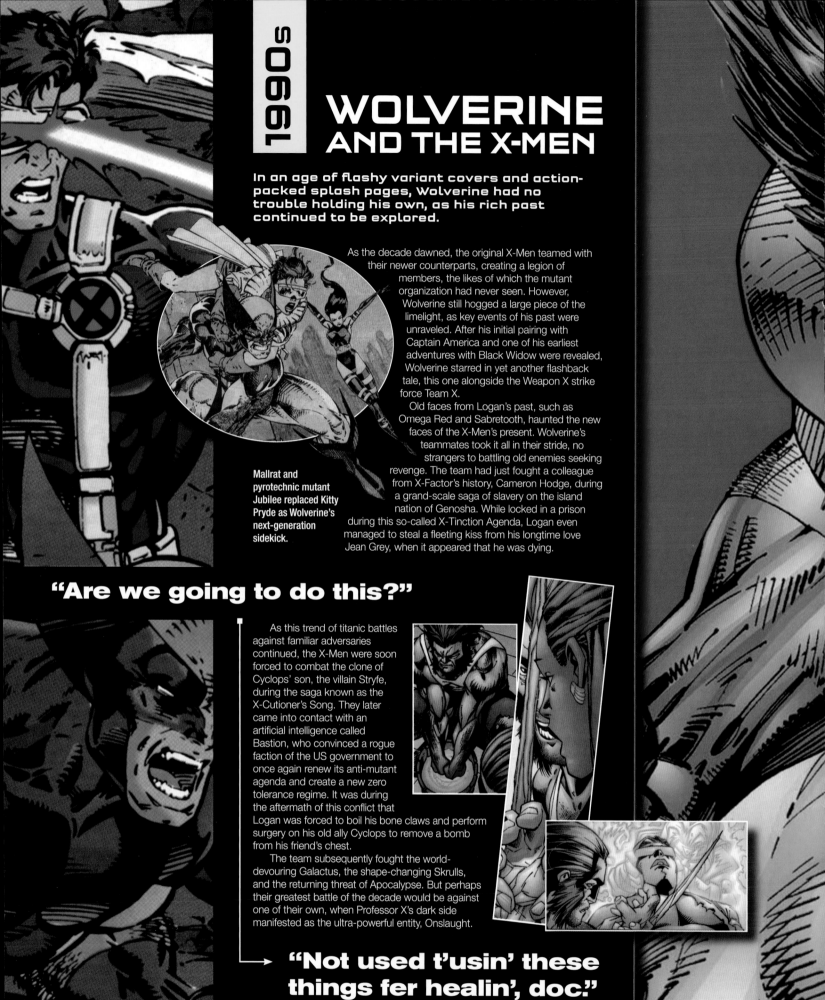

# WOLVERINE
## AND THE X-MEN

In an age of flashy variant covers and action-packed splash pages, Wolverine had no trouble holding his own, as his rich past continued to be explored.

As the decade dawned, the original X-Men teamed with their newer counterparts, creating a legion of members, the likes of which the mutant organization had never seen. However, Wolverine still hogged a large piece of the limelight, as key events of his past were unraveled. After his initial pairing with Captain America and one of his earliest adventures with Black Widow were revealed, Wolverine starred in yet another flashback tale, this one alongside the Weapon X strike force Team X.

Old faces from Logan's past, such as Omega Red and Sabretooth, haunted the new faces of the X-Men's present. Wolverine's teammates took it all in their stride, no strangers to battling old enemies seeking revenge. The team had just fought a colleague from X-Factor's history, Cameron Hodge, during a grand-scale saga of slavery on the island nation of Genosha. While locked in a prison during this so-called X-Tinction Agenda, Logan even managed to steal a fleeting kiss from his longtime love Jean Grey, when it appeared that he was dying.

Mallrat and pyrotechnic mutant Jubilee replaced Kitty Pryde as Wolverine's next-generation sidekick.

## "Are we going to do this?"

As this trend of titanic battles against familiar adversaries continued, the X-Men were soon forced to combat the clone of Cyclops' son, the villain Stryfe, during the saga known as the X-Cutioner's Song. They later came into contact with an artificial intelligence called Bastion, who convinced a rogue faction of the US government to once again renew its anti-mutant agenda and create a new zero tolerance regime. It was during the aftermath of this conflict that Logan was forced to boil his bone claws and perform surgery on his old ally Cyclops to remove a bomb from his friend's chest.

The team subsequently fought the world-devouring Galactus, the shape-changing Skrulls, and the returning threat of Apocalypse. But perhaps their greatest battle of the decade would be against one of their own, when Professor X's dark side manifested as the ultra-powerful entity, Onslaught.

## "Not used t'usin' these things fer healin', doc."

The Uncanny X-Men #268
(Sept. 1990)
Wolverine fought against the
Hand both with Black Widow
in the present and with
Captain America in the past.

X-Men #1 (Oct, 1991)
The original X-Men joined
forces with their newer
recruits during a fierce battle
against Magneto.

X-Men #70 (Dec. 1997)
In the wake of the Zero
Tolerance event, the X-Men's
ranks were increased by
several new members.

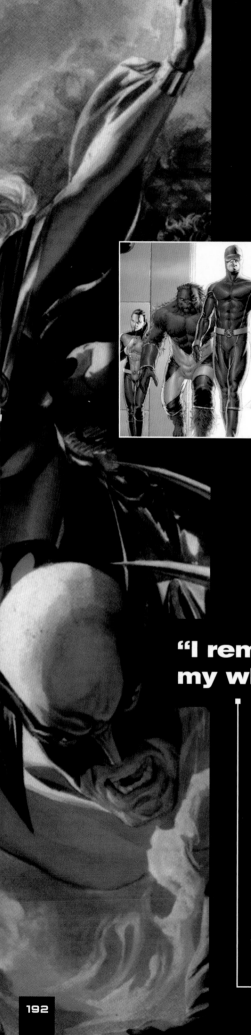

# WOLVERINE
# AND THE X-MEN

A cultural icon in the present day, Wolverine has quickly become the most famous of the X-Men and a dedicated and loyal member of the team.

Kitty Pryde and the recently resurrected Colossus would later join the X-Men's core team.

The decade began with the X-Men in the same state of convoluted organization as at the end of the 1990s. However, the team soon received a facelift and complete restructuring. Xavier's Institute once again became a place of learning, its focus switching from being simply an X-Men complex to a school once again, one that would train the next generation of mutants for the roles that awaited them. With a core group of so-called New X-Men on the teaching roster, including Professor X, Wolverine, Cyclops, Jean Grey, Beast, and even Emma Frost, the White Queen, the mutant children of the world flocked to this safe haven, especially when Professor X publicly announced that he was a mutant.

Despite their newfound passion as professors of mutant studies, the X-Men nevertheless found time to save the planet on a few occasions. During this era, the X-Men faced the likes of Professor X's evil twin Cassandra Nova, the disturbed turncoat Xorn, and even a few renegade students. Meanwhile, Wolverine learned a bit more about the scope of the Weapon X project, and once again lost his love Jean Grey. She was killed by Xorn, when the powerful mutant came to believe the delusion that he in fact was Magneto.

As more changes rocked the X-Men's universe, including a permanent move to California, the group's roster altered a few times, yet the faithful Wolverine always remained a constant.

## "I remember... my whole life."

When the Scarlet Witch returned the world to the way it had been, she used her chaos magic to reduce the number of mutants to 198. Wolverine still remembered all of his past that he had recalled during the House of M saga. Now Logan was awake in his world, remembering everything.

## "Everything."

# 2000s

## KEY ISSUES

**Astonishing X-Men #1
(July 2004)**
As Xavier's school reopened for business, Wolverine and Cyclops had it out, both grieving over Jean Grey's recent death.

**Uncanny X-Men #500
(September 2008)**
The X-Men set up their new digs in San Francisco, alongside old friends Angel, Storm, and Nightcrawler.

**X-Men: Deadly Genesis #1
(January 2006)**
The team discovered that Professor X had led a secret group of X-Men years ago, one that didn't survive past its first mission.

# THE NEW AVENGERS

## "We'll find out who did this. And then we'll avenge it."

## MISSION NUMBER 1

The Avengers had been disassembled. After former member Scarlet Witch had gone insane and killed several of them, the legendary team had become a thing of the past. They would have stayed that way if the Raft hadn't exploded.

As Luke Cage and Spider-Woman Jessica Drew toured this maximum holding facility, the criminal Electro attacked and freed all of the dangerous super-powered inmates. Iron Man, Spider-Man, and Captain America rushed to the prison to lend a hand, then embarked on a mission to the Savage Land, to track down Electro's employers. There they joined with Wolverine, already hot on the same trail, and the New Avengers were formed. The team took down the powerful mutant Sauron, and a corrupt branch of the government agency SHIELD.

## REGISTRATION

When the Super Hero Registration Act was passed, a Civil War broke out between the nation's masked crime fighters. As torn as any other faction of heroes, the Avengers split into two divisions: the Mighty Avengers organized by Iron Man, a staunch supporter of registering heroes with the government, and Captain America's Secret Avengers, a team of heroes operating from the shadows, and protesting the government's involvement in their lives. Although he was busy tracking down the villain Nitro during the majority of the Civil War, when the dust had settled, Wolverine resumed his role alongside the Secret Avengers, believing in the group's noble cause. Continually on the run from the law, this new batch of Secret Avengers was later augmented by new members Echo, Iron Fist, Dr. Strange, and the second hero to call himself Ronin.

## THE OLD AVENGERS

It began with a ragtag mismatched group of heroes: the armored Iron Man, the shrinking Ant-Man and Wasp, god of thunder Thor, and even the rampaging Incredible Hulk. United together by circumstance, and kept together by necessity, the team wouldn't quite blossom until they unearthed World War II hero Captain America, who was frozen in a block of ice at the ocean's floor, trapped in suspended animation at his prime. Once revived, Cap quickly became the uncontested leader, and served as a constant inspiration to the rest of the team. As members came and went, the team took up residence off Manhattan's Central Park in an impressive mansion supplied by Iron Man's alter ego, billionaire Tony Stark. It was there that the team quickly became the lauded guardians of all mankind and Earth's mightiest heroes—the Avengers.

## ECHO

The deaf Maya Lopez possesses photographic reflexes that allow her to mimic physical movements she sees others perform. She utilized this talent as a crime fighter called Echo after being manipulated by the criminal Kingpin into hunting the hero Daredevil.

## RONIN

Originally Echo in disguise, the identity of the wandering samurai Ronin was passed on to former Avenger Hawkeye when he returned from the seeming grave. Though master of the bow and arrow, as Ronin, Clint Barton now relies mostly on his martial art skills.

## IRON FIST

Danny Rand is the newest in a long line of martial artists possessing the ability to channel their chi into a rock hard fist of fury. He uses his powers as well as his bank account to aid the Secret Avengers, even funding a new hideout for the clandestine team.

## DR. STRANGE

The former Sorcerer Supreme of the Marvel Universe, Dr. Stephen Strange recently abandoned his title after using a darker variety of his magic powers in battle. However, before leaving the New Avengers, Strange had been offering his mystically shrouded home to them as a refuge.

## SPIDER-MAN

When Peter Parker was bitten by a radioactive spider, granting him the proportionate powers of the arachnid, his life was turned upside down as he became the wall-crawling hero Spider-Man. Originally a supporter of Iron Man's registration act, Spidey realized the error of his ways and went on the run with the Avengers.

## LUKE CAGE

Assuming a leadership role in the New Avengers after the death of Captain America, Luke Cage uses his intelligence, tough attitude and near-invulnerable skin to become an influential voice in his team's secret operations. A reformed criminal who was granted his powers in an experimental operation, Cage has been on both sides of the law before, and therefore is unwavering in his opposition to the Super Hero Registration Act.

## WOLVERINE

Despite being a mutant and exempt from the Registration Act, Wolverine has stuck by his fellow New Avengers until the present day. Always exhibiting a fierce sense of loyalty, Logan wholeheartedly supports the Secret Avengers' cause, and will do everything in his power to fight against this new form of government oppression.

*The Scarlet Witch had gone insane. A former Avenger and the daughter of Magneto, Wanda Maximoff had been spiraling away from sanity for years, and hit rock bottom when she single-handedly disassembled the Avengers, killing several of their members and destroying their home. As the other heroes decided what to do about their old friend, Wanda stretched her reality warping abilities to their fullest, and recreated the universe in her own image.*

# THE HOUSE OF M

**No longer the hated minority, mutants were now the abundant majority in a brave new world led by Magneto's royal family.**

Awaking in this new World of M with all his old memories intact, Wolverine discovered that he was now an agent of SHIELD.

Wolverine had been mind-wiped before, and he had no intention of repeating that fate. Abandoning his position in the Magneto-run government organization SHIELD, Wolverine traveled to Manhattan, deciding to seek out past allies. As he hunted for Charles Xavier, Wolverine was being hunted himself by his old government colleagues. He narrowly escaped the agents with the help of the sudden appearance of the teleporter Cloak. Logan stumbled upon the Human Resistance Movement, led by strong man Luke Cage. As Magneto's human-hunting Sentinels pursued the underground team, Wolverine and company successfully recruited Spider-Man, Daredevil, the X-Men, and a host of others, and then stormed Magneto's Genoshan island home.

Hitching a ride inside a commandeered Sentinel, the heroes struggled valiantly against Magneto's forces, finally showing the villain the truth of the situation. With his past memories restored, Magneto realized that his daughter had been coerced into creating this new reality by her brother, the former Avenger Quicksilver. Magneto attacked his son and to avoid further conflict, the Scarlet Witch restored the world to its true form, with one major difference: she removed the powers of nearly every living mutant on Earth.

With all of his past memories restored for the first time in his entire life, Logan escaped SHIELD by literally throwing himself off their helicarrier.

The World of M was overseen by Magneto and his royal family, consisting of his daughters, Scarlet Witch and Polaris, and his son, Quicksilver. His rule was looked upon favorably by the vast majority of the mutants under his thrall, however this was not a sentiment shared by their Homo sapiens relatives. Humans were oppressed in this new reality in much the same way that mutants had been in the previous one.

When staging their attack on the House of M, the Human Resistance had hidden inside a Sentinel. Magneto easily halted it with his magnetic powers.

# WOLVERINE'S CIVIL WAR

**It was an epic conflict that pitted brother against brother. A battle between heroes the likes of which the Marvel Universe had never witnessed. It was the Super Hero Civil War, and Wolverine was caught right in the middle.**

It was a choice the heroes never thought they'd have to make. When a conflict between the young heroes known as the New Warriors and a group of Super Villains escalated into the destruction of a school and the surrounding small town of Stamford, Connecticut, civilians became infuriated, and needed a place to direct their anger. Soon Congress provided the answer and passed the Super Hero Registration Act, creating a law that required all superhumans to register their powers with the United States government or face incarceration. Those willing to expose their secret identities to the authorities would be placed in the Initiative program, and be trained to serve their country as part of a government sponsored Super Hero team. Needless to say, this controversial new law divided the Super Hero community in half, the pro-registration side filing in behind Iron Man, while the dissenters rallied behind the voice of freedom, Captain America.

## "LOOKS LIKE THE, SHORTEST OF THE X-MEN'S GONE THE WAY OF ALL FLESH."

Wolverine's feral anger helped him survive an explosion akin to an atomic bomb.

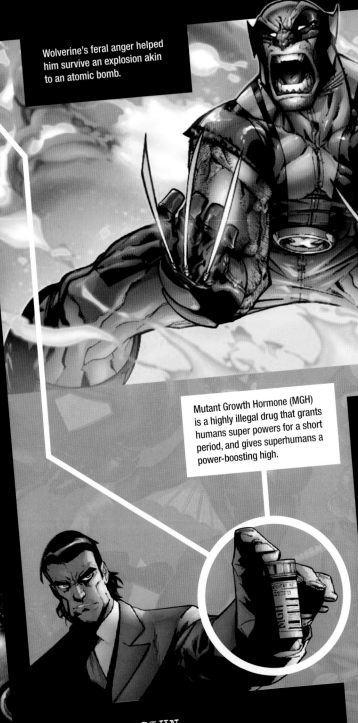

### NITRO

But in Wolverine's eyes, this whole mess was the fault of one man—Nitro. After all, he was the Super Villain who had detonated his explosive powers, killing hundreds of Stamford residents. So instead of participating in the deadly war games with his fellow Avengers, or sitting on the sidelines with his fellow X-Men, Wolverine began to track Nitro, following his scent to Big Sur, California.

When Logan attacked him, Nitro immediately unleashed his powers, engulfing Wolverine in a lethal fireball, and reducing his body to little more than a metal skeleton. Using his healing factor, he knit himself back together, and viciously assaulted Nitro, prepared to kill the villain for his sins. But Nitro had information: Someone had supplied him with Mutant Growth Hormone, aka steroids for the super-powered set.

Captain America finally ended the fighting and turned himself in to Iron Man, after seeing the devastation they had caused in New York City.

Mutant Growth Hormone (MGH) is a highly illegal drug that grants humans super powers for a short period, and gives superhumans a power-boosting high.

### NAMOR

Before Wolverine could learn the name of Nitro's drug supplier, he was attacked by Namor, the King of Atlantis, and two of his sleeper human agents, Janus and Amir. Knocking Wolverine out, Namor departed for Atlantis with Nitro, determined to punish the villain for the death of his cousin, the New Warrior Namorita. Though Logan followed the sea king with the aid of an Iron Man suit, he later decided that Nitro's fate should be left up to Namor.

### WALTER DECLUN

After learning from Namor that successful businessman and head of the Damage Control Super Hero clean-up service, Walter Declun, had given Nitro the MGH, Logan headed to the corrupt CEO's Manhattan office. Learning that Super Hero fights meant big money to Declun, Wolverine killed the scheming businessman, despite Declun trying to even the odds by taking the very drug he peddled.

Gaining an Iron Man suit from Tony Stark, Wolverine used the armor to journey underwater to Atlantis.

# The DEATH of Wolverine

He was a walking dead man, and didn't even know it. As the dust cleared on the Super Hero Civil War, Wolverine's life returned to its usual insanely fast pace. On a favor to his new love, the blue-skinned Atlantean warrior Amir, he traveled to Iraq and encountered the Scimitar **(1)**, a secret terrorist organization that was attempting to rival similar sinister groups such as the Hand, AIM, and Hydra. Discovering that Scimitar was targeting SHIELD director and Super Hero Iron Man, Wolverine boarded a SHIELD helicarrier in order to rescue his old ally, only to discover he had been tricked into boarding a Scimitar air vessel instead. Forced into battle with a masked man clad in adamantium armor, Wolverine watched helplessly as Amir was killed by the warrior's throwing star **(2)**. He blindly charged his opponent, enraged at the all-too-familiar sight of his lovers being butchered. Wolverine then felt something being stuffed into his mouth, but reacted much too late **(3)**. He had just swallowed a bomb, one his attacker did not balk in detonating.

While Logan's physical body lay brain dead, recovered by SHIELD agents, his soul was enjoying a few beers at an empty bar in a purgatory of sorts. There, the astral form of sorcerer supreme Dr. Strange paid the mutant a strange visit, explaining to Wolverine exactly how and why he had been brought to such a place **(4)**. It seemed that back in World War I, Logan had faced a threat on a German field of battle after being dosed with chlorine gas. The threat was a lone man, dressed in a red cloak and armed with nothing more than a broadsword. Logan brazenly charged this new enemy with nothing more than the blades of two bayonets, and actually bested the foe, running the mysterious man through with his own sword. What Logan didn't know at the time was that the man he had killed that day was Lazaer, an anagram for Azrael, the angel of death himself.

Even though he had beaten the angel of death Lazaer once, Wolverine wasn't the type to shy away from a rematch. Since his original duel during World War I, every time Logan suffered a life-threatening injury, his body would mend itself while his soul would travel to purgatory to do battle with Lazaer, and win the chance to save his soul and keep it from passing into the afterlife. However upon his last duel with the angel of death, Wolverine's will had been sapped by the death of his newest love Amir, and Lazaer was finally able to defeat him **(5)**.

After being briefed on his history with Lazaer by Dr. Strange, Wolverine decided to escape his purgatory saloon life and exited out the front door. However he found himself battling different versions of himself **(6)**, from when he first learned he was a mutant, to his time as a guinea pig in the Weapon X program, to when he had been run through by the murderous Hand agent Gorgon. It was during this last encounter that Wolverine realized something about himself had changed. On this occasion, the Hand had used an ancient ritual to bring Wolverine back to life. Present at the ceremony was a woman who had stolen something vital from Logan, something that had made it harder for him to defeat Lazaer each time they fought. Wolverine realized he had to find this woman. At that moment, his soul was reunited with his body in the physical world.

Milking the Hand for information, Wolverine soon learned this female enemy was named Phaedra **(7)**, and that she now worked closely with Scimitar. Following her back to her home, Wolverine attacked Phaedra, only to discover that what she had stolen from him was a piece of his very soul. As Lazaer stepped out of the shadows, revealing he knew Phaedra quite well, Wolverine realized he was outnumbered but not outmatched. Phaedra's frequent resurrections plagued the angel of death's very existence yet, for some reason, Lazaer was unable to kill her. Wolverine did not have the same restrictions and made a deal with the angel of death. He would kill Phaedra **(8)**, and free Lazaer from her meddling if Lazaer would return Logan's soul to him in full. This price Lazaer was glad to pay, making Wolverine a whole man once again. There was only one catch: the next time Wolverine died, it would be for good.

**Wolverine did the unthinkable to regain the missing piece of his soul.**

# INDEX

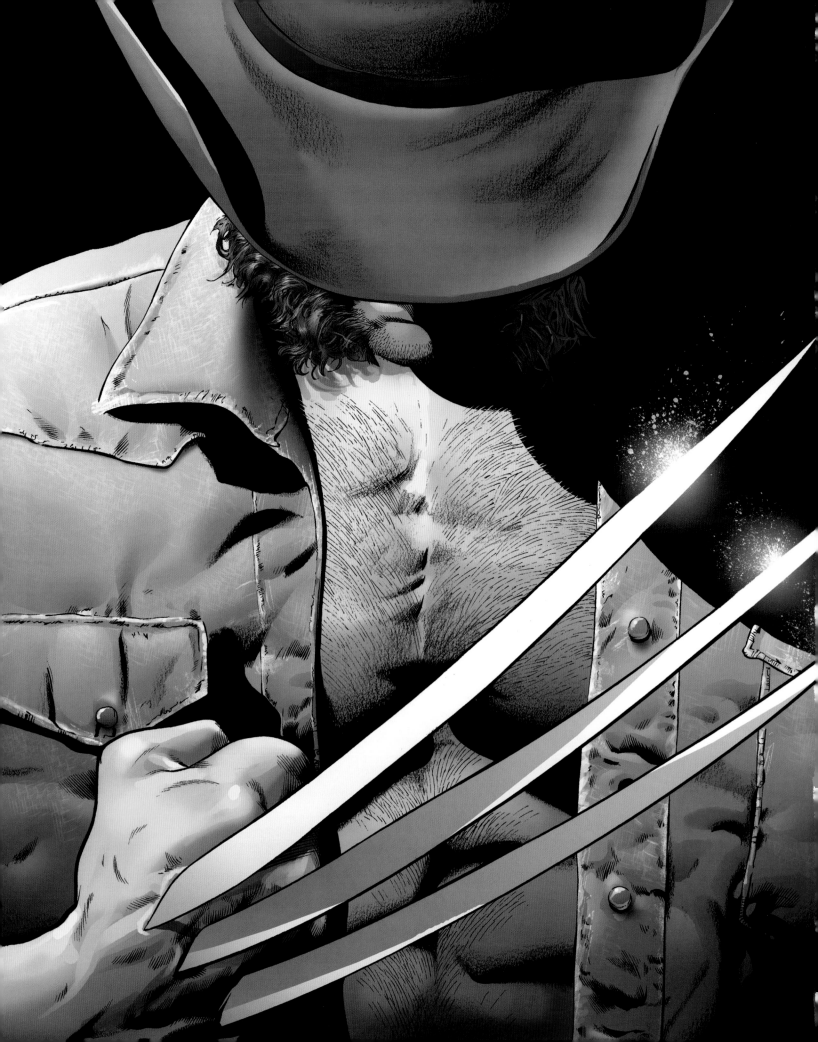